The albums of Dr. John include:

Gris-Gris *(Atco)*
Babylon *(Atco)*
Remedies *(Atco)*
The Sun, Moon, and Herbs *(Atco)*
Gumbo *(Atco)*
In the Right Place *(Atco)*
Desitively Bonaroo *(Atco)*
Hollywood Be Thy Name *(United Artists)*
City Lights *(Horizon/A&M)*
Tango Palace *(Horizon/A&M)*
Dr. John Plays Mac Rebennack *(Clean Cuts)*
The Brightest Smile in Town *(Clean Cuts)*
Live in London *(Sprindrift)*
The Ultimate Dr. John *(Warner Bros.)*
In a Sentimental Mood *(Warner Bros.)*
On a Mardi Gras Day *(Great Southern)*
Goin' Back to New Orleans *(Warner Bros.)*
Mos' Scocious *(Rhino)*
Television *(MCA/GRP)*

The Life of Dr. John the Night Tripper

**Dr. John (Mac Rebennack)
with Jack Rummel**

ST. MARTIN'S GRIFFIN NEW YORK

Grateful acknowledgment is made to the following for
use of the lyrics of songs by Mac Rebennack in this
book: Skull Music; Warner/Chappell Music; Rondor
Music; and Ten East Music. "For All We Know" by
Fred Coots and Samuel Lewis courtesy of C.P.P./
Belwin, Inc. All Rights Reserved.

DESIGN BY JUDITH A. STAGNITTO

Library of Congress Cataloging-in-Publication Data

John, Dr.
    Under a hoodoo moon / Dr. John (Mac
Rebennack) with Jack Rummel.
        p.   cm.
    ISBN 0-312-13197-6 (pbk.)
    1. John, Dr., 1941–   . 2. Rock musicians—United
States—Biography.   I. Rummel, Jack.   II. Title.
ML420.J725A3   1995
781.66′092—dc20
[B]   95-2219
                                            CIP
                                            MN

D10 9 8 7 6 5 4 3 2

For all the New Orleans musicians
and for Karla, Tara, Jessica, Jennifer, and Max

Mac Rebennack thanks Mr. G., Cosimo Matassa, Red Tyler, Lee Allen, Jessie Hill, Mrs. Lastie, Allen Toussaint, Earl Palmer, Edward Frank, and Danny Barker for their help.

Jack Rummel would like to thank Julian Bach, BB—Barbara Becker—Bill Bentley, and Cal Morgan, whose help was essential in writing this book. Also thanks and love to Ann Lowe.

PRELUDE

The chicken and the fightin' rooster had a fight.
The fightin' rooster knocked the chicken out of sight.
The chicken told the fightin' rooster, "That's all right.
Gonna meet you in the gumbo tomorrow night."

—*Traditional New Orleans rhyme*

U.S. Public Health Hospital, Fort Worth, Texas. The mid-sixties. No new suit or ten-cent cigar, just a letter in the pocket of my jeans: "Do not go to or through New Orleans." In the bat of an eye, I'm out on the bricks of the fonky streets of Fort Worth, smelling rawhide and cow pies, heading for the airport and the blue skies.

After wearing an NP ("Narcotics Patient") suit for a time, as a result of violations of the Boggs and Harrison acts, I was cut loose. I was looking west toward California, but my mind was concerned about New Orleans: about a wife and child, and about the home of rhythm and blues, where a gang and a half of hits came out of Cosimo Matassa's studio on Governor Nicholls Street—hits like Little Richard's "Tutti Frutti" and "Long Tall Sally," Huey Smith's "Rockin' Pneumonia," Fats Domino's "I'm Walkin'," Shirley and Lee's "Let the Good Times Roll." I was concerned about my home.

A twenty-four-hours-a-day happening city was being closed.

1

Shut down by a gangbusters DA who padlocked the gambling dens, whorehouses, juke joints, and temples of tricknology that had kept the New Orleans music scene alive. No matter to Jim Garrison: The lights had gone dim in the joints, the music slammed into the gutter. Up at 35,000 feet on my way to LA I couldn't help wondering: What would happen to the 4:00 A.M. cutting contests? The all-night jam sessions? The clubs were out of biz, the record industry running to Memphis, to Muscle Shoals, to anywhere else it could, carrying squabbling record execs and leaving a panicked musicians' union in its wake.

Was this the end of the piano professors like Longhair, Tuts Washington, Huey Smith, Herbert Santina, Allen Toussaint, whose tradition went back before Satchmo or Buddy Bolden, back to Yoruba and Bakongo grooves from Congo Square that they'd kept alive and funky?

Broke, busted, disgusted, being shipped to the sunny-California City of Angels, I wanted to scream out: All you hustlers and hobos, rustlers with your mojos, all you life actors and care-ack-ters—the odds may be in the graveyard's favor, but there ain't no way you can kill the flavor.

From that day, I have crossed many a river to get to where I am now.

Be then ready, in reading the words that follow, to jump over the fault line, knowing you got to find the fault within yourself before you find a fault in me. It ain't about blame, it's just a music game.

This is a testament to New Orleans funk—to funksterators, tricknologists, mu-jicians, who got music burning in their brains and no holes in their souls. Like the tail of a comet blowing through galaxies, these tales are my tribute to them.

And one last word of warning: You can't shut the fonk up. No, the fonk got a mind of its own.

So saith Mac Rebennack, who some of y'all might know as Dr. John the Night Tripper.

THE THIRD WARD

Big Chief Tuddy
Played some Tee na-na
All on a Mardi Gras Day.

Saying He la Bah Bene Mo Cha.
Did you heard what I seen,
Did you heard what I saw.

We going down and dig the Mardi Gras,
All on a Mardi Gras Day.

—*"All on a Mardi Gras Day,"*
Mac Rebennack

Music is something no one person owns. Like a field
holler or a second-line rhythm, it hovers in the air for a lingering
beat and passes away, living through us only for a moment. We
can give it our spin, but then we have to let go and pass it on.

My maternal grandfather, who sang and hoofed for a while
for the Al G. Fields minstrel show operating out of Mobile,
Alabama, was the one who passed the music on to me in a down
way for the first time. He was an Irishman from Mobile who at
a certain point moved with his family to Algiers, just across the
Mississippi from New Orleans. Later he moved again, this time
into New Orleans proper, and for a while all of us lived together
in his house on Ida Street near City Park.

3

When he was very old, long after he had turned in his last act, he used to sit with me on the front porch and sing the charts he had worked in his day. He was confined to a wheelchair; he had doubled as a strongman in the minstrel act, and one day got himself messed up when a safe he was lifting fell on him. I remember him, old and thin, smoking a pipe, singing in his froggy voice:

I been hoodooed
I been hoodooed
I been hoodooed
Somebody done put the jinx on me . . .

I don't know why, but that memory stuck with me like a remembered dream. Later, I took it and (with a few changes to cut out the racist lines that came with my grandfather's version) recorded it on my album *In the Right Place*. It was my turn to pick up on it and I passed it, with my twists, into the AM/FM wind.

My grandfather ran the hoodoo song and other numbers down during tours around the South at the turn of the century, which was the height of the minstrel and vaudeville era. There was scores of minstrel acts, black and white, crisscrossing the country back then; unfortunately, the race stuff came down thick and heavy in lyrics on both sides of the color fence. But each song usually came with at least half a dozen different, alternate lyrics too—some risqué, some sad, some funny, some crazy, however you might want to go, and if you didn't like none of them you could make up your own.

Another of my grandfather's favorites was a song called "Jump Sturdy." Jump Sturdy was a home-brewed liquor popular in New Orleans and along the Gulf Coast that tasted like lemonade; it was supposed to pep you up so you could dance or jam or boogie or jook to your heart's contentment. One of the lines of my grandfather's version went like this:

If the devil was born without any horns
He must have been the furniture man

. . . or the insurance man or the dago man or the Cajun man or whatever group or type y'all wanted to knock. I took the melody of the song, changed Jump Sturdy from the name of a liquor to the name of a girl, and put it on my *Gris-Gris* album.

To this day, I think he used to smoke a little herb to put himself in the mood to run down these numbers with me. He kept his tobacco in a can of Prince Albert, and inside the can he had another leather bag. He'd be sitting out on the porch smoking tobacco out of the can, then all of a sudden he'd take his little bit of something else out of the bag, and soon enough he'd get to laughing and cutting up. That's when he'd sing me these songs and tell me stories about the minstrels.

Oh just save me the leavings
Save me the leavings
Leftovers is just good enough for me . . .

It went on and on like that for night after night, the beginning of my learning about what it is and what it ain't—important stuff for a kid or a grown-up to know.

I was born in New Orleans just before Thanksgiving 1940. I was a big baby, checked in nearly a month late. Because of my size and my birthday, my mother took to calling me her Thanksgiving turkey, a term of endearment I was glad she dropped well before I began going to school.

We lived with my grandfather and grandmother until I was five or six. During those years my father owned an appliance store, but sometime during the war he got into a tangle with the appliance company and the place went bankrupt. After that, we moved around the city quite a bit, until finally we ended up in a more-or-less permanent place on Jeff Davis Parkway in the Third Ward.

Between my father's hustling to make a living and our constant moving from one shotgun house to another, life was up and down around my home when I was young. But there were compensations. One of the first things I remember about my childhood was a white baby grand Kimball piano in the living room. My sister, who was ten years older than I was, used to practice on it, and I was hypnotized by its beautiful white sheen and the way it glowed like a ghost in the evening light.

The streets of the Third Ward were alive with characters back then. One of my first encounters with street music came from a guy named Bugling Sam DeKemel, a peddler who sold waffles and Roman candy from a mule-drawn wagon. He used to come down the street, blowing a bugle from his wagon real loud. Bugling Sam might not have been a great bugle player, but he was one cranked-up loud one. When the kids heard him blowing his horn they came running from all around to fix their candy and waffle joneses.

There was another cat who came around in a mule-drawn horse buggy, selling seafood and game. He had his own special chant to hawk his wares:

> I got oyster, I got oyster, lady . . .
> I got quail, I got swumps [shrimps]
> I got watermelon, good to the rind
> Buy mine, lady, have a real good time
>
> I got watermelon, good to the seed
> I got all the watermelon you need
> I got watermelon . . .

And there was a third man who used to fascinate the shit out of me. He was one of the many Italians who had moved to New Orleans in the early part of the century. This fella had a vegetable hustle, which he worked off a hand-pulled cart in the neighborhood, and he also ran a scissor-sharpening business. As he came through the neighborhood, he made his presence known by rubbing a piece of metal against his sharpening device, which made a fierce grating sound. If you was within a hundred yards of him while he was putting down his grinding signal, it would cut through your body something awful. He had a funny call that ran like this:

Sharpen' sharpe-na, sharpe-na, sharpe-na . . .

Over and over, and never once did he end the call with *scissors*.

These were just three characters in our Third Ward neighborhood. There were lots more wandering the streets, all over the city.

My grandfather and grandmother both loved to scare the daylights out of us little kids; my grandmother got her particular charge from throwing us really wicked curves right when we was going to sleep. She'd come in and tell us stories about this guy who'd go around New Orleans slitting people's throats. She'd run through her story and have us crawling in our beds, only to stop at the scariest point, telling us she'd keep the rest for the next night. We'd beg her to tell us some more and she'd make a show of giving in—then she'd get us even more terrified. The next day she picked up right where she'd left off—that story might run for weeks.

Because my grandfather couldn't get into our room in his wheelchair, he told us scary stories during the day. One of these was about a cat he called the Needle Man. The Needle Man would wait till he passed an innocent stranger alone in the street, then he'd poke the person's eyes out with his needle, and jut the needle in the victim's throat and arteries. After one of these stories, my Cousin Gail and I would be just absolutely scared shitless, which gave my grandparents all kinds of kicks.

My grandmother was a woman who possessed unusual powers, and she passed on to me my curiosity and inclination toward spiritualism and voodoo. As I think back, I realize that if she had been born under different circumstances, she could have been a root doctor or what we in New Orleans call a reverend mother— a female spiritual healer and community leader. She was just a little woman, and a real sweetheart, but she had the touch.

One night—I was too young to remember this—Grandmother did something that really freaked everybody out. She was sitting around our dining room table when suddenly she began to "walk" the table. It was a big, heavy oak table, carved with leaves and vines and lion's-claw feet, that was made in Angola Penitentiary. The inmates used dow pins to put the table together, constructing it with the same caliber of craftsmanship you'd see on all the gambling tables and roulette wheels they made for Boss Perez's gaming houses out in Plaquemines Parish and the Marcellos' clubs in Jefferson Parish. It was one heavy table; no single guy, no matter how big, could pick it up.

According to the story, my grandmother got up from her chair and put her fists on the table, and the table lifted off the ground and began wobbling across the room with Grandmother following after it. My mother and her sisters got so scared that one of them ran off to get the priest to come and exorcise her. The exorcism may have chilled her out for a minute, but I don't believe the rite really put her right.

Later, when I was in my teens, she'd say strange, foreboding things to me, and I still remember them with a chill. One time I came by our house with a girl I was hanging out with, and Grandmother told me under her breath: "You'd better get rid of that girl. She's nothing but charity ass." And I knew if I didn't get rid of her, she'd say it loud enough for the girl to hear it. That would wipe it out right there.

Once or twice, when I tried to sneak another girl into my bedroom without my mother knowing it, my grandmother stopped me and gave me high warning. "If you try sneaking that girl in here behind your mother's back I'm gonna bust you." She did that kind of thing on the side, and was always real cool about it. In the last year or so of her life, she took to walking around the house singing "What Am I Living For?" When I'd tell my mother about some of the things Grandmother said and did, she wouldn't believe it, but they wasn't no joke. She wasn't the kind of human most people could laugh at; she was the kind of human who put the horrors creeping up your back.

Through all this, my mother kept on with her business. She

liked to stay around the house and cook for me, my sister, and my father; she was very religious, and worked a lot for the church. Beneath it all, though, she liked to cut up and have fun. She's always been industrious and thrifty; when I was a kid, she started a business with another lady, making hoopskirts for the girls and ladies who went to the carnival balls. My mother hit upon a profitable gig with these: She'd take sturdy wire, wrap it around itself to form a frame, and cover it up with cloth. Then she'd sew the cloth on and fix the hoops up so that you could wear them around your waist. Later she went to millinery school and learned to make hats—she loved to wear them, too, and almost always wore one of her jobs whenever she went out of the house.

When I was eight, my father used to send me down to Rappolo's Bar, a neighborhood joint, to get beers and sodas for him. There was an old guy named Gutierrez who used to hang out there, drinking his pluck, and I knew I could hustle him for a few quarters for the jukebox. My favorite songs now were the Joe Turner records with Pete Johnson on the piano, playing "Piney Brown" and "Jump for Joy." These songs, and later "One Room Country Shack" by Mercy Dee Walton, just used to gas me and thrill me right down to my toes. I'd listen to those records over and over, because I didn't yet have my own.

The old guys who'd talk to a little kid was few and far between. Most of the old-timers would say "Get the hell out of my face, kid," but a few of the old cats, seriously in their load, would take the time to rap with me. Mr. Gutierrez and another character named Mr. Pierson were among these. Mr. Gutierrez had worked with carnivals and minstrels and fascinated me with his stories. Like a lot of carnies, Mr. Gutierrez made everything rhyme, and he used a lot of words that were mysterious to me. I first heard about reefer, which he called "steam," from him. He called his reefer roach his "cocktail." "Yeah, this is my little steam dream," he'd say.

Mr. Gutierrez apparently used to work for the Rabbit Foot Minstrels and another minstrel group. Minstrel shows used to travel with the carnivals, and Mr. Gutierrez loved to go into great, long detail about his favorite routine, the geek act, during which a guy bit the head off a chicken—one of the things you did to draw a crowd. Also running with this gang of traveling vagabonds—they was like early rock and rollers—was one of the black street gangs/social clubs from New Orleans, called the Indians on account of how at Mardi Gras they dress up in Indian costumes to celebrate.

Whenever Mr. Gutierrez brought up the Indians, Mr. Pierson jumped into the conversation, and their long, old argument taught me a lot about New Orleans history. Mr. Pierson would say something like, "Man, the Indians who hung out with the Rabbit Foot Minstrels used to make their change selling beads."

And Mr. Gutierrez countered, "No, man, the Indians always got their bread off blankets and charms."

And so forth and so on, while Pete Johnson pounded out a stompdown boogie from the juke in the back of the bar.

Back at home, my mother and father didn't step out much. My father took me and my sister out to a boxing match every now and then. But my mother didn't go out in the evenings unless there was something particular that interested her—like a carnival ball, for instance, regulation stuff in New Orleans at the time. I never got off on these balls myself. They were always too formal, jive and stuffy for my taste, but my mother dug them. They always were one of the high points of her year.

My father was a real workaholic who slaved around the clock. After his appliance business folded, he scuffled hard to make a living, and he finally opened up a small record shop, repairing radios, phonographs, and PA systems on the side. He was so good-hearted, he'd fix anybody's radio or TV, and if you didn't have the money he'd take chickens or fish as payment. He took a lot of pride in his work: If you got him to fix something, he'd spend however long it took to do it. Unfortunately, I think that's one of the reasons he always had cash problems.

From the time I was really little, about five or six, I got to go hang out at his place, which was a hole-in-the-wall joint on Gentilly Road, right next to Dillard University. My father wasn't a musician, but he dug all different kinds of music. The stuff he liked, he stocked in his store—so-called race records (black R&B and blues of the time), gospel, bebop, jazz, hillbilly, and pop records. Generally, he had some tune playing when I was over there—if he didn't, I made sure he put something on. By the time I was seven or eight I had built myself up a collection of favorites for the record player at home. Before long, I was listening to records six hours a day on top of what I heard when I hung out at the store.

Once I started I couldn't get enough of those sounds. I remember one summer especially, when my whole family used to go out to the arcade on Lake Pontchartrain. This spot was a sort of open-air gazebo inside of which was rigged up a booth where you could record your own funky little songs and listen to records on a jukebox. I made a demonstration record saying I was crazy about three songs in particular: Gene Autry's "Blueberry Hill"; "Give Me That Old-Time Religion," a gospel song by Edna McGriff; and a schmaltzy version of "Long Ago and Far Away" by some band or other. Those are pretty strange songs for anyone to dig, but go figure why kids like anything at a given time.

My father was an easygoing guy when I was young. Things got rougher when I got older, but when I was a kid we got along fine. My mother was cool, too, although she was always pushing me to be with society-type people. One year she finagled to get me into a kids' Mardi Gras ball. She did me up a costume, a little prince's outfit or some such thing: I was getting into the get-up, but when she hit me with a wig I freaked. I hollered, threw the wig across the room and refused to wear it; she had to do a lot of calming me down before I let her put it back on.

My mother had her ideas about how things should be. She was always trying to get me dates with society-type girls, the good girls, all-right kinds of girls. But before too long I had turned in another direction. Once I got my bands together and she saw a whole different kind of girl coming around, she got the picture that things wasn't exactly working the way she had imagined. She wasn't too thrilled, but when she realized that her concept wasn't happening, she backed off. It's funny, too: Since then, I've met some of them same girls she used to lay on me, and it's the same thing now as then. I still can't relate to them. She meant well, but it just didn't make it. That's motherism for you.

Bit by bit I began to listen to all different kinds of sounds, everything from Roy Rogers to Roy Eldridge, Perez Prado to Prez, Hawkshaw Hawkins to Erskine Hawkins. My father somehow got his hands on old radio-station victory records from the war years; they spun backward, so the needle would move from the inside to the outside. I especially remember going nuts over Cab Calloway's songs. I spent a lot of time listening to the music, and watching the needle run backward on those old records.

Pretty soon, I began to hone my tastes and made a line for jazz and R&B. I listened to the old New Orleans riffs by King Oliver and Louis Armstrong and R&B and blues from Memphis Minnie and Big Bill Broonzy. I even remember copping to the jazz that was coming out on the first Blue Note 78s. At a certain point, when my father started selling bebop records, I picked up on bits and pieces of that kind of jazz. It wasn't so much that I was interested in the jazz sound itself; what I liked were the piano parts and the drums. I remember when I first heard Art Blakey, I thought, Man, I bet this guy's from New Orleans—I didn't know he was from Pittsburgh. I had a thing about New Orleans music, even though I didn't know exactly what it was about.

Guys like Art Tatum petrified me and made me never want to play the piano. He was such a two-fisted, twenty-fingered musician that I thought I could never equal the stuff he was putting down. On the other hand, pianists like Albert Ammons and Pete Johnson made me want to play. Their fast boogie shit— "Roll 'Em Pete" and "Swanee River Boogie"—excited me, and I thought, I want to be like that; that's what I want to do. I fixed in on that vision of myself playing the piano when I listened to those songs.

My father wasn't the only one who liked music. My mother,

sister, aunties, and uncles all gathered around to play; they took turns on the piano and sang together. Aunt Andre was real tough—she knew all the hip tunes of the time, whether it was the "St. James Infirmary" or "Everybody Loves My Baby." My Aunt Dottie Mae and Uncle John got good musicians together over at their house. Whenever he was around, my Uncle Gene, who was a boxer, would show up with my Aunt Andre, and everybody would jam off her piano. My Uncle Joe, who was married to my Aunt Myrtice, also played great boogie piano; he used to love to pound out them real hip Texas stomps. Aunt Dottie Mae played piano, too, and her old man John played a mean bass. Even my older Aunt Louella used to get into the act. She was the only real professional musician of the group: During the twenties and thirties she had held down a gig as a piano player at one of the silent movie theaters in town. Now she's a church organist in San Francisco.

Aunt Guerneri, who was married to my Uncle Johnny Guerneri, was another of my favorite aunts—but of the culinary rather than the musical variety. Aunt Guerneri lived around Carrollton, but we often walked to the French Quarter, a round-trip of several miles, to get ingredients for her meals.

Almost every night of the week she cooked huge six- or seven-course dinners. Every course left you stuffed and satisfied; I often couldn't get through it all. There was all kinds of things that people just don't make anymore: vinegar with blackberries, all kinds of pickled treats, and all made from scratch. One of my favorites was a strip of steak she wrapped around eggplant with shrimps and stuffed merliton (a green squash) with crawfish, which she then encased in a thin pie dough. I've asked the Alcia-toiles, the Brennans (both of whose families regularly ate at Aunt Guerneri's house), and other New Orleans restauranteurs if they ever have it on their menus, but none of them know it. This dish has disappeared—another little bit of vanishing New Orleans.

But Aunt Andre was my special partner. She knew everything, and that used to tickle me. She knew how to play "Texas Boogie," and took the time to teach it to me—that was the very first song I learned to play on the piano. I also learned from her how to listen to records over and over. Once, when her old man had left her and she was feeling bad, she listened to this Billie Holiday song, "Till the Real Thing Comes Along," over and over and over. I really dug that. Everybody else came around and said "Don't do that," because she was also way off into a crying jag. But I would get off when she played them records, because that's what I did when nobody else was around my house. We shared something secret. We were hypnotized by the riffs that were just right for whatever mood we happened to fall into.

Sometimes, if the jams couldn't be held at Aunt Dottie and Uncle John's house, Aunt Andre would have them at her pad. Auntie Dottie and Uncle John lived just six blocks from our place and Auntie Andre lived only five blocks away, so I was out on the streets a lot, running back and forth from one house to the other. It was the first time I was with a bunch of musicians with bass and drums and horns, my first experience being right in the middle of a jam session, and it opened up my head.

Some friends of mine also happened to be champion piano players. One of them was a girl named Earlie LeClaire, and she played a truly fine piano. Her dad, who was a friend of my parents, was also a killer. He stomped down on that classic New Orleans stride piano, and he knew all the stuff: Jelly Roll Morton, Albert Ammons boogie-woogie, Pinetop Smith, and all the rest. Earlie picked up a two-hand rhythm style from him that just scared the hell out of me. I got to know her pretty well, and later I used her as a backup singer on a number of recording dates. She was just as good a background singer as she was a piano player. She sight-read vocals and delivered them in perfect pitch. My sister Barbara was a fine singer and pianist, too; she played great versions of Pearl Bailey songs, with a killer sense of humor.

The Third Ward at that time was a racially mixed place, and it seemed to be busting with music. Everybody around town would be playing those songs my aunties and uncles played, but everyone did it just a bit differently. The music came from all kinds of sources, but one of the most interesting for me was laid down by the black Indian tribes. The tribes hung out together on the streets and in local bars; they usually formed small groups— tribes—of anywhere from half a dozen to a couple dozen members. Many of the Indians worked together, whether on the docks, at the brewery, or around the refineries. These neighborhood outfits maintained a real sense of pride about themselves, about being black, and about the black New Orleans heritage.

In the old days, there must have been several dozen tribes in the city: the Wild Squatoolas; the Yellow Pocahontas; the Red, White, and Blue; the Golden Blades; the Monogram Hunters; and others. Now there aren't quite as many, but every Mardi Gras those that are left still put on a parade like the old days. During their rambles, they played a real funky kind of street music, and got down seriously on that syncopated percussion beat known as the second line. The second line came originally from the rhythm of the music played in New Orleans funeral marches. It's basically a 2/4 beat with double-time accents that can be played a million different ways. The tribes got together throughout the year to practice their singing and percussion, so by the time Mardi Gras rolled around, they were ready to roll with it.

They would start to drift up to their clubhouse the night before Mardi Gras, and by sunup you could find them getting together in the street outside. Someone would have built a little fire outside, and they huddled around it, banging out the beat on bottles, sticks, and cans. Most of the Indians weren't professional musicians, but that didn't matter; the tribes weren't about professional-quality musicianship, they were about individuality. That's what was so wonderful about them. They went their own way and didn't give a shit about what anyone thought.

The tribes were tightly organized from top to bottom. The head man of each tribe was the Big Chief, who was the elder of the group. Next in line of authority came the Second Chief, then the Trail Chief; finally you got down to the Wild Man, who was in charge of clearing the streets so the tribe could parade and strut without obstruction to their destination. But when the tribe headed out on their parade, the lead man out front was the Spy

Boy, followed by the Flag Boy and the Wild Man. Last came the Big Chief and the rest of the tribe. One of my first memories of the tribes was of a Wild Man from a tribe called the White Eagles coming down the street on horseback, firing double-barrel shotgun loads of colored glass pellets into the air to get everyone's attention and clear the way—which he definitely succeeded in doing.

To keep an eye out for other tribes roaming around the city on Mardi Gras day, a tribe sent out the Spy Boy as a runner. If one Spy Boy bumped into another Spy Boy from some other tribe, they'd have an exchange like so:

"Om bah way," the first Spy Boy might say.

And the other Spy Boy, if everything was cool and there wasn't going to be no confrontation, answered: "Tu way pocky way."

This talk was the Indian's own Creole language, part French, part Spanish, part Choctaw, part Yoruba, and part mystery to an outsider like me. What the first one said basically was, "Where yaatt, bro?" or the like. And the second one said, "Everything's oaks and herbs"—which means everything's cool because they had smoked lots of herbs. If the second one responded "No om bah way," then y'all had problems, and a challenge by way of each and other had been issued. If neither backed down, the word was passed on to the rest of the tribe by the Flag Boy, who carried a banner, a spear, or some sort of emblem representing the tribe. After a while the main bodies of the two tribes finally came together for a confrontation, which centered on the Big Chiefs. They wouldn't get it on right away, because first the two tribes mingled, said their how-you-dos, and in general stopped in the nearest bar to party for a while. After a time, though, the good-natured ribbing built up to a crescendo that could be settled by only the Big Chiefs.

One Big Chief and his whole tribe tried to out-attitude the other Big Chief and tribe, engaging one another in their own brand of stylized language. One might say: "Big Chief come in thunder and lightnin'. Big Chief come and the strong be frighten'." And the first would come back: "Mighty Big Chief have fire and thunder. If the fools don't move it make you wonder."

Then the game was on, each and other talking this rumbling poetry and moving around in a kind of dance. While all this was happening, the chiefs were dressed to the nines in their special costumes with long feathered headdresses, glass bead patches, and all kinds of ribbon and glitter. I mean, it was like Sunday High Mass, but more soulful.

It used to be that these exchanges got violent, and it wasn't uncommon for tribes to end up shooting and shanking their way downtown. But by the time I came around, most often they were peaceful: The chiefs just tried to see who could outjive the other, like playing the dozens to see who could outdo whom in exaggeration.

Back in the late forties and early fifties, there were twenty or thirty tribes in New Orleans, so on Mardi Gras you'd have hundreds of tribesmen out on the street all over town. Each tribe had a different route through town, but the uptown tribes often started in Shakespeare Park and ended at twilight around Robertson and Dumaine streets. St. Roch Park was another favorite spot for some of the downtown tribes, because it had a lot of voodoo vibes attached to it. In any event, by the evening the tribes had decamped at one of the city parks, where they built bonfires, or stopped at a bar and played music and danced. Then the tribes had another big to-do on St. Joseph's Day, when the Queens of the tribes danced and jumped over bonfires, which was another part of their ritual.

One of the gangs was made up of all the whores and pimps from Perdido Street; their parade was called Gangster Molls and Baby Dolls. Everyone in this group dressed as outlandishly as possible: The women wore eye-popping dresses; the ones who looked highest-priced wore ultra-sharp women's suits, but with see-through bras underneath. Others wore slit miniskirts showing lace panties, stiletto heels, and flowery low-cut blouses. The pimps got decked out in acey-deucy Stetsons with cocked brims, jelly-roll-peg zoot suits, one-button roll coats with wide lapels, and zebra-skinned shoes; not infrequently, they'd strut down the street with canes made out of bull dicks.

They were ridiculous and funny all at the same time. They'd come busting out of their dives during Mardi Gras, their dresses and suits lined in satin and glitter, real sharp-looking and hilarious. They'd march down the greens, that broad strip of grass that separates one side of the street from the other, cutting up, shakin' the bacon and carrying on, and everyone would back off to let them start high-steppin'. And you had best back off, too, because they took their kicks seriously. They were real rowdy. Cats would brandish switchblades, and whip them out in your face if you got too close. The tribes always drew a big crowd of black and white folks, but this kind of thing seemed normal to me as a kid. Didn't every town have tribes? I thought so.

The Third Ward back then was a real livable place—not always peaceful or safe, but it was comfortable. Like every city in the South, it was segregated into its black and white neighborhoods; generally, the uptown side of the ward was black, the downtown white. Because we were white, my family lived in a white neighborhood of the Third Ward. But this pattern of segregation didn't follow no strict line: The area around my house was arranged into a funky checkerboard of races, a couple of black blocks side by side with a chunk that was white. And even within the white and black neighborhoods, you'd find families here and there of other races. In spite of the best efforts of segregationists, the races had a natural tendency to mingle and mix, jook and jive, rock and roll. Wherever you went—black neighborhood or white—there was a real feeling of community.

This isn't to say that it couldn't get rough out on the streets. The Third Ward had its share of street gangs, and occasionally guys got shanked and killed in gang fights. This action wasn't necessarily racial. Most of the time, it was just one gang against the other. I can remember a kid named Chattanooga who was a partner of mine when I was real young. One day a couple of the kids from one of the gangs opened up on him with BB guns or zip guns and put his eye out, blew a hole through his face. I was on the horrors from this. Every time some action started, it always seemed there was some bully pushing some other guy to do something he wouldn't have done on his own. That always bugged me. I mean, if this one guy was such a badass punk, then how come he couldn't pull it off himself? I stayed away from the really rough stuff when I was a kid. My scene was the music, not the gangs.

Around my eighth birthday, my father began to take me and my sister, Bobbie, along with him when he went out to fix PA systems at the clubs around town. Bobbie was crazy about the music, too, and since she was older she'd been going with him for a while before I ever went. Pop didn't want to bring me along at first, but that didn't seem right to me, so I let my attitude be known: I bugged him so much that he finally gave in and let me hang with him.

Even then, though, he was careful to make sure we didn't actually go inside the clubs. I'd sit in the car while he worked, listening to what was going on—the only way I could hear the local bands. When the PA was working, I heard the music real good. The sounds blew out into the street from places like the Pepper Pot and the Cadillac Club, and I got high on the riffs. It was at these places that I got my first taste of local acts such as the Papa Celestin band, Dave Bartholomew, the Basin Street Six, Professor Longhair, and a hundred others.

My father was always on my case about staying in the car, but if the band was on a break, I'd try to go meet them. If they were sitting on a crate outside, I'd jump out of the car real fast and go rap with them. Dad didn't consider this cool; he figured I was too young to be hanging out. He was right. He caught me, kicked my ass.

But I was fascinated by those cats. Professor Longhair, Roy Brown, and Dave Bartholomew were heroes of mine. I knew their records, and saw posters all over town bearing their names and pictures. Professor Longhair, in particular, moved me. His songs "Tipitina" and "Bald Head" were being played all around town.

I remember one time peeking into a window and watching him from the back as his long, thin fingers ran across the keys.

Being around that environment had a lot to do with my deciding I wanted to be a musician. Listening to those cats made me dream of being like them, of being one of those guys who had loads of flash, fancy pianos, and a lot of dough. All that flash looked good to a kid. But I had a few illuminations real fast. Around the time I began sitting in on my aunties' jam sessions and hanging around in the clubs, I began to get hipped in a little more to reality: There were an awful lot of good piano players, and not nearly enough jobs to go around. How was I ever going to compete with killer players like Tuts Washington? Salvador Doucette? Herbert Santina? Professor Longhair himself? And the list only began there. So I began to pick up on the guitar players. I became a fan of Walter "Papoose" Nelson, who played with Fats Domino. And after thinking about it for a while, I decided to take guitar lessons; I figured I might as well play something I could get a job at.

What finally pushed me into taking up the guitar was a long stint of illness. Around my seventh birthday, I'd been laid up with a touch of malaria; for months, I couldn't play with kids my age. I must have driven everyone crazy, because finally, when I had begun to recover, my mother had arranged for me to take guitar lessons from a guy named Al Guma at Werlein's music store, a well-known place in town. Mr. Guma was a respected New Orleans musician; he gigged around town some, but mainly he dedicated himself to teaching. His brother Paul was a little better-known: He played with Pete Fountain, and from time to time so did Al.

Al tried to teach me to read guitar music, but I faked it. I had this ability to take a run that I heard and play it back—instead of reading, I was copying. Finally, he said to my mother, "Mrs. Rebennack, I don't think your son is learning how to read music. He's got a good ear, but he's not learning how to read. When he hears something, he just picks it." That was it for our short-lived connection.

He was right: From the minute I got a guitar, I sat in my room listening to records and copying licks. I fixed in heavy on Lightnin' Hopkins and T-Bone Walker; I played their songs day and night. That was my serious thing. I mean, I wanted to *be* T-Bone Walker, and I said to myself, "If I can't make it as T-Bone, I'll try Lightnin'."

After Mr. Guma gave up on me, my father talked to Papoose Nelson, and Papoose agreed to take me on. The first lesson, Papoose listened to my chops and said, "Hey, man, you can't play that shit and get a job. What are you, crazy? That outta-meter, foot-beater jive. You gotta play stuff like this." Then he started playing me legitimate blues, which I was on the trail of with T-Bone Walker. It was the Lightnin' shuffle that was off the wall as far as Papoose was concerned.

Papoose got down to rearranging my licks in a hurry. He knew his R&B and jazz inside out; it came from the source. Not only did he play guitar for Fats Domino; *his* father, Louis Nelson, had played guitar with Louis Armstrong, so Papoose had deep New Orleans roots. He was a real soulful player, probably the most soulful guitar teacher I had.

To point me in the right direction, Papoose insisted I learn to read music, and got me to listening to other guys, like Billy Butler and Mickey Baker. These two were defining the sound of rhythm and blues guitar at the time. Mickey played on millions of R&B records, everybody from Ray Charles to Little Willie John. He affected a style that guitar players copy even today. Billy had a real classy and hip sound that was still bluesy and deep. Papoose, just like Huey Smith and James Booker later when I was learning more about the piano, tried to get me to grow, to learn something a little more sophisticated. I didn't even know what sophisticated meant at the time, but I was open to suggestions.

Papoose played a style that was akin to Billy Butler's. He could play bluesier when he worked with guys like Professor Longhair, but when he worked with a band like Fats Domino's, which was most of the time, he slipped into a smoother sound.

And Papoose wouldn't let me listen to just the blues. I had to key into other things, like pop and jazz. I had listened to that stuff before, but I hadn't *really* listened. I hadn't clued into the guitar parts. As I got a little older, Papoose insisted that I learn jazz, even though I wasn't feeling it in my soul yet. And then, all of a sudden, I'm not learning traditional jazz, but a little progressive, too. He would run me through a tough jazz piece, just comping chords for him while he stretched out. Papoose busted my balls, but this routine began to give me some musical discipline. "You got to learn something in the first guitar position," he'd say—then, right in the middle of the tune, he'd yell out "Second position!" and I'd have to scramble my way up the fretboard. It was a funny setup; I didn't really appreciate what he was doing for me until much later.

After I had studied with him for a while, Papoose started going out on long road gigs with Fats, so he turned me over to Roy Montrell, who became my longest-running teacher. Roy played a strong guitar, not as soulful as Papoose, but hard-driving.

Before my first lesson with Roy, my father took me out to buy a brand-new guitar. I had been hitting on him for a new one for a while now, but he had resisted my pleas because he didn't have all that much money, and wasn't sure how serious I was about the music business. When he finally took me downtown, I picked out a cheap but flashy-looking green-and-black Harmony. I was just thrilled to death with it, couldn't wait to try it out with my new teacher.

My first lesson: Roy took one look at the guitar and croaked, in that always-raspy voice, "Why'd you bring this piece of shit over here?"

"It's my guitar," I said.

"Give me that guitar." He took it, walked outside into the backyard, laid it down on the ground, picked up an ax, and split it right in half. Then he broke it to pieces and threw it in his neighbor's yard.

I stood there in a state of shock, staring at the crazy bastard I had as my teacher, and wondering what I was going to tell my father.

After Roy had finished decomposing my guitar, he called up my pa at work and told him, "Hey, nobody can play on that jive piece of wood your son brought over here. You want me to teach him guitar? Come on, we'll go get him a guitar." All three of us went over to a pawnshop, and Roy picked out a Gibson for me. My father didn't say a word until later; apparently, Roy had taken him aside and told him, "I taught your son a lesson, that you don't get things because of the way they look. You get them on how they work." My pa told me I'd have to work off the money he'd spent for the Gibson by putting in more time at his shop, so for a long time after that I worked extra hours over at his place.

Once we fixed the matter of what kind of guitar I was going to play, Roy got down to basics. He was a pretty slick con artist, and he had a way of teaching that kept me coming back for more. During the lesson, he strung me along with ordinary riffs—but then right at the end he'd play some killer lick, his back turned so I couldn't see his fingers, and say, "Hey, wanna learn that shit, kid? Come back next week. Now get the fuck outta here." The tricks worked. I became a regular student.

I used to go over to Roy's for my guitar lessons. Roy lived in a peculiar arrangement with his auntie at her place on Kerlerec Street. The auntie had a building that was partly a storefront church and partly her house. She had a little room with a few chairs and an altar in the front, and she lived toward the back. Roy's little pad was even farther back in the yard, behind the church and the woodshed.

His aunt's name was Sister Elizabeth Eustace; they made a strange pair. Sister Eustace was a missionary lady; Roy was a stone jazz and R&B player. She'd laid a number on Roy, and somehow kept him in line for years, helping her out on guitar in her gospel performances. By the time I came along he had grown tired of this situation; con man that he was, he managed to slide me into Sister Eustace's gigs as a sub.

Now, I mean, I still barely knew the guitar at this point. One day I'd be scuffling with some twenty-year-old rum-dum tune, the next I was struggling with her arrangements at a sanctified church across town. She had one style of arrangement that she'd do just at her church, another set when she went out on missionary work, and a third set she'd lay down when she spread the gospel stuff with a Dixieland band.

She was a presence. By the time I came onto the scene, she had already cut a lot of albums and was very much a known quantity on the gospel circuit. She dragged me around here and there, and each time it was different. I never knew what I was going to get into with her. I had to learn on the run; it got so I could follow tunes like "I Shall Not Be Moved" through alleys inconceivable to man. I heard songs from her that I'd never heard before or since, though I figured they were there somewhere in a hymnbook.

Once she took the band out to some tiny almost-town in the bayou. They set up in a little striped tent, and it commenced to pour down rain. Everybody in the tent—band members and congregation—got soaked. Somebody had brought along a set of batteries for the guitars and her mike, because there wasn't no electricity to plug into. About the middle of the service, the batteries got all wet from the rain, and we lost the juice. The sound just slipped away like water going down a drain, but nobody stopped playing or singing. The spirit was so high in that little tent, the loss of the amps didn't faze nothing.

You would think with all the pandemonium of the spirit swirling around, she wouldn't have paid much mind to the music—but that wasn't how Sister Eustace operated. She had a sharp set of ears, and if I blew one chord in a song she knew it. She was always on my case. Every now and then, she'd call me aside after a gig and tell me that if I didn't get my act together she'd have to let me go and start up with Roy again, 'cause Roy knew her music. That kind of sermon hurt my feelings, because I was beginning to enjoy some of the gigs. They'd always have good food at these affairs, and a little wine, and lots of soft drinks. I guess I'd begun to feel like part of the family.

We never got paid a dime for working with Sister Elizabeth Eustace; she wouldn't even reimburse us for expenses. She was about helping people, but she was also a fanatical zealot. At first she scared me half to death, but then, bit by bit, I grew to dig her. But I didn't really have a chance to play with her very long, because after a time I got off into something else and left her far behind. A fella I'd met had put me into his own schemes, figured me into his plans in a big way. In short order, I left Sister Eustace and her sanctified music to become Shank's regular little gofer and running partner.

JUNKO PARTNER

> I got a woman in the Parish
> And another in the House of D;
> Another one in San Gabriel
> Doing my time for me.
>
> —"Junkie Blues"
> (traditional)

By the time I made it to the third or fourth grade, I had developed a taste for hopping the train and riding out toward Gentilly Road instead of going to school. I had a friend out there, and we'd go round up a few other kids to hang out with. One of us would go into a hardware store and steal a sinker, another rustled up some bait, and we'd go fishing. That was fun while it lasted, but I wasn't long into innocent kid stuff before I found better things to do.

Among the discoveries I made were the rhythm-and-blues clubs down on Canal Street—and the cutting contests that went with them.

There were so many killer piano players floating around in those days that an unwritten law of the jungle had come down. It was simple, and went like this: You had better be able to cut somebody—beat them at their own piano game—or you wouldn't get a club date. To get and keep regular club gigs, you had to be a bad motherfucker. In a cutting contest you'd have a band playing, with four or five piano players sitting at the table next to the bandstand. The regular player would work his stuff, and after a while the band leader or club owner would call up the guys known as the "cutters." The first cat would come up, slide onto the bench, and keep it going. And he had better cut the original guy, or he sure wouldn't last long. If he did real bad, the band would just end the song on a key change. It could be that cold.

The guy who blew everybody else away ended up being the one who kept the gig with the band at the club. The guy whose job it had been usually ended up with a two-week notice, if he was lucky, and a case of the chronic sweats. That kind of shit happened all the time—and it wasn't just the piano players who had something to fear. When they had cutting contests, the focus could change suddenly to any guy on the bandstand.

The contests started all kinds of ways. It might be just one guy wanting to steal another guy's job. The actual cutting most often happened after hours, when musicians got off other gigs. Two or three players might get around and start conspiring against the guy holding the slot the others coveted. I saw this kind of action all over town while I was growing up. I mean, you'd see cats get annihilated so bad the poor suckers would never find a good gig again. People could make you look so lame you'd be plexed forever after.

Usually the flashiest guy—but not necessarily the hippest player—would come out ahead in a cutting contest. It could be a real sad scene: You'd see some piano player with all kinds of flashy hand stuff draw musical blood. The guy'd look great, even if he didn't always sound that good. But that's show biz.

I didn't know anything about all this back in the days when I was hanging around outside the clubs with my father. Later, I realized I must have been hearing cutting contests all the way back then. I remember one sax contest at the Norwegian Seaman's Hall that stayed with me: When I got there, I saw one tenor player up there really cooking. I was hanging near the doorway of the club, and my father didn't glimmer me for a while, so I got to see a second guy glow and get serious house. He'd cut the first one. My father saw me while the joint was still raisin' sand up, and scooted me out of there fast.

Later I saw a lot of these showdowns. Some clubs had a real attitude about them. Paul Gayten had regular cutting contests at his club, the Brass Rail on Canal Street. Canal Street was a happening area at the time; in a couple of blocks you could find three or four jumping juke joints—the Monkey Bar, the Texas Lounge, and the Brass Rail being the hottest.

I got to know Paul when I was in fifth or sixth grade. I'd skip going to Mass at Sacred Heart, jump on a streetcar, and slide down to the Brass Rail first thing in the morning to hear their last set. About eight in the morning was prime cutting and after-hours time. The clubs had been open all night and everyone was burning hot before they crashed for the rest of the day.

Hearing this last set was heaven for me. Paul had the best singers, musicians, and entertainers in New Orleans. He had a chick named Annie Laurie who was the house singer for the band; she had a hit called "Since I Fell For You," and she used to blow me away. Most of the guys in the house band were the same cats who became the standard studio musicians for Cosimo Matassa's J&M Studio later on: Lee Allen on sax, Frank "Dude" Fields on bass, and Charlie Williams, whom they used to call "Hungry," on the drums.

Usually, I wouldn't have to hang around outside the club for very long. Pretty quickly, I got to be tight with the band members and a drummer named Frankie Parker, who would call for me to come inside and listen as soon as I showed up. I would just take a seat in the back of the club, where it was dark, and watch. I didn't want to stand out too much; I was afraid the police would come in and throw me out.

Gayten was a piano player with his own band at his club. Naturally he had figured the rules of his contest real carefully. He'd get up first and run through a set, then he'd step aside and emcee while the rest of the cats blew one another away. He wasn't as cold-blooded as some cats, 'cause everything he did was seasoned with class.

I first heard tenor saxman Sam Butera, who later worked as a sideman for Louis Prima and Frank Sinatra and just about everybody else, at a cutting contest with Lee Allen there at the Brass Rail. This was at a time when Sam was real popular locally. He had a couple of hits out, "Easy Rockin'" and "Chicken Scratch," which naturally I knew. He was a big thing. I remember how he walked in the bar and caught everyone's attention immediately with his personality. He got up onstage, grabbed his tenor, and blew his ass off. He *was* show biz, as far as I was concerned. The whole scene was so sweet it was almost sugar diabetes, and I just couldn't get enough of it.

Right down the street was a place called the Texas Lounge, where I occasionally popped in to hear Roy Montrell play—I met him for the first time there at the Texas. Since I was crazy about the music scene and Roy was a friendly guy, before long I was welcomed in there, too. When he was out in the world, not just helping me along in my picking, Roy played a really far-out guitar style. Some of the stuff he played reminded me of some bebop turned avant-garde sound; it just wasn't the kind of thing guitarists do, even to this day. That was his personality coming through in his music—he liked to push things to the limit.

Listening to Roy, I also got to know Red Tyler, the sax player in Earl Williams's band who later got to be the leader of Cosimo's studio group. So it was a very small, very intimate little scene at the time; it was easy to slot into, but at the same time competitive as hell if you were a musician.

Roy used to drag me into the Texas Lounge. I was just starting to learn guitar, and Roy used to put a bug in my ear with the things he would say, like "Hey, kid, to play guitar, you gotta learn a lot of shit. I don't know, maybe you'd be better off learning piano." That opened my nose real wide. It made me determined to understand the guitar.

I liked to hang out with the musicians as much as I could. At the Texas Lounge, I'd go all the way to the back of the club to the dark little booth where the white club owner made the black band members sit. The idea was that they were supposed to disappear after showtime. It was a jive situation, but the cats took their little area and got their partners to sneak in and they ended up doing what they wanted without too much hassle. I just sat there, quiet as a mouse, and listened to them cutting up on their break.

I loved hanging around them guys, and I learned a lot from them. They played every standard in the world; they had moves for songs that transformed them into another dimension, and I thought: Oh, my God, they actually make this shit-music that I hate sound good.

Paul Gayten did the same thing, but in a whole 'nother way. He never played a song the same way twice. One time it might be a ballad, the next time he'd turn it into a cha-cha, the next a meringue, the next a mambo. It would change. There was no standard arrangement. They took any request the audience threw at them, but if they didn't like it, they'd mock it. That's what got me hooked on Gayten's band. They didn't look at no music like it was sacred. They just fucked with it, and that was so hip to me.

Paul was also progressive—and tough—about his views of race. He was instrumental in breaking up the strict color line that prevailed at that time in the clubs and recording studios in New Orleans. He got Sam Butera a gig to record with his outfit on a radio show he hosted for a while in the early fifties, and later he helped me get some of my first recording sessions with the studio cats, many of whom were black. He also helped other white musicians, like Jimmy Clanton and Bobby Charles, break into the R&B scene. At his own club, he ignored the segregation laws as much as he was able to and still keep the place open. Paul just didn't go along with the program of keeping blacks and whites apart. If you came out publicly with this view in the fifties, you were putting your ass in a sling: He had to take all kinds of flak from folks, especially the black music union 496 and the vice squad. But in his own soft-spoken way he saw that battle through; eventually, his way won the battle, but not the war, which still continues.

I think what got Paul through all this was his funny sense of attitude. Nothing would faze him. Somebody would come up and insult the band, and he'd turn around and make a rib out of it. He knew how to keep things from getting uptight, because he didn't let nothing get next to him. I think Paul's attitude revealed one of the real important secrets of why the New Orleans music scene in the fifties stayed alive. Guys played music and didn't get caught up too much in ego battles among one another or in the jive-ass race-hatred that intruded from the outside world, and even from some of the so-called free-and-easy set on the inside. Today, now that all of this is completely turned around—at least in the music business—it's hard to see that back then musicians had to maintain this cool in order to survive.

I made the club scene part of my life. By 1952–1953, when I was in sixth or seventh grade, my running schedule read like this: Skip Mass and hang down at the clubs on Canal, but try to make it back for the morning classes at Sacred Heart. After school, go over to hang out at the house of another musician I had met on Canal Street, a guy named Shank. Gradually, my hangout time began to intrude with school. A lot of the reason for this, besides the music, had to do with dope.

I started messing around with narcotics when I was about twelve. First I tried a little reefer; I liked the way it made me feel, and I liked the lifestyle that went along with being high and feeling good. I had a lot of junko partners, but Shank was the cat who turned me on to drugs in a really serious way. Shank needed plenty of tending to. He liked to move around only when necessary, and sooner or later the question always came around—who was going to go get him his sandwiches or his beer, or his reefer?

Before long, he had me running all over town copping narcotics for him. I got to know the projects—Magnolia, St. Bernard, and others—pretty well. They hid stuff there in the 'jecks, or else, if one of his dealers had another connection to make, the dealer would leave Shank's stuff at some drop-off point. One time I was supposed to go over to an alley in the Magnolia 'jecks and pick up a bag of reefer wrapped in butcher paper that was hidden under a trash can. I made that run three times before I found the stuff; by then people were peeking out their windows and whispering to one another, wondering what a little white kid like me was hunting for under garbage cans in the alley.

My mother and Shank had an interesting relationship. My mother always used to tell me how much she trusted him. Naturally, she was curious about who I was hanging with and didn't want me going off with dubious characters—which, of course, Shank was. Yet he charmed the socks off her, even though she knew he wasn't wrapped perfectly straight. One Christmas we went over to his house and found his tree decorated with joints of reefer. My mother knew what it was, but she thought it was the funniest thing in the world. If anybody else had done that, she would have got uptight.

I was pretty loose with my habits, and my mother and father used to find decks of reefer and pills in my pockets. I told my parents that the stuff wasn't mine, that I was just holding for friends. At first, my mother got upset with me, but after a while all she did was warn me that I'd get busted if I didn't change my ways. My father stayed upset, and we had a lot of arguments, but he never pushed me to the wall about the issue; maybe this was because I'd learned to stash a little better.

All of this drug activity was made even worse in my parents' eyes because of race. A lot of my friends at the time—musicians I had met in the clubs, and others—were black, and a lot of them were somewhat older than I was. Now in general, for their time my parents were pretty loose about race. They didn't mind me hanging out with my black friends as long as these cats didn't start hanging on the stoop of our house. They didn't actually object to having my friends inside; what bothered them was the flak they would get from the neighbors because of the commotion my black friends made. One of the problems was that they were all dressing outrageously for the time—wearing zoot suits, big old hats, and the like. These kinds of outfits were considered unacceptable by a lot of people. At one point, my father even told me to bring my friends through the back door. But I didn't give in, and gradually they stopped hammering on me about that.

With all this happening—strange-looking cats coming and going, dope and powders being discovered in my pockets—I always thought my mother, in spite of her protests, got a little charge out of it. The truth was, I think my mother unconsciously dug reefer, or at least enjoyed the idea of a marygeranium high. I remember there were times when my partners and I would sit around in my room, smoking mootahs, and the room would be full of smoke. After a while, my mother would come in, and before long she'd be laughing and cutting up because she was getting a contact high. I don't know if she ever knew what we were doing to her, but she sure got high, and all she could do was caution us to be careful.

Before long, Shank began sending me out for heavier stuff than marijuana. One day he told me to go out and get works for him. I knew about heroin, but I didn't completely understand what it did or how you went about fixing and shooting up. Shank told me to go to this particular drugstore and ask for a certain pharmacist. His instructions were exact. "Go get me two sets of D.B. 23's"—a specific type of needle—"and get me some eyedroppers and some baby pacifiers. . . ." The procedure for shooting up was a lot more complicated than it is now, but those rigs, if you put them together right, were actually safer than the ones people use now.

I went in, asked for the pharmacist, and laid down my order. A couple of customers were waiting for prescriptions to be filled, and I remember heads swiveling around and the pharmacist leaning over me, inquiring as to whether I had somehow got hold of the wrong list. I explained that it was for Shank and he filled the order, no questions asked.

When I got back to Shank's house, I asked him if I could watch. I'd seen my Cousin Snake fix before and I wanted to hang around to see how Shank did it.

"No!" Shank said, real indignant-like, "go into the other room, kid."

I was pissed. I figured he at least owed me a lesson for going to get him the stuff. But in spite of Shank's slightly good intentions, it was just a matter of time before I learned the system. Later I even got to be friends with the same pharmacist when I was going for myself.

After that trip to the pharmacy, I hit the narcotic trail for Shank with a vengeance. He didn't have to use any cons on me to get me to do it—I jumped into the game wholeheartedly. What people sometimes don't realize about the whole drug scene is that it can thrill as well as chill and kill. I was getting my kicks off running around with Shank.

There was this place in the St. Bernard projects where he used to send me to get him coke sometimes. Going there was a charge for me. He used to send me with this other kid, another young musician; we would slide over there at night and it was a little creepy. One time, we got to the dopeman's pad and knocked on the door with the right code knock, but the guy wouldn't let us in. He kept wanting to know who we were and what we wanted. "You police, ain't you?" he said again and again. Police, shit. We were only kids, thirteen or so. And meanwhile people had come out into the hall and were staring at us real hard. These folks weren't necessarily thrilled to see white kids on their turf. They were hanging out and signifyin' and we were just stuck there, praying the guy would let us in quick. We could have pissed in our pants, we were so scared. This was something hip and uncool at the same time—raw excitement like a DA's indictment.

Finally the guy let us in. It turned out that was just his way of ribbing us, but I didn't see it that way at the time. Later, when I knew this guy better, I saw he was good people, a funny cat. I guess making us stand out in that hallway was just his way of running us through changes, to see if we'd panic. Who knows?

Occasionally, I had to make fairly serious marches to get some of this stuff, and from time to time I'd be late showing up back at Shank's. If I came in too late, he'd be pissed off. He needed to get his sick off. His habit was an oil-burner, and he expected me to fly across town double-time for him. He'd bitch and moan, but—slick con that he was—he always had a way of making me laugh after the excitement had died down and he was in his load.

And if Shank's narcotics operations wasn't enough, he capped it off with the way he maneuvered my girlfriends. By the time I was fourteen or fifteen, I had a few girls I'd bring over to meet my guru and partner, the man who was showing me all this streetside action. Sometimes the girls was older than I was—say, seventeen or eighteen. Some of them wanted to be singers, some just liked hanging with musicians. Now, Shank would take them aside and tell them that if they wanted to be *really* good singers they'd have to give him head, because his come would make them sing sweet and rich. The strange thing was, a lot of them went for the okeydoke.

This went on for a couple of years. The music and narcotics business took more and more of my energy away from school. By the time I was fifteen, I had been studying guitar for several long years, and had played the piano for even longer than that. During that year, 1955, I moved from Sacred Heart grade school to high school. My parents were Catholics, so I had always attended parochial schools. To get into the best of them, Jesuit High, you had to take a special test; it was a tough joint, with high academic standards and a strict reputation. I didn't think I had a chance in hell. So I was shocked when word came back that I'd copped a high score and would be accepted.

I'd done well enough in school before then. I always was good in reading and history, but at Jesuit they threw Latin at me, and I couldn't even fake the French I knew with those people. On top of that, it was an all-guys' school. I had always been around girls, but all of a sudden all I could see was a bunch of guys. I made one or two friends, but that was it. All of these changes had a lot to do with why I just gave up on it and didn't give a shit about anything—especially after I got kicked out of Jesuit.

Trouble was, I'd sit in class and spend my time reading

comic books like "Tales From the Crypt," and writing songs. When school was out, I hustled over to Specialty Records, a major R&B label with an office in New Orleans, and gave them what I'd been working on at school. I scored with them on a bunch of these songs: a few with Little Richard, who was in and out of New Orleans a lot during that time, and Art Neville, who was still pretty much unknown, playing with the Hawkettes. I didn't make much off these songs, maybe thirty or forty dollars each. But that was decent pocket money for a high school kid, and having my songs recorded and published was pretty heavy stuff.

So I was in a trick bag. On one side, I had one foot in the free-and-easy money--or so I thought at the time—of the music business; on the other, I was stuck in the shuck of high school. I hated the regimentation of Jesuit, the khaki uniforms and short haircuts they forced on you. At Sacred Heart, I had begun to get into a certain kind of look—a slicked-back ducktail cut with a lick coming down in front—and I couldn't get behind what the padres and the penguins were laying down at all. I didn't like it from the jump.

Around that time, I had joined a band with a group of my friends, called the Spades. One of our gigs was for a talent show held around Christmas at Jesuit High. I came in there loaded, playing R&B covers of Fats Domino, Lloyd Price, all the rest. All the winners before us had played stuff like Glenn Miller swing and Dixieland jazz. The priests were outraged enough by our songs, but it was really our style they hated. One of the teachers put me down like a dog; he had me kicked out of school because of the way I played guitar. This cat claimed I was tickling my testicles and scratching my scrotum with my guitar. I don't know about that; I was just putting on a show, and I think he didn't appreciate the fact that we won. My father got real salty over this accusation; he told the cat to take off his collar and come into the street. The result, for me, was probation. That was the final straw for the band. I remember that soon after this incident, it snowed. Snow don't come often in New Orleans. Leonard James, who played sax in our band, and I saw these snowflakes coming down like some kind of illumination. We looked at each other and said: "That's it. Let's go on the road." And that was the end of school for me.

A little bit before this happened, I had become curious about junk. Besides Shank, my Cousin Snake also did opiates, and I always used to tell him, "Man, you'll never see me do what you do. I'll never use myself for no pin cushion." But as I got older, my thinking changed.

Not very many white musicians were into heroin back then. On the white side of the dope-and-music business it wasn't considered cool. A lot of them went for goofballs: Nembutal, Seconal, tuinal, phenobarbital. The nals, we used to call them—the junk-a-dope-a-nals. The ones who were into the opiates usually copped drugstore stuff, everything from Dilaudids and morphine to codeine in some of its better forms and tincture of opium. But that was all watered-down crap as far as your really hip dope fiends were concerned. Especially tincture of opium. Tincture of opium was viewed as low-class, strictly for low-riders.

I had tried Dilaudids with my Cousin Snake, but they didn't get me off. I suspected him of shorting me by giving me a cotton shot; that made me mad, and I was pissed bad for a while thereafter. Finally, I went over to Shank's and demanded that he give me a taste of some good shit. I'd seen him fix loads of times by this point, so I knew how it was *done*; what I wanted to know was how it *felt*. Looking back, my perspective on my father had a lot to do with this new attitude; he hated dope fiends, and was warning me to stay away from them—but when I looked around, most of the famous musicians I'd heard of were junkies. That was a heavy influence on me: It was my way of turning away from him, and joining the set I dug.

Shank, as usual, bad-mouthed the idea. "No, man—what are you, crazy? Stick with your weed and goofballs. They make you high. This shit don't make you high. It make you dope-sick." But I wouldn't let go of it. I explained to him what had happened with Snake, and eventually he broke down and cooked up some of his stuff for me. I was sitting on a stool strumming a guitar, and I remember what he said: "Okay, you want some of this? You're going to get it today. You've finally pissed me off. Now let go the guitar neck." He took a baby pacifier and tied it with thread around the large open end of an eyedropper. He fitted the needle, or what we called the point, into the narrowed end. Then he secured the eyedropper by cutting off the cuff of a dollar bill, the little white part on the corner, and tying it with thread tightly around the outside of the dropper. That was real dope-fiend works. Hypodermics were considered strictly amateur-night stuff.

He gave me a mainline hit right there. The high I got was immediately satisfying. I had never felt that way off reefer or hash and never got that kind of high off goofballs. I felt like I was thirty feet tall, like everything made sense. The high didn't really make much difference in my playing; it was for my heart and soul. The music some days might have been better, others worse. But that's life. That's how it would have been with or without the junk.

One of the reasons those highs were so tremendous was that the stuff that came through New Orleans was real, 100 percent Corsican junk that came straight off the boats from Cuba uncut. To check the purity of the dope, you fixed up a little pinhead of it for a test. Once you had gauged its purity, you did a little more. The good stuff was tasty—I mean it literally had a taste all its own that you could sense in your mouth. Low-quality stuff had an almost medicinal taste, and gave you a morphine flash, which is like the sharp pricks of pins and needles in your skin and makes your hands feel like they're going to sleep. High quality comes on slowly, and you get a ginger taste on your tongue just before you nod out. The smooth, slow feel was what we were looking for. It's funny what you remember about those times: I recall that dope that originated from the Corsicans was sometimes molded in hard cakes with the face of a little boy on it—an innocent face, indicating purity.

I quickly started to do it every day while I was in what would be my last year of high school. Back then, dope wasn't that expensive—a fifty-cent cap lasted for days. Shank cautioned me to do it just a little bit at a time. For him and the others, heroin was primarily about maintaining a habit. To maintain it and live, you had to be careful; back when I first started, a match-head's worth of dope shaken up in a little bit of water could kill you in a second. It could be that high-grade.

Later, when I got to know him, Professor Longhair warned me against heroin. He'd say, "Those narcotics you doing is just going to get you where you trying to keep from being sick. Smoke the reefer and you'll be high, but that stuff is going to turn on you." I thought, Man, this guy's crazy. He likes his reefer, and that's his high. So why should he push his load off on me? I ain't hurting nobody but me, if I'm hurting anybody.

There was a whole language and lifestyle that went along with being a stone dope fiend, and you were schooled into it by the old-timers if you wanted to be accepted by them. For instance, no self-respecting fiend ever cooks up their business in a spoon, like I've seen done in certain movies. He'll use a bottletop, or anything but a spoon, because the kind of metal in a spoon eats up dope. Likewise, the homemade rigs—eyedropper, baby pacifier, dollar bill, and all—was considered to give a safer fix, unmatched by a hypodermic.

We used to have dozens of those rigs and caps of dope stashed around town. A favorite spot to put this stuff was under the stairsteps outside people's houses. In New Orleans in them days almost every house had an opening under the stairsteps so you could crawl under the house. We got so we hid our stuff so well that it was never stolen, although sometimes we forgot where we stashed.

I used to carry only enough dope on me that I could eat it in an emergency and not kill myself. The heroin came in capsules, which I wrapped in cellophane and foil or rubbers and kept in the side of my mouth. I knew guys who were supposed to be hip who carried dope in a hole they cut in their zoot suit lapel or in their drawers or socks. But, as the old-timers taught me, the guys who survived always carried dope, whether it was reefer, pills, or junk, in their mouth so they could flip it over with their tongue and swallow it without a narc noticing. You never knew when narcotic agents would be around. If they saw you throw something in your mouth, they'd slam you down and one of them would strangle your throat to make the stuff come up quick if it was high, while the other would kick you in the stomach to get it up if it had gone down. This happened to me once, and it was the only lesson I needed about that particular subject. From then on, I always carried my stuff in my mouth.

The cops figured me out pretty quickly and began to stop me regularly to see if I had tracks on my arms. Since I did, they almost always picked me up and took me down to the precinct house to hold me for "investigation" for seventy-two hours. Usually the cops would just book you on suspicion long enough to get you sick, then they'd let you go. When they interrogated me and I'd become belligerent and uncooperative, as usual, they'd transfer me after seventy-two hours to another precinct house or central lockup and hold me there for another seventy-two. They could hold you up for days this way, moving you from precinct to precinct, and your lawyer or bondsman would always be one or two steps behind in tracking you down.

While they were holding you, they often applied a little of their third degree to you. They liked to beat you on the head above the hairline with rubber hoses: The hoses didn't leave any marks, so they could beat the shit out of you and not have to worry about your appearance when they hauled you to court. If they saw you had scars from another scrape or earlier police beating, and most especially if these were above the hairline where they'd be hidden, then they'd work on you with nightsticks.

Needless to say, even the ASPCA wouldn't have approved of this treatment, and the beatings weren't the worst of it. As your habit came on, you had to get something to keep you from going into withdrawal. If you were lucky, you could score some phenobarbital the first night to knock you out. Heroin was almost impossible to come by in the precinct jails, and if you could get it you had to sniff it, which I never could do anyway. Most of the time, you had to take what came your way.

Once I'd been inside for seventy-two hours, I was more determined than ever to tighten up as soon as I hit the streets. I hurt so bad on release that even though I wanted to kill the narcs I had to run to cop a stash first. Later, when the sick had been dealt with, I'd sit back and think about killing the bastards who had been fucking with me. Then I always realized it was a bad— a very bad—idea.

A particular cop had it in for me and always threatened to bust me and my new wife, Lydia. He came through on his threat, too, but we both had learned how never to get caught with anything on us. The more he hassled us, only to see us released soon after, the angrier he got. Finally, he told us he was going to see to it that we were put away for a long time, the suggestion being that even if we weren't holding he would plant something on us. He finally did try to frame us one day when we were out on Decatur Street. He came up and stopped us, and I saw he was fingering a bag in his pocket that he was going to put on us. Luckily, some people had gathered, and we were protected by witnesses, which made this narc retreat. If he'd gotten away with his fonky-monkey business, we'd probably still be gone today.

This was just the beginning of my problems with narcotics. I had cut a tight deck for myself, but I didn't care. This was how I wanted to live. I felt straight-up alive and ready, willing and able to deal with whatever might be coming down the road. Another couple of decades would pass before I began to reject my attitude, and took those first halting steps out of the junkie twilight.

PECULIAR REALITY

Peculiar reality,
Where have I heard it before?
It wasn't on the radio
Or a TV show.

—*"Familiar Reality,"*
Mac Rebennack

In 1954, about a year before I got booted out of Jesuit High School, I began to get seriously involved as a player in the New Orleans music business. For a while, I gigged with my school band, Henri Guerineau's the Spades. Our outfit mainly stuck close to the school dance scene, playing the Holy Father circuit. Around the same time I slid into a different, more serious groove, when I hooked up with a great tenor player, Leonard James.

Leonard was a student at Warren Easton, a public high school across the street from my school. Often, after I had finished up at Jesuit, I went over to Warren Easton to hang out. There was always a bunch of cats in zoot suits and greased-back hair hanging out there after school. One day I heard this band playing Sam Butera songs in the school gymnasium and I thought, Man, that's really hip. I wouldn't mind gigging with them. The sax player turned out to be Leonard. Leonard knew all the cats at Paul Gayten's Brass Rail club. Like me, he loved Annie Laurie,

Roy Brown, and Larry Darnell; both of us were wild about New Orleans's R&B. I got to talking with him and the others, told them I played guitar and piano. One thing led to another, and before long I was jamming with Leonard all over the place, wherever we could pick up a gig. This materialized into a permanent way of life.

Leonard turned out to be a great hustler of gigs for the band. He managed to get us jobs anywhere and everywhere in town, out in the sticks and on the road. We didn't have no representation at that time, just Leonard. Later, after he was gone, I got us a booking agent; but when Leonard was in the band, he talked us in and walked us out. He hustled us gigs in clubs that were so far over our head it'd make us sick—real fancy joints. We'd walk in the place looking like garbagemen and the people would all be in tuxes, and we'd be wondering how Leonard got us into that set. But that was only part of the routine; we played whenever we could.

After a while, we began holding a lot of our rehearsals in Leonard's pad, which was up near the St. Roch Park section of New Orleans—a pretty tough part of town. Leonard's daddy owned a bar and knew the game; he hipped him to the fine points of hustling gigs. He also was a tough-as-nails character who didn't take no shit off nobody.

One day, Leonard and I got into a fight with two guys in St. Roch Park. These two kicked the shit out of me and Leonard. We went home and Leonard's dad said, "What happened to you two?"

"Two guys in St. Roch Park beat the shit out of us," Leonard said.

He says, "Well, goddamn it, beat the shit out of them."
And I said, "Oh no!"

So Leonard's father called my father, and they got together and said, "Yeah, we're gonna make them go out and fight those guys again."

Well, we went out there, and those guys kicked our ass again—and all the time with Leonard's dad rooting us on. When we got stomped the second time, he got pissed off and told Leonard he was going to beat his ass. We had to go out there a third time and get whomped for them to decide, "Well, they couldn't beat them guys after all."

One of the special things about Leonard I remember from our hours of practicing was that he loved to play songs in different keys; he always made us learn to play a song in more than one. This helped especially with the vocal parts, because we couldn't always sing the songs in their original key. Later, we used this tactic to drive out rotten singers who were working with the band: Leonard would yell out, "Flight 36," and we'd start changing keys every chorus so the guy would eventually have to cut out and leave the stage before he busted a blood vessel. Leonard had a way of putting things he was good at to odds and ends.

Leonard also had a great ear for talent and brought a lot of fine players around to jam with us or even join the band. He copped to some great young piano players around town at that time—people like Al Johnson, who later made "Carnival Time," and James Booker, who had a big R&B hit for Don Robey on the Peacock label in the early sixties called "Gonzo," and later teamed up with me as a keyboard man in some of my Dr. John bands. Booker was a child prodigy who had begun playing at something like age three or four. His father was a preacher from Texas and his mother hailed from Mississippi; he used to go into long, brilliant raps about his father, calling forth everything in him of the black preaching style. Booker never actually joined our band, but he was always around on the scene, and we all became jam-up partners later.

Our first piano player was a cat named Hal Farrel. The first singer was a fellow named Deadeye, and the guitarist was Earl Stanley. Even though I wanted to be the guitarist in the band, I started off as a bass player because Earl already held down the guitar spot. Earl was a kicks character, one of those originals hanging around town at the time. His father was a Yaqui Indian from Mexico who had ended up in New Orleans working as a chef wherever he could land a job. The whole family played

Mexican music a lot at home, which was how Earl had first learned the guitar. They played really low-down norteños and other Mexican stuff, but in New Orleans at the time there was just absolutely zero calling for Mexican music, so Earl branched out into R&B.

Stanley's pa was an interesting character. He set himself up a migratory pattern that had him working in New Orleans for a year or so, putting money away as fast as he could; then, when he had made enough dough, he'd buy a pretty good used car and a lot of stuff and drive it back to his hometown in Mexico, where he'd sell the car and all the stuff and kick back for a while. When he got tired of Mexico or ran out of green, he'd head up the road again to New Orleans, work for a while as a chef, then turn it around again.

Earl might have gone with his pop a couple of times, but mostly he and the rest of the family stayed in New Orleans. By the time I met up with him, Earl was billing himself as King Earl, after Earl King, one of the hot up-and-coming New Orleans guitarists at the time. Before too long, I had connived to trade places with Earl by arranging for him to buy an electric bass at Werlein's music store, the place where I had taken my first guitar lesson from Mr. Guma when I was younger. The electric bass had just hit the market, and ours was one of the first in a New Orleans band. The electric bass made our band something special, sliced us a rocking sound and gave us an edge on other New Orleans bands, who still used upright basses or none at all. Earl got real excited about this new bit of equipment. But most of all, the new electric bass appeased Earl and left him feeling okay, even though I had his chair as guitarist.

The band started out as a floating group of musicians, so it wasn't unusual that on my first gig I played with a lean-and-mean trio. That night, Leonard dropped by my house and took me down to a strip joint on St. Charles Avenue, near Lee Circle Square. St. Charles was nothing but back-to-back strip joints, clip joints, and gin mills. I thought, Man, if my people find out where Leonard's taking me, I'm in deep shit.

That night I met Paul Staehle, a cat who would become my good friend and our drummer. Paul was a bit older than I was, and had already been working a while at another club—the Blue Cat or the Jet Lounge or the Club Leoma, all of which were just down the street from our gig. Leonard took me into this club before our gig and I listened to the drummer, who was just killing me. With the drummer was a blind piano player; it was just the two of them, and they were great. As I listened to Paul, I thought, I'd really like to play with this guy—he's got some chops. Before I could say a word, Leonard says to me, "This cat's the drummer I hired for our band." That night, after he finished his set with the piano player, we shanghaied Paul and took him down the street to gig with us. He was our drummer from then on.

Because our group was a loose tribe of musicians, we varied our act from night to night. It was a scramble to get gigs in them days, and the lean times had a definite motivating effect in getting us to do whatever was necessary to raise a few ducats. In order to keep working, we developed into about eight bands rolled into one. We invented a bunch of different names to suit any occasion: Mac Rebennack and the Skyliners, Frankie Ford and the Thunderbirds, Jerry Byrnes and the Loafers, Leonard James and the Night Trains, the Shadows, on and on. But mainly we were known as the Night Trains. All these bands were basically made up of the same musicians. Paul Staehle put together a bunch of different banners to fit on the bass drumhead, and he used the banner to match whatever group we were that night. We also varied our stage dress depending on who we were. One night we wore white shirts, the next blue suits; sometimes we even pinned polka dots on our suits—whatever it took to get around being passed off as the same band that had played crosstown the night before under a different name.

Most of our repertoire consisted of covers of songs from R&B acts: Ray Charles's "Funny (But I Still Love You)," Bobby Bland's "Further On Up the Road," Junior Parker's "Driving Wheel," Roy Brown's "Good Rockin' Tonight," Little Willie John's "Need Your Love So Bad," Fats Domino's many hits, and the like. There was a certain kind of music that was really popular in New Orleans, and we tried to play in that groove. It could be shuffle, it could be rockin', it could be bluesy, but mainly it had to be danceable, and in a lot of the places we played, the dancing got way down. In the strip joints, for instance, between shows the strippers danced with the tricks; folks was doing every different kind of dance—the belly rub, the dry hump, funky stuff generally. We sprinkled a lot of original songs in our act, too, and we played around with different arrangements to songs, depending on the venue.

Still, even though there was a lot of work available in New Orleans during those years, the game wasn't easy to break into. You had to hustle and scuffle to keep a gig happening. We had a couple of maneuvers to grab the attention of club owners. Through Papoose and Roy Montrell, I had managed to break in as an occasional sideman at Cosimo Matassa's studio, which was *the* studio for R&B in New Orleans. I persuaded Cosimo to let the band cut demo records of our songs there during off-hours. We took these demos around to the clubs, and if things weren't going well, Leonard would "accidentally" drop one of the discs on the floor. The boss would ask, "What's that?" "That's our new hit record," he'd tell him. Now, we knew it wasn't going right onto his jukebox, but he might be curious and give it a listen. If he liked what he heard, he'd hire us. If not, on the way to the door, Leonard James would turn a con where his sax case popped open mysteriously, allowing him to snatch up his horn and start playing. If that didn't work, he'd try something else.

A lot of musicians in New Orleans back then took whatever job they could just to keep them in food and drugs, and a lot of the gigs you ended up with were peculiar, to say the least. I got turned on to some of the more extreme clubs when I was a little older—around my sixteenth birthday. One night Huey Smith, the piano player for a popular band in town called the Clowns, took me down to a place called the Dew Drop Inn. The Dew Drop was primarily a black club, but it attracted a small white audience too. Because of the segregation laws, whites and blacks were supposed to be separated inside the club, though in reality whites would usually just congregate in one corner. The Dew Drop was one of your prime pit stops on what was then called the chitlin' circuit, which was the string of clubs in the South that featured the main R&B (and early rock and roll) acts of the day. Virtually every current star, faded star, and future star in the business passed through the Dew Drop, from Joe Turner, Joe Tex, Charles Brown, and Big Maybelle to Ray Charles, Bobby Bland, Sam Cooke, and James Brown—just to name a few.

These were the headliners, who usually played on weekends. On the off nights, a different kind of action was featured. During these evenings, the Dew Drop was taken over by extravagant drag-queen revues, backed by a big, seven-piece house band with a horn section. The show was choreographed down to the last high kick, and the costumes were ultra-sharp. Now, I went there to cop on the music. But, man, when I hit the door, I knew I had encountered something else again.

We sat down and I guess I was trying to act like this was all just another night in Babylon, but I wasn't faking it very well. That night, the Dew Drop was turned out totally drag. Black Beauty and her Powder Puff Revue started things off by hitting the stage singing "I'm a woman trapped in a man's body. I live the life I love and I love the life I live. . . ." Then another Queen came out, with the star singing the "St. Louis Blues," with its tagline "I hate to see the evening sun go down"—only he would change it a little so it came out "I hate to see my youngest son go down." The headliner was an act called Sir Lady Java, who came out, flashed tits, then at the end of the show flashed a dick, too. I had a hard time handling it. Huey and the other guys laughed their asses off at me because I was so innocent. But this was just Huey's way of hipping me to show biz in New Orleans.

Now while this awful-scented show was going down, the musicians would be cranking away at the back of the stage, behind the revue. Sometimes I had to play one of these gigs myself. Even if the material wasn't what many of the musicians were into, you had to hand it to the drag performers. Most of them were dynamite singers and entertainers. Still, the musicians in the house bands weren't necessarily thrilled to be up there night after night. We were doing it because that's all there was sometimes, and we had to pay some tough dues just to keep life and limb hanging more or less together.

Another popular place where we'd hang out in those days was a joint called Leroy's Steakhouse. Musicians gravitated there to be close to the wire about gigs. If you were looking for another musician, or wanted the latest information about anything relating to the music business, Leroy's was the place to be. Leroy's was right next to the Dew Drop, which wasn't so great for me because the police knew me around that area. The cops were thick around the Dew Drop because they knew a lot of hot property was fenced around there. As a rule, they didn't want to see no palefaces with no obvious means of support lingering in that part of town. As a result, I was harassed and chased a lot by certain police, but after a while they let me alone because they got to know my face. I guess they figured I must have been completely psychotic, showing up there no matter how much heat they laid down on me.

Throughout all this, my band worked wherever anyone would pay us to play. One of our regular spots for about a minute was a grocery store in the Ninth Ward; sometimes, it was a hardware store. You wouldn't get much at these joints, maybe ten dollars a night for the whole band; at the clubs, we often made union-scale wages, about forty dollars a night.

We played this one grocery store every Wednesday or Thursday night—off nights, so they didn't interfere with our regular club gigs. It was a little mom-and-pop storefront-type place, and the owner moved his stock to the side when we came and put some of it in a back room so it looked like a little roadhouse joint. This went on for a while, until one night a couple of the rumdums got into a fight and started throwing cans of corn and tomato juice around and busted up the store, making a hell of a gumbo in the process.

By and by, we slotted into a habit of constant gigging in New Orleans and its environs. Whenever we had a night or a day off, we shedded, sometimes for as long as seventy-two hours straight, in order to learn new songs so we could work new gigs. After one of these marathon sessions we were so fried we could hardly see straight, and our gigs probably suffered for a few days hence.

We lived high and crazy, and pretty soon we'd picked up a bad rep around the clubs because of the drugs. But back in them days, we all ran hard all the time—especially Leonard, even though he never shared the drug kick with the rest of the band. Leonard just didn't have the stupidity to become a dope fiend or a weed or pill head; he was never anything but a stone character.

For starters, we almost always showed up late. And just about everywhere we played, we came back from our break loaded. After the gig ended, the owner would come up to us and say, "You guys were fucked up." We'd look at him like we were astonished. "What, you crazy?" we'd say. Then he'd hit us with, "When you came in here, everything you played was fast. But after the break, every song was slow." And it was true. We were burning the black candles at both ends.

Paul Staehle, our drummer, was a real loose character. If I've met anyone who was a genius besides James Booker, it was Paul. I say that about Paul because he was a creative, inventive cat. Not only did he literally wire his house for sound in the mid-1950s, but a little later he built a small submarine that worked. He also put together a model flying saucer that actually flew. He used to love to go out to the beach on Lake Pontchartrain and send it way out over the water, running it by remote control. Paul had a giant shortwave set in his house; he used to tell me he was in touch with Mars and Venus and shit. He'd sit around and hear voices, too. We were all out there a ways back then, but Paul had gone a lot further than most of us.

For a while, Paul played this crazy set of drums he had rigged up for himself. He painted his sticks black and wrapped silver tape around them, so that when he was working out it looked like silver spirals in motion. He painted his drumheads black on top to make them look invisible, and he put lights in the drums so that when he played them they all lighted up in different colors, syncopated to his beats. To top it off, we stole water softeners—devices that looked like big radio tubes—and put Christmas lights inside them so they went on and off. When he played his solos, he hit a button and that shit all came on. He'd be playing the drums, they'd light up, and it was something to behold. This was all a good decade before the appearance of so-called psychedelic music. I had never seen any drummer do anything like he was doing. It wasn't Mickey Mouse; it was real pro. He was a show all unto hisself, scary and awesome and powerful, and it drew a crowd.

One night Paul got Charlie Maduell, one of our sax players, so tripped out that Maduell walked out onto the bar with his tenor and thought he was doing the Dance of the Seven Veils. Maduell ended up putting on a total strip. This might have been the night Charlie got on my back so bad bugging me for goofballs that I gave him roach poison instead. Whatever it was, Charlie was as passionate as he was crazy, and he got wrapped up in whatever was going down.

Paul also often slipped into the role of comedian during our act; he'd take a pratfall off the stage, then come up laughing and do it all again. We wondered what the hell was the matter with this guy, but he always carried it off. This was in keeping with the southern R&B tradition back then, which stressed the entertainment aspect of music. Musicians were expected to put on a show, to create a fuss. That was excitement; that was show biz. And the audience went nuts for it.

Another routine went like this: At a particularly climactic part of the set, we'd get Leonard James to jump off the stage and walk the bar. He'd hop up, playing his ass off while he danced among the Jax beers, cheap pluck, and cut brown whiskey. When he got to the end of the bar, he'd jump down and run into the ladies' room. Then after a moment he'd come out with a big set of women's drawers hanging off his tenor. He'd be playing a real fast tune, "Hand Clapping" or "Flying Home" or something. Taking his time, he'd come back onstage, all the while burning the house down—until, suddenly, he'd collapse. He'd be laying there, the drawers on the floor, and his horn, too. Most of the band would stop and we'd get this big prop bottle of whiskey and pour him some—nothing. We'd take a big paper shoe that we'd gotten from a shoe store and wave that in front of his face. That wouldn't work. Then we'd have a huge joint and blow a hit at him. He'd still be out cold. Then we'd take the drawers and wave them at him, and he'd come up playing like crazy. The house loved it; from that point, they were in the palm of our hand. That's old show biz shit. We'd finish up the set by doing a little second-line through the audience, old New Orleans style. Nobody could ever top that.

You'd see these kinds of routines in all the clubs in New Orleans, put on by all types of bands, white and black. Guys like Edgar Blanchard's band, whether they were playing black or white clubs (they were a black group), would do their own bits: They would change song lyrics around, stop and go within a set or even a song, change into Mexican costumes or dress up like a woman, or whatever. This stuff wasn't necessarily as sharp as the acts put on by black comedians like Pigmeat Markham or Moms Mabley, but it was funny enough because it was about a band playing with its image. It was a traditional thing to do, and it got over.

But that kind of burlesque routine died during the days of integration because it was considered Uncle Tomish, especially when it was performed by a black act. And soon it seemed Tom for a white act, too. Those routines finally just got lost in the shuffle, which was too bad because they could be real funny, and great for what they were.

The survival rate from all this craziness on- and offstage wasn't high. Our first singer, Deadeye, got sent up to Angola for manslaughter. The second singer, Jerry Byrne, got shipped on a trumped-up rape charge. Our third singer, Roland Stone, also found his way to the joint on a narcotics rap. Jerry's fate was especially sad. He had recorded one of my songs, "Lights Out," which had turned into a hit for him. He had a follow-up record that was also starting to hit, and he was beginning to tour with the Big Bopper when he was arrested; things had been about to break wide open for him, but after that his record company dropped him like a hot potato.

Our last singer was a real young cat from the other side of the river named Ronnie Barron. Ronnie was an innocent kid who was a natural singer and soon proved he had a good ear for music. I started teaching him a little piano, and was surprised to see how quickly he picked up on what I showed him. Before too long, when I was playing organ, he was able to play vibes and sing. Later, he became a member of several of the Dr. John bands.

Our drummers didn't fare much better than the singers. Out of the first group of drummers, all but one or two died from OD's. (Unfortunately, this included Paul Staehle, who overdosed in the sixties.) It got so bad that guys were scared to take a drumming gig with us—and you had to be crazy to want to sing with us. A band can build up a certain mystique from this action and the word going around was that we was jinxed, which might have been fine for the audience PR but didn't help us much with some club owners.

At a certain point, our band began going on the road to play venues here and there around the South. This was the wide-open chitlin' circuit, and it took us to auditoriums, juke joints, chicken shacks, and roadhouses as far east as the Carolinas, along the Gulf Coast from Tampa to Galveston and inland up to Monroe, Jackson, Shreveport, Texarkana, Dallas, Oklahoma City, and back to New Orleans.

These were always grueling ordeals; the band packed into one or two cars and flat-out blew nonstop for as long as six weeks. Promoters and booking agents could get away with a lot in those days, and the rules of the game were made up as you went along. I can remember doing mixed-race gigs in places where you knew it wasn't going to be cool. When you blew into a hamlet in Mississippi that had a big sign announcing UNITED KLANS OF AMERICA WELCOMES YOU, you knew you weren't exactly in God's country. One time we went up to do a gig in Hattiesburg,

Mississippi, with a mixed show, which was also a fraud show—
a New Orleans act known as Sugar and Sweet, passing themselves
off as Shirley and Lee, a very popular New Orleans act of the
day. We also had a kid named Ricky Ricardo passing himself off
as Frankie Ford, and James Booker and a band passed themselves
off as Huey Smith and the Clowns. The whole show was a fraud.
Everything went fine until Ricky went up to be Frankie Ford and
it blew the whole scam—the real Frankie Ford had been on
"American Bandstand" that night!

When the local promoter found out what was going down,
he pulled us into the back room and said, "Look, I'm giving y'all
half the money and you're lucky to get that. Now get the fuck
out of town." I was thinking, Oh my God, we're going to get
killed. We're in Hattiesburg and it's all over. I think it was Earl
King who said, "Man, don't worry. Just give us the half. I'll
explain it to the rest of them later."

We were leaving town when a police cruiser pulled us over
to the side of the road. I was starting to get seriously worried,
thinking the promoter might have claimed that we stuck him up.
Visions of a Mississippi dungeon were passing before my eyes
when James Booker jumped out the back door and told the state
police, "Now look, don't you worry 'bout what the man told you.
We threw the weed out the car miles back."

We were all freaking, going through the roof now, looking
at one another, thinking, What the fuck is Booker telling the cops
something like that for? But the cops started laughing at him, he
was so crazy. They didn't even look in the car good; they just told
us to get out of town and not come back. That was part of
Booker's creativity, his insanity, this way he had of knowing just
what to do, just how to mess with the police to get us out of a
jam.

Back before the images of stars were stamped into everybody's mind by media overkill, this kind of bogus road act wasn't
uncommon. On another tour, Sugar and Sweet not only came on
during one show to pass themselves off as Shirley and Lee (as
they had done in Hattiesburg) but came on again *later in the same
show* and passed as Charlie and Inez Foxx!

When we went out with the real people—Huey Smith, for instance—we also got hassled over the race issue. More than a few times, we backed Huey playing behind a curtain so the audience (and the police) couldn't see we were a mixed group. Some of these things were so inconsistent, they were off the wall. In Mississippi, which was dazzlingly racist, we got away with a lot of mixed shows and fraud shows; meanwhile back in New Orleans, which was relatively tolerant, we often couldn't jam with black acts in black clubs. We played a gig in Mobile and someone had turned the band on with hash just before the set. We started off with a slow piece, something like "Stormy Monday," and the club owner came running up to bitch us out. "What is this slow shit?" he starts screaming, right in the middle of maybe the second song. Just stops the act and gets down on us. Then, after whatever it was we said, he pulls a gun on us and tells us to pack the fuck up and get out of the club—we wasn't even going to get half out of him. Now, we didn't have gas money to get to the next gig. We had dope-fiended our way to the gig; now we had dope, but no money.

Finally, Lydia (my girlfriend and later my wife) conned the guy into a deal where we would play extra hours for free if we could have another crack at the gig. We got up there, still messed up, and played a gang and a half of hours for chump change. The next day, as we were pulling out of the rat-hole motel where we were staying (which was owned by the same guy who ran the club), the police tagged us and said the guy had complained we hadn't paid our motel bill. Well, the bill was supposed to be included in the gig. We got stiffed. Somehow we managed to make it to the next spot on a single tank of gas.

After a time, we cut back on the road dates and began working more in Jefferson and St. Bernard parishes; these places were less hot and consequently less threatening to our lifestyle than New Orleans, and less demanding than being on the road. One of our favorite clubs was a little place out in Jefferson called the Club Forest.

It was around this time that I began to get hipped to the once-in-a-lifetime names carried by some of the characters in the dark-and-dirty nightlife world. There was a bartender at the Club Forest called Nubs. It was amazing to see this guy, who sported just the first joint of every finger, working as a bartender. Every so often, someone would ask, "Say, Nubs, what happened to your fingers?"

"I owed some money," was his standard reply.

I guess they figured they'd put him out of work as a bartender. But this guy kept on, mixing drinks and doing everything a bartender's supposed to do, without nothing but that first joint on his fingers.

There were other guys at clubs and bars around the projects in New Orleans with amazing names: Louie Lump Lump, Billie Bell, Harmonica Al, Papa Lightfoot, the Reverend Utah Smith. Then there were the Indians: Big Chief Jolly, Big Chief Tuddy (whose real name was Allison Montana). There was a little guy, Ooney Bebbels, who always used to come by the gigs. Ooney Bebbels got so well known that Larry McKinley, a big-time R&B deejay in town, used to talk about him on his radio show. There were serious name freaks who used to go to the Poppa Stoppa radio show, another very popular local production, and give him long lists, pages and pages of funny-named cats. It was just a New Orleans thing that everybody had some sort of funny name, whether it was Iron Jaw or Chicoo or some other name. Chicoo ran around with a guy named Hatchet Head, Hatchet Head Bumarita. And I remember plenty more: Two Weed, Marblehead, Ratty Joe Jinks, Sweetblood, Ears, Big Dick Jim, Tangle-eyed George, No-toed Joe, Izzycoo, Seven Come Eleven, Duck Lady.

By this point, when we played in New Orleans at all, it was in the more protected clubs, where we wouldn't get hassled. When the whole Jimmy Smith organ-trio scene became hot in the early 1960s, I slotted into a different musical groove: James Booker taught me to play the organ, and I began working regular gigs more on Bourbon Street itself. But in the late 1950s, I hadn't figured that hustle yet; I still had some basic dues to pay, one of which was to back up the traveling rock and roll shows that came to New Orleans. These extravaganzas were thrown at the Pontchartrain Beach Amphitheater, or at the Municipal Auditorium. From 1956 to 1959, they were wildly popular in New Orleans and nationwide.

Back then, the stars of the moment just hit the road without a band and played shows with pickup bands in each town. Because we was the only band in New Orleans that played both R&B *and* rock and roll, and could read music, we managed to become the major backup band for all these acts. These were good gigs for us: The wages were union-scale, and we got to know a lot of people who probably wouldn't have known us otherwise.

Normally, the stars would blow into town in the afternoon; we'd rehearse together that evening and be ready for showtime at night. Since I was the band leader as well as the guitarist, it was my job to put together the package each star was looking for. If he needed four trumpets, four trombones, five saxophones, I knew who to call—the cats who could cut all the charts and more. I had all the best players there were in New Orleans. They could transpose violin parts for their horns if they had to.

Most acts were supposed to be strictly segregated in New Orleans, but our band managed to play with both white and black acts on the road. On the white side of the fence, we were the house band that backed acts like Jerry Lee Lewis, Bobby Darin, Frankie Avalon, Freddy Cannon, and Fabian. Usually a black band, like Tommy Ridgley's, backed the black acts. But we'd do gigs on the road with some of the very same black acts that we couldn't do at the big segregated gigs in New Orleans.

Musicians' unions in New Orleans at the time were segregated: There was local 174, the white union, and 496, the black union, and each one put in their two cents whenever they could. New Orleans was a much stronger union town in those days, and both unions were trying to keep black and white musicians apart. We got in a lot of trouble one year backing Bo Diddley when his band didn't show: We played part of his set, and then they stopped the show. Somebody came up and pulled the plug on us; Bo had to finish up with just Bo. He did a great job anyway, because Bo is a pro, and he killed them as we watched from the side.

Once we did a thing with Jimmy Reed that for some reason was okay—which just shows you how haphazard the racial code was way back then. A lot of times, the scene came from the opposite direction: If we sat in with a black band, we got *them* in trouble. There were a couple of places on the West Bank and Jefferson Parish where we'd go sit in with local acts like Sugar Boy and the Cane Cutters or Lee Allen's band (people we worked with in the studio all the time), and all of a sudden the club owner would pull a gun and tell me to get off the stage. It was that heavy.

Soon after we hooked up, I started cowriting songs with Leonard. On top of being our booking agent and co-bandleader, Leonard was also a damned good funky tenor player. Our band made an album of instrumental tunes called *Boppin' and Strollin'* for Decca Records in 1956. Leonard and I wrote all the songs on the album. Danny Kessler, who we did the album for, got us in the union. That was one of the nice things Danny did. He didn't give us no money, but he got us in the union.

I got my break with Danny during a stint auditioning singers at Cosimo's—my job was just to sit around at the piano playing tunes while singers ran through their stuff for producers—when Danny blew into town from LA looking for New Orleans talent. I was auditioning some people, and Danny came in and told me he liked the way I played piano. I told him I was really a guitar player, and I guess that impressed him, too. So he talked to Cosimo and Cos said, "Yeah, they got a little band." Danny said, "Well, bring 'em over." We ended up cutting more than two dozen instrumentals, which Decca cut down to fourteen songs and decided to title *Boppin' and Strollin' with Leonard James*, which was released in 1957. After we had done the album under Leonard's name, Danny cut four sides with me for Capitol Records, including a version of "Storm Warning," a tune that later became a regional hit for me. Most of these songs were in the Bo Diddley vein, which was popular at the time; Leonard was working out behind a Lee Allen tenor sound, and we even copied Paul Gayten by using a samba beat to one or two songs. We used to make up instrumentals all the time. We were such a young band— I was seventeen, Earl Stanley was eighteen, Leonard was nineteen.

After Decca cut the record, they sat on it for a while, until the Stroll became a popular dance and Decca saw their main chance. The album didn't do shit in the United States, but for some reason it went down big in Europe; all over Europe cuts from it were used in commercials, and for years I collected BMI chump change from that.

We were already embarrassed by the record by the time it came out, because our playing had changed so much. We hardly ever played any of those songs during our gigs; that instrumental session was just a quick-change job we did for the chance to get something out on a disc. Oh, there was some nice things on it; on the song "Strollin' Home" we put a kind of "St. James Infirmary" riff on top of the Stroll dance rhythm, with a bass line Leonard had stolen from an opera called *The Pearl Fishers*. Presto, y'all got y'all's Stroll. But you always progress faster when you're young; when we finally heard the album, we said to ourselves, "Wow, did we do that shit?"

Boppin' and Strollin' didn't do us much good. It was hardly played at all below the Cotton Curtain. I don't recall hearing it ever in New Orleans, or anywhere else for that matter (even though I was mostly in New Orleans during the times it would have had airplay). But there it was, our first record.

Around 1958 or 1959, Leonard James called it quits with our band, and the music biz in general, when he started losing his hair. Leonard was always proud of his ducktails and his hair. He and Ronnie Barron took more time to look pretty than most guys I know. Leonard always put a bebop hat on his head after he had done it up perfect, and by the time he took it off to play, it would be a little messed up, so he had to go through the whole deal all over again. At a certain point, though, Leonard noticed he was beginning to lose his mane; he freaked out when that started coming down, and one day out of the blue he just up and joined the air force. All he left us with was his newest invention, a one-man band machine that I never did get to see work. Long before electronic drummers came onto the scene, Leonard had devised a setup that let him play the sax with one hand and the organ with the other, laying down an electric drumbeat all the while.

When Leonard evaporated out of the picture, Charlie Maduell took his place as lead tenor. Charlie had always wanted Leonard's gig, and for quite a while the two of them had a real competition going between themselves. Charlie fit real easily into the band—in a way even better than Leonard, because Leonard never got loaded. Charlie did. To our way of looking at it, he was perfect.

Our whole band was a bunch of dope fiends, but Charlie Maduell was the most serious junkie of us all. Charlie's in the joint right now, doing forever-and-one years. Back then, on the road or off, Charlie was our point man for the procurement of drugs. I had a certain drugstore where I usually cashed phony scripts to get my narcotics, but since it was always a good idea to vary your routine, Charlie and I often worked other places. He was the guy who went inside to cash the goods. If we had any doubt about the moral turpitude of the pharmacist, we rounded up a wino and sent him inside to handle the transaction. We told the rum-dum to go in and get the stuff without delay. If the pharmacist gave the guy the drugs, he was to come right on out; if he told the rum-dum to wait, we told him to come out anyway so there wouldn't be no chance to call the narcs.

There was other ways of obtaining narcotics besides that scheme, and since Charlie liked to get his drugs free, we'd set it up so he could slip into drugstores after hours. On these occasions, we'd drive out into the country, looking for places to burglarize. We'd leave New Orleans late in the afternoon with me behind the wheel and Charlie riding shotgun. Charlie had one fine set of antennae out for this kind of business; I mean, his instincts were always in key. We'd be ripping and running through some little town and he'd say, "Slow down." Sure enough, right up ahead would be some little Shady Grove–type joint. We'd slide around the hamlet for a while, casing the territory, and when we was sure everything was okay, I'd pull over somewhere and let Charlie go to work. Meanwhile, I waited behind the wheel, nervous as hell, hoping Charlie would get out of there soon.

After a while, all this scamming—and the rise in temperature surrounding the band, whose rep was getting badder all the time—began to get to Charlie, and he became a little crazy trying to beat the heat. First he went with these loony disguises. He dyed his blond hair red, then silver; he wore capes and masks to the gigs. He changed his stage name to Charlie Cobra, Count Maduell, and other names to try to pass himself off as somebody else. Sometimes this stuff worked; other times it didn't.

To keep close to narcotics he took a gig in a drugstore, and that was Charlie Maduell's downfall. See, Charlie's kicks was being right under the man's nose and getting away with his scam, and for a minute he had set himself up a smooth operation stealing narcotics from the pharmacy. After a few months, a couple of kids who were working with him at that place lost their cool and fingered him.

But with Charlie or without him, the show had to go on. I was still spending most of my stage time on the guitar, although I would play piano on pieces that our regular piano player couldn't do—Professor Longhair stuff and more complicated numbers like "Body and Soul," which Eddie Hynes, our trombone player, liked to do later at night.

The band began cutting more records now, although most were backup gigs for other artists. Our second recording shot after *Boppin' and Strollin'* was a vocal showcase for an act called Little Choker, on Aladdin Records. Eddie Mesner at Aladdin had recorded a number of big-name acts, including Charles Brown, Amos Milburn, and Floyd Dixon; the year before I hooked up with them, Aladdin had a monster hit with Shirley and Lee's "Let the Good Times Roll."

Eddie ended up messing me over real bad. I'd met him the same way I had met Danny Kessler at Decca, hanging around Cos's studio helping with auditions. One thing led to another, and eventually my parents came down to sign a songwriter's contract on my behalf for a handful of songs to be used on the Little Choker album and other records. Where the contract read "rate of royalty," Eddie had inked in a big zero, though I consoled myself with the three and a half cents I got per sheet of music sold. The joke of it was, nine times out of ten they didn't even make sheet music for this kind of music.

When Leonard left, I became by default the bandleader and straw boss. We were still driving hard, and were real proud of our seventy-two-hour rehearsals, an enduring tradition. We'd learn more songs in seventy-two hours than some bands ever knew in their whole existence. But because we were always getting high, it seemed like a lot of these sessions ended up in fistfights. Eddie Hynes was always the one who got things chilled out by being just an all-round crazy motherfucker. Eddie was one of my favorite trombone players; he was probably our oldest member, and had been around more than any of the rest of us in professional bands. Eddie was there through all of the changes in our band: He was a killer trombone player and brought a lot of hip tunes our way, tunes like "Señor Blues," "Blue Prelude," bits and pieces of this and that from Duke Ellington and older songwriters.

We had a couple of hot trumpet players. First came Warren Leuning, fresh from Tony Almerico's Dixieland band. Tony Almerico was considered a real character. He had a radio show of his own, played at the Parisian Room all the time. He loved his New Orleans food; he used to give free plugs on his radio shows to places where he'd eaten the night before. I remember watching him do his radio show one night; he loaded up one side of a full loaf of hot French bread with sliced bananas and poured a can of condensed milk on it. On the other side of the loaf, he piled up a mound of peanut butter—all while he was on the air. One of the last of the truly original down-home characters.

Warren Leuning had almost as much shine as Eddie Hynes when he came into the band. In Tony's band, Warren had been featured as the trumpet prodigy. He played with us for only a minute, but he brought a sense of hipness along with him. Warren's being in our band shows what kind of crossbreezes were blowing through the New Orleans music scene then: There just weren't a whole lot of established categories that anyone was paying much mind to. You could have a guy like Warren with lots of Dixieland background, or a guy like Eddie Hynes with a big-band jazz orientation, decide to sit in with what was basically an R&B and rock and roll group like ours. It made for a lot of interesting live music, because no one was trying to pigeonhole anyone else into this or that exclusive groove.

Charlie Miller, who replaced Warren, was another super trumpet player. Charlie, like Warren, did arrangements of very hip tunes that normally we wouldn't have played; he dug more contemporary tunes, especially Horace Silver jazz pieces. Charlie played with my band for years, until he got disgusted with me on account of my narcotics use. He contributed arrangements to the band, always writing great stuff. He had not only great taste, but an understanding of New Orleans music that ran deep.

Trying to bring home the bacon, we kept gigging around town wherever we could. One of the places we used to play was a joint called Spec's Moulin Rouge, in Gretna. There'd be three bands there: the Kid Thomas Dixieland band, Clarence "Frogman" Henry's band, and us with Frankie Ford. I remember one week we played a Sunday afternoon gig that was broadcast live on the radio; the deejay said, "Here we are, live at Spec's Moulin Rouge," and all of a sudden you heard three shots: *bam, bam, bam!* A gang fight had broken out, and the little rent-a-cop hired to look out for the place had panicked and fired into the crowd. Then it all fell apart into a real badass free-for-all. When it was over and the Gretna police were all over the place, trying to take everybody off, there was one last guy who wouldn't leave. "Man, you can't make me go, motherfucker. Leave me alone. Let me finish my beer." The guy had two bullet holes in him.

The kicks of it all was that when all of this went down, the deejay, who was known as Jerry the Hound Dog, fainted, and old man Spec took over the mike. "Ain't no trouble here at the Moulin Rouge," he says. "It . . . it . . . it . . . it's just that drummer making noise over there. Come right on down to Spec's. You can have a good time anytime." The way he said it, everyone knew something bad had happened.

There were other places like that around. The Wego Inn on the Hill in Westwego, which was owned by Happy Cuchero, was one of them. That cat's name was appropriate, at least regarding firearms: Old Happy was real gun-happy. One night, during something called the Cane Cutters Dance, we were playing our set to a packed joint until Happy got mad at somebody for something and started shooting his guns—both of 'em! He emptied his own joint and then got mad at us, claiming we had run people out because we hadn't started playing a fast boogie when the bad action had gone down.

Happy ran a peculiar place. By and large, it was a white club—that is, the audience was white—but it ran to very black music. Even the black bands who played there played the kind of music they'd play if they was gigging in a black club. But it was a rough, rowdy place. One evening two Indian tribes, the Choctaw Boys and the Cherokees, had a fight out in Happy's parking lot. After it was over, the police fished somebody out of the river, and they found another boy's body up in the branches of a tree.

When you got over there into Jefferson Parish, things just got much dicier—and more racist—than in Orleans Parish 'cross the river. I'm not saying there wasn't racist places in Orleans Parish, but there was more of these joints in Jefferson. They loved black music; they just didn't love blacks.

The source of their bigotry seemed to be that the West

Bank ofays were scared that black guys would take off with their women. This fear caused some weird permutations around town: In more than a couple of the strip joints, for instance, if a black band was playing behind a white stripper, the club would put a screen up between the girl and the band. There were a handful of cool club owners, though, guys who just let you play without putting you through changes. One of the great things about New Orleans clubs in the fifties was that club owners booked the kind of music they personally liked: If a guy liked Afro-Cuban, that's what he booked. Another had a thing for blues, then he went with that. Hog-wild about Dixieland, book the motherfucker. Same for progressive jazz, legit big band, Tin Pan Alley, and all the rest. Our band—whatever we were calling ourselves—worked in almost every different kind of place except for the big-band scene. We played blues in the strip and shake-dance joints; we worked backup for magicians and lounge singers; we jammed with Afro-Cuban groups from time to time; and later, for a while, I even worked as a bass player for some of your traditional jazz artists like Murphy Campo at the Famous Door. It was a great time and place to build your chops, and I was lucky to have fallen into it—or most of it—the way I did.

FOUR

SITTING IN

Let me hear you sing
the same old sweet little singalong song.
The one we used to sing when
everything was all wrong.
The one that used to pull us together,
The one that we could sing it forever.

—*"Singalong Song,"*
Mac Rebennack

Specialty Records, one of the biggest labels out of New Orleans, had an office on Claiborne Avenue on top of the Houston Music Store. When I first started songwriting, I got my kicks hanging over there, and in short order I met Larry Williams and Little Richard at the Specialty office. The first time I saw Larry, he had just bought a Cadillac; it had gold letters on the side that said "Short Fat Fannie," the name of the hit that paid for the Caddy. That just blew me away, it was such class; leaving that car there on Claiborne Avenue and not getting nothing ripped off impressed the hell out of me, too.

At a certain point Johnny Vincent, who had been Specialty's A&R man, left to form his own Ace label, and Harold Battiste, a local musician, songwriter, and arranger, took the A&R job. This was when I really got to know Harold, and I quickly realized that he brought a good head to Specialty. One of the things he did was grade the material we songwriters brought in, which was real helpful to me. Harold had certain categories set up to judge a song by; he might tell you the melody needed improvement, or that a bridge was needed at a certain place. Then you could take the song home, revamp it, and go back to Specialty to see if they'd take it on the second bounce.

When I started out, I wrote songs with particular artists in mind, and at first the artist was almost always Little Richard. Just a little bit later, I branched out to writing songs intended for Art Neville and Lloyd Price. What was funny was that Specialty very rarely gave songs to the artist you'd written them for; instead, they'd dole them out to any artist who needed material at the moment. I might write a song for Little Richard, but he and Larry Williams would pass on it. Then the song would filter down the roster, until it ended up with a lesser-known singer. If a guy blew into the studio and didn't have any songs, they'd begin pulling songs out of the files and cut whatever was on hand. If your song was there at the right place at the right time, you'd get it cut.

I used to bring singers over there all the time. Leonard James and I brought our first singer, Deadeye, over to Specialty to audition, and also took him over to Dave Bartholomew at Imperial. I always took my songs and singers to Specialty or Imperial first because they were bigger-time in those days than, say, Ace Records. Imperial had Fats Domino on its roster, as well as Smiley Lewis and T-Bone Walker; Specialty had the best of the rest in gospel, rock and roll and R&B, acts like Roy Milton, Percy Mayfield, Lloyd Price, and Guitar Slim. But I learned early on that Dave Bartholomew would pretty much ixnay stuff I brought to him, so I began to lean toward Specialty. Dave iced me out because he himself was a songwriter; he just didn't need the amount of material Specialty did, because he could cover most of their catalog.

I'd bring singers to my pad before an audition in order to run through a new song a few times. When I thought the singer was ready, we'd roll over to Specialty and audition singer and song at the same time, with my piano accompaniment. In them days, songwriters were such second-class citizens that if your song became a record, the record company wouldn't even give you a complimentary copy; you had to go out and buy your own. They were really cheap, but at least Specialty was fair. They paid us royalties, unlike some other labels.

When you got a song published in those days, you didn't get any up-front money; all you did was sign a contract. You had to be very careful about checking these pieces of paper out; I learned this the hard way over a song originally titled "Try Not to Think About You," which I wrote for Art Neville or Willie West to cut. The song never got recorded by these two. It just laid around the Specialty office for a while, until Lloyd Price noticed it. Lloyd ended up stealing the song—which he pulled off because it hadn't been copyrighted. Specialty usually didn't copyright a song until it had been recorded; around that time, Lloyd moved to ABC Paramount, and he must have snatched this song when he left. He changed the name of the song to "Lady Luck" (after the first line of the song, "Lady Luck turned her back on me") and in 1960 it became a big, big hit.

I had no idea Lloyd had recorded the song until I heard it on the radio in New Orleans one day. I was all excited—thinking I'd written a hit—until I got a copy of the record, on which Lloyd was listed as the songwriter. I wasn't steamed at Specialty; by that time, I had worked around a while, and I knew the score about record companies. The one I wanted to kill (and I mean literally) was Lloyd Price. I heard through the wire that Lloyd was scheduled to appear in New Orleans, so I went out and got a gun on the street. My plan was to show up at the venue, wait for Lloyd to finish, and blow him away after the gig, but at the last minute the gig was canceled. I wasn't put off; I kept waiting. Fortunately for me, our paths didn't cross again until much, much later, and by then I'd had time to cool off.

If that kind of treatment wasn't bad enough, an even worse condition came down the line later when I discovered that the attorney my parents and I had hired to sue Lloyd Price to get my money and rights to the song back was Lloyd's own lawyer, a conflict of interest if ever there was one. My family didn't know nothing about no conflict of interests, and we got taken. The lawyer, who was the only music-business attorney in New Orleans at the time, pocketed the change and did nothing. For a minute, I was afraid if I ever ran across that bastard, I'd kill him, too.

Still, I did score with a couple of hit songs in my name back in those days. "Lights Out," which was recorded by Jerry Byrne, one of the singers in my band, sold pretty good in the late fifties and has since been covered by Be Bop Deluxe, Johnny Winter, Ronnie Barron, and others. A lot of my other songs from that period, like "Carry On," which Jerry also recorded, have also been covered by all kinds of people. None of them was in itself a huge record, but they became pretty big in their own way because of how many times they were covered. A song like "Losing Battle," which Johnny Adams cut, was covered right away by Junior Parker, the Sims Twins, and other people, and it keeps right on coming.

In the fifties and into the early sixties, nobody paid much attention to albums; the business was all about singles. When an artist had enough singles, they put an album out and stuck all the trash they could on it until it was filled up. One of the first artists I remember making an album with was Jimmy Clanton, who was coming off a big hit single, "Just A Dream." Jimmy was a white prettyboy who'd copped a lot of Earl King's style, and they thought he could be another Elvis. That was what they was always looking for. When they found a new contender, it would turn the heads of the producers, arrangers, and other artists at places like Specialty or Ace; the record executives would put out the white boy's single, book him on "American Bandstand," and sit back and pray.

Johnny Vincent of Ace and Joe Ruffino of Specialty had both started out aiming to make records; they would put out as good a record as they could by whoever, this whoever usually being black. By the late fifties, though, even they became obsessed with finding the next Elvis. When Jimmy Clanton began to sell,

Johnny Vincent went crazy. He sent Jimmy all over the country, spent money like he never had before. Huey Smith, who had all these other hit records for Johnny with no money spent, but who was black, got shit on left and right. It was an ugly situation.

I don't hold nothing against Jimmy. He was a talented cat. What happened wasn't his doing; it was the doing of the record executives' obsession with latching on to that lean, mean green. To show how weird it was, his brother Ike Clanton, who was a bass player with Duane Eddy's band, also got picked out as an Elvis impersonator, and made some sides for Ace. Both Ike and Jimmy got the push, and both held the spotlight for a minute, but the second Elvis never rose from the ground. There was only one Elvis; that's all anyone ever needed.

There was a time when New Orleans radio backed New Orleans records so big, you'd think the records was national hits. Poppa Stoppa, Doctor Daddy-O, Jack the Cat, and Ernie the Whip were all deejays who backed local artists. Those cats and Larry McKinley were some of the most heartfelt disc jockeys I've ever met anywhere. They played records by local acts not because of payola, but because they really liked the music and wanted to help the musicians in any way they could. They even helped musicians get gigs, and their airplay helped new acts break throughout the region, because a lot of New Orleans stations could be heard as far as Texas, Mississippi, and Arkansas.

Hearing local stuff in New Orleans was so regulation that it wasn't until you were on the road that you'd really pay attention when you heard one of your songs on the radio. I remember around 1958, when Jerry Byrne's recording of "Lights Out" was taking off. I was getting reports that it was going up the charts—to 60 to 40 to 30. At the time, Specialty had us on a package tour with the Big Bopper. Jerry worked his way up from being close to the bottom act on this tour to being second to the Bopper himself as the record rose in the charts. I knew the record was happening, and Jerry was killing the audiences because the promoters couldn't hold him back. The Big Bopper couldn't handle the heat, because Jerry was a tough performer. I got a thrill out of him, because of all the singers who worked in my band, there were some who could sing better, others who could perform better, but none who had all those talents rolled into one like Jerry. When he hit a gig, people remembered him real strong. He lifted from everybody: James Brown, Hank Ballard, whoever was popular and had that something extra that Jerry could turn to his own advantage. He sure could get house.

Around the time I first began hanging at Specialty, I met Joe "Mr. Google Eyes" August, who in the late forties and early fifties had busted out of the New Orleans pack as a R&B singer. Joe got his name when he worked as a busboy at Dookey Chase's, a popular New Orleans restaurant, where he loved to eye the ladies; one night a waiter told him he was "the googlest-eyed motherfucker" he'd ever seen, and the name stuck. Back then G was billed as the youngest blues singer in America; he was probably about fifteen when he had his first hits, and by the time I met him in the mid-fifties he had become a seasoned pro. The first time I ever laid eyes on him, he was luxuriating outside his club in a purple Buick with leopard-skin upholstery and leopard skin covering the dash and lining the trunk. It was some eye-popping car, but G had the style to drive a set of wheels like that.

G ran a couple of clubs around town, many of them set up on up-front money from various members of the police force. These were hot spots, joints known for their sizzling after-hours music and the variety of the characters they attracted. There were other hot spots in the neighborhood that attracted police attention, but no matter what might be going down outside, you were cool and safe from the police if you made it inside of G's club.

On top of providing an after-hours venue for almost all the out-of-town acts, plus a lot of regular-hours Latin bands, G played his club with his own badass, low-down, bebop scat-jazz R&B act. I used to go and watch G because I knew he knew how to work a house. I'd bring the singer with my band along and tell him to keep his eyes on Mr. Google Eyes. G would get down there, pull his coat back, rear back on the crowd, talk shit, and work 'em. That's an art form; people don't know nothing about that today.

Cosimo Matassa was another important person in my life then. I first remember Cos working around the little studio he had on Dumaine Street, across from a place called Johnny's Restaurant right off of North Rampart. Cos had *the* studio for recording R&B and rock and roll in New Orleans from the late forties until the mid-sixties. Even as a kid, when I was just coming by with my pa, I was fascinated that this was where records were made. Long before we started sitting in on sessions, James Booker, Leonard James, Deadeye, and I were skipping out of school to hang at Cos's studio. We'd sit outside and wait to try to get into the studio. At other studios, kids like us would get thrown out, but Paul Gayten and Johnny Vincent would let us hang.

At the time, Booker had already done a session or two himself, and he acted like an old hand at the studio business; we followed his lead. When a regular session was over, one of us would jump on the piano, another would get on the drums. We didn't jam exactly; we played things for each other. I might show Booker a little tune I was writing, and he'd turn around and flash some classical stuff he'd just learned. Before too long, I was doing sessions with Eddie Bo, Bobby Charles, and a bunch of other cats. Soon after, Lee Allen and the fellas in the regular studio band (Red Tyler, Justin Adams, Frank Fields, Earl Palmer, and Lee Allen) came in and announced, "Now you're in the funk club." I felt honored that they would make an issue of my being accepted.

All of this was a real mind-opening thing for a youngster like me. A lot of days, I'd go in there without a clue; they'd tell me "Do this, do that," and I was just glad to be there learning it all. We worked with so many hip artists back then, performers like Joe Tex or Bobby Marchand I'd admired from afar not long before. I remember the first time I met Bobby: He was in drag, and Huey Smith introduced him to me as Roberta. Later I met him as Bobby, and had no idea it was the same guy.

Another time, I got my head turned around by Little Richard. On one of Richard's studio dates, he had a bagful of money with him; I watched him as he threw it at Lee Allen's feet, trying to get Lee to go to bed with him. Lee kicked the bag over by where Leonard, Booker, Deadeye, and I were. Deadeye wanted to grab the bag and run. We said, "No, man, Cosimo would get pissed." So Deadeye threw the bag back and Richard started hitting on Deadeye. I was floored; I had never seen that kind of action before.

We was there when Richard cut "Tutti Frutti" and when Ray Charles dropped by to cut stuff, as well as peeping in on sessions by local giants like Fats Domino, Smiley Lewis, and Professor Longhair. This was just so hip to me—all these great musicians, in the flesh, doing it right then and there in Cos's place.

It was a real special scene back then. On some of the sessions, I'd get to play guitar with Justin Adams or Edgar Blanchard; these guys were heroes of mine—and now I was getting to work with them, not to mention with the whole rest of the studio band, a whole flock of heroes. Piano players would change almost session by session. There was Edward Frank, Huey Smith, Allen Toussaint, even my buddy James Booker. At first, I didn't play piano that much on sessions because of all these other killer players. Later, though, as I began producing records, I played piano more—especially if I couldn't get the guy I wanted, which happened a lot. Back then, aside from doing a bunch of boogie-woogies, the only style I could half-ass copy on the piano was Huey Smith's, with a little Professor Longhair thrown in. On one date, when Booker couldn't make it, he sent Allen Toussaint to sub for him, which was nice because by watching him so closely, I began to develop a real special feeling for Allen's playing and style.

I began my stint as a record man with Johnny Vincent's Ace Records, where I worked from 1956 to 1958 or 1959. Johnny was paying me three hundred dollars a week as a producer, plus usually another two hundred a week for all the extras I was giving. By extras, I mean whenever I found somebody who was good, I had to find material for him to record if he didn't have any usable songs. If I found material, I had to get the song arranged, then I had to supervise and often play on the cutting of the tune. It was my job, in short, to deliver finished product—even though, soon after I took the job, Johnny told me that if I earned over three hundred on sessions he wouldn't pay my salary.

Johnny tried to pass off as Johnny Vincent the country bumpkin, but his full name was Johnny Vincent Imbragulio and he wasn't no kind of bumpkin. He was a hustler, and he used that country shit to get over on us and other people. Johnny would eat them uppers and smoke them cigars like they was going out of style. He had two accents he used for whichever occasion fit: One was his backwoods bit from the sticks (which wasn't a total act, because he was from Jackson, Mississippi); the other was Italian gangster patter. He had one major talent: When he was at a session, he'd latch onto one thing, his mantra of the day, and repeat it over and over. For instance, if the session was with Huey Smith, he'd say "Huu-ree, put some *shit* in it." And everybody would respond and, sure enough, put some shit in it. That was it; that was the compiled wisdom of Johnny Vincent's approach to making records.

After a session sometimes, he'd ask me, "Do you think this guy's it? Is this guy any good?" And he really didn't know. But because of the way he asked you, and because he was such a conniving son of a bitch, he could make you feel like you were part of the big time—a big time that wasn't.

Johnny had a couple of fellas who would hit the highway to spot talent for him; if they found something, which was rare, they sent them my way. But most of the real action went on down in New Orleans itself, and my job was to sit in Cos's recording studio with a little piano and audition new acts that came in—one after the other after the other after the other. There were some guys who wouldn't give up. One particular guy auditioned every day I was there. Got turned down every day, came back the next to try it again. There was some acts you wouldn't have believed.

One guy had this fucking two-word song he'd say over and over, so fast you'd want to run out of the room and puke. Something like "Beautiful, baby, baby . . . beautiful, baa-by, baa-by, baa-da'by . . . beautiful . . ."—real fast, trying to imitate Little Richard. He'd be spitting on the mike. When you got to a solo break, he'd start trying to make these animal noises, these screams, but when it came out of him it sounded like a gorilla dying of ptomaine poisoning. I'd invite Dave Dixon, a New Orleans songwriter I got real tight with later in LA, and other cats over to get their kicks off these guys.

There was one little group that featured a midget singer. The singer was cool (we ended up recording them later for either Ace or Ric and Ron), but another guy in the group was so out of it that, whatever the harmony was, he sang a fifth or a fourth away from the key. Why the other members of the group didn't notice, I'll never know.

Occasionally some good ones came through, though, and we'd cut them right away. Al Reed, known as Pharaoh Al Reed, was one of these. He wasn't exactly a novice, because he had recorded for Imperial before he hit our audition. And his experience paid off for us: He touted me on other talented people to check out, such as Earl King's brother-in-law Raymond Washington, who we did some sides with, as well as two great songwriters named Eddie and Flip, who Johnny probably buried or blew the deal with.

When Johnny Vincent hired me to do producing for Ace, right away I got into the whole other side of studio work—things like contracting musicians for the sessions and hiring arrangers, all the functions of a producer. Back then, the title of producer was a whole different kettle of fish. What would really happen was that an act would come in the studio, make up a song (or decide to record one that was already in their repertoire), run through it with the tapes spinning, and listen to the playbacks. That was that. There wasn't any elaborate arrangement or engineering involved; you just worked out a head chart, and cut the tune.

All this business I learned haphazardly; only later did I really get to study the art of producing, from Red Tyler. Red was always the studio bandleader. He was the straw boss, the arranger, everything. Red was in charge.

We had this dumb practice that probably was kind of unusual at the time. We was so naïve about making money on sessions that we used to pass around the role of leader (and thus the right to a double rate) on any given session. This was unfair to cats like Red, because he was really the leader on most of these dates. But that's how unbusinesslike we were about it all.

This loose arrangement was a real financial drawback within the New Orleans recording scene at that time. In other places producers, arrangers, and contractors were paid; in New Orleans, I was making bottom-line three hundred dollars a week. But there was nothing you could do about it; none of the record company owners in New Orleans were about to get generous and offer us, out of the kindness of their hearts, a real live producer's fee.

If record labels paid for solos on hit records, Lee Allen would be a rich man; he played more sax solos on more hit records than anybody I know. Herbert Hardesty also had a lot of hot sax solos on other people's records, and even Fats Domino played piano for hire (check out Lloyd Price's "Lawdy Miss Clawdy"). The great Huey Smith, who should have been an international star himself, always felt obliged to add a particular stamp to another artist's record—he called it putting an "ID" on it— that would make it unmistakably that artist's own. This kind of attitude went way beyond the call of duty. They could have just come in and played the gig, but usually the studio musicians went to a lot of extra trouble to give people's records an identity. Earl King and Billy Tate (who played bass guitar and accordion) did the same.

It was from these cats that I learned my tricks, and I began to copy this attitude, too. If a guitar solo was called for, I would try to put a touch on it, at least phrase it differently for one artist than I would for another. When you got it right you knew it, even if the producer didn't always agree. We might hit something right on the money on the sixteenth take, but have to go on through forty takes before he decided we were done. But at the end of the session, we'd tell Cos: "Cos, take sixteen was it. All this other shit is downhill." Usually, he'd agree with us.

The most grueling sessions were when we tried to cut a follow-up to a hit; we'd have to do as many as a hundred takes, trying to capture that magic again. By the end, the trumpet player's lips would be gone, and we would have played ourselves into insanity, all over this *one* song. After a while, the guys would tell the producer, "Listen to take three again." He'd hear it and that was the one.

Most of the time, our schedules would be crazy. We might cut a session in the morning, do a gig in the Quarter that afternoon, cut another session that night after the gig, play a late-night gig after the session, then get up the next day to make a gig somewhere up in Mississippi or Arkansas. The roads in them days were so bad that if it rained there was a real possibility you couldn't make it back to New Orleans in time for whatever else you had to do. I mean, the road up to Jackson, Mississippi, once you hit the Mississippi border, wasn't nothing more than a one-lane dirt cow road. If he wanted me to make it to Jackson for sure, more often than not Johnny Vincent would have to put me on the train.

I remember more than once getting off a gig at two or three in the morning and going straight to Cos's for a session. Cos had sessions going around the clock, because for a while he had the only studio in town. When Shelby Singleton came into town with guys like Jimmy McCracklin or the Isley Brothers, he liked to book dates after hours because he felt the best time to get the session players was after their gigs, instead of early in the morning when everybody was in rotten shape.

Cos engineered dates by setting all the controls at a particular point, and then splitting. It was up to us then to get the sound down; all our mixing was in our playing itself. If a guy came up with a saxophone solo, he'd have to eat the mike with his horn; if it was a guitar solo, the player had to turn his guitar way up. If it was a piano part, the guy had better play pretty soft till the solo, and then hammer down or he'd get buried. Early on, we even faded down ourselves at the end of a record without the help of electronics. Very soulful stuff came out of that.

One of the flusturations of this job was that when I delivered something I thought was good, many times Johnny didn't put it out. Instead, he'd try to hand me another tune, saying, "See if you can put this on top of what you've got and disguise it—put some new words on it." That way, you could steal somebody else's song, so the money ended up back with Johnny. There would be times when Johnny called me up and said, "Call a session for eleven; I'll be there at three with the money." We'd do the session—Johnny wouldn't show up. This happened so many times that me and Huey Smith and a bunch of us had to go stick Johnny up at the record distributor's office to get the money he owed us. We held a gun on him while we went through his shoes, drawers, and trousers. This didn't seem to phase Johnny; it was nothing personal, and he'd try the same shit on us a few weeks later. And a few weeks after that, we had to track him down and stick him up again for our dough.

He could get over on us because he was the guy who had the money; we could get over on him because we was the guys who could deliver the music. He fired me more than once, in a manner that wasn't very businessfied. He never even did the dirty job himself; he got the guy who ran his books to do it. The guy would call me and say, "You're fired." I'd say, "From what?" Guy would say, "From Ace Records. You no longer work for Ace or Vin Records." I'd say, "Well, who is this?" (I didn't even know this accountant.) When I got rehired, as usually happened, Johnny told me himself (like he did the first time, by buttonholing me after a session, slipping a few dollars in my shirt pocket, and saying, "There's a session tomorrow at eleven. I want you to run it"). Everything was real casual and slippery with Johnny; nothing was on paper, and you had to pin him down before you'd find out how much you were supposed to be getting for your work.

I didn't know why I was hired in the first place, much less why I periodically got fired. But when he hired me back after firing me I'd feel much better, and forget all about being fired in the first place. Johnny Vincent was a good con artist.

He wouldn't think twice about selling guys down the river; there was one time he had two records out by Earl King at the same time, competing against each other—one under Earl's real name on Ace, another under the name of Handsome Earl on Vin Records, one of Johnny's other labels. It was the same way he set up two gigs under the name of Huey Smith on the same night: Huey would play one with his band, the Clowns; James Booker, passing himself off as Huey, would do the other with another band.

But on the other side, we didn't pay him his commission for these phony gigs he set us up with, which amounted to maybe fifty dollars. That's how we rationalized working with Johnny— through these nickel-and-dime ripoffs.

Johnny Vincent always claimed to appreciate songwriters; I'm told he hired me originally because I was a songwriter, though he was too busy thinking of ways to con me to level with me on that score. The funny thing is, though, he never got wise to how Specialty, his rival label, groomed their songwriters. Johnny never did appreciate what he had—a pair of hot writers in Earl King and Huey Smith. Some of Earl's best-known songs are "Come On" (recorded later by Jimi Hendrix, Stevie Ray Vaughan, and others), "Trick Bag," and "Those Lonely, Lonely Nights." Huey wrote "Rockin' Pneumonia and the Boogie Woogie Flu," "Don't You Just Know It," and "High Blood Pressure."

Johnny always figured Huey Smith could bail him out of anything because Huey was so hot for a while as a songwriter. Yet, at the same time, he mistreated Huey terribly. He took Huey's great song "Sea Cruise" and promoted the version by Frankie Ford, turning it into a hit—for Ford, not Huey. I know Huey wanted to do that song bad. He also took tracks away from Huey and gave them to Jimmy Clanton and other acts. Johnny never thought twice about what this did to his main guy.

Huey was so good to play with in sessions. His attitude was laid-back and funky, and he was always coming up with little groovy riffs that got the band even higher on the music. Huey inspired Allen Toussaint, me, and a lot of other musicians. Like a lot of us, Huey wanted to be like Professor Longhair; but when Huey played Fess's shit, it was Huey's, not Fess's. We all got along well. We loved each other, truth be told, and looked after each and other. For instance, Allen Toussaint would often sub for Huey on a date and play just like Huey; the other way around, Huey also subbed for Allen and laid down a sound just like Allen's. Me and Booker did the same thing; we were all at each other's beck and call.

Huey just had a knack for writing killer songs at the time. I learned more about writing songs from Huey than just about anybody else. He clued me into nursery rhymes as sources for songs; he also took lines off the streets, used Indian chants and slang, put it all into his songs. His song "Don't You Know, Yockomo" uses a famous Indian chant, "Oom bah way, tu way pocky way," in the very first line. People in the greater United States didn't know what that was, but Huey made it into a hit record.

One of the real scumbag things that happened with record companies back then was this: I'd write a song and bring it in, say, to Johnny Vincent. He would take it, put his name on it beside mine, and then a lot of times add the name of a disc jockey I'd never met but who he wanted to get to promote the record. This gave this deejay a third of the royalty rights to my song. So right now, there are gangs of songs I wrote back in the fifties that's got the names of people I never even met on them as my cowriter. Two of the worst offenders were Hoss Allen and John Richberg, who ran an operation out of Gallatin, Tennessee. Richberg was a deejay on this powerful radio station in Gallatin that could reach as far north as New York and Chicago and as far south as Jamaica and as far west as West Texas. Allen ran a mail-order R&B and blues record business in conjunction with the station and could move a lot of records. I was so glad they were recording my songs that I didn't realize I was getting fucked.

This kind of thing happened to all the New Orleans musicians and songwriters.

During the time that Johnny Vincent was investing so much time in Jimmy Clanton or Frankie Ford or any white singer who sounded like Elvis, I heard Jessie Hill doing his act at a place called Shy Guy's. The highlight of the act was a song he had written called "Ooh Poo Pah Doo." I came to Johnny and said, "Man, you should go check out Jessie Hill. The audience goes wild at this one song every time it's played." Johnny shrugged me off; later, when Larry McKinley and Joe Banashak got interested in Jessie, it was too late. He had signed with Joe Banashak's Minit label, and blasted off with "Ooh Poo Pah Doo," which Allen Toussaint did one of his typical great fonk productions on.

After a while, I threw in the towel on Ace because I got a better offer from Joe Ruffino at Ric and Ron Records. I did well for Joe Ruffino, so well that he offered me a job as president of the Ric and Ron label. I was just a nineteen- or twenty-year-old kid at the time. Joe was a spontaneous guy, but I thought he had real balls to offer me a job like that. My family thought he was nuts.

I might have had the title of President and A&R man, but as I had at Ace, what I was really doing was writing songs and producing. With Ric and Ron, I produced Martha Carter, Chris Kenner, Johnny Adams, and Tommy Ridgley. On my own and on the side, I also did a lot of scab productions at the same time with a trombone player, Leo O'Neil. Most of these sessions were done for Huey Meaux, and the artists themselves were mostly Texas acts that Huey shipped into New Orleans to be recorded— people like Barbara Lynn, Joey Long, Wayne Talbot, and Prince Charles.

Among all those acts, Johnny Adams was one of the biggest inspirations for me. Joe Ruffino was always tickled that he was the one who had Johnny Adams, who had some big hits with records like "I Won't Cry," "Losing Battle," and "Release Me." I always considered Aaron Neville and Johnny Adams the premier singers floating around the area.

In the late fifties and early sixties, producers were flying into

New Orleans by the planeload. During the time I worked for Ace I would also be doing sessions for Paul Gayten, who worked for Chess, Checker, and Argo Records. I remember doing a date for Paul and meeting one of the Chess brothers (I don't know which one it was). I remember this guy coming in with Paul, wearing a bebop hat; I thought, Wow, a record company president with a bebop cap—he must be pretty hip. Those were big deals for us in them days—having the Chess brothers or Jerry Wexler or Ahmet Ertegun coming down from New York for Atlantic to do a session in New Orleans.

Art Rupe's wife Lena also came to town to start her own label. Art owned Specialty Records; when Lena divorced Art, she came to town and cut Professor Longhair, Tabby Thomas, and a bunch of gut-bucket blues players from around Baton Rouge. I'd be on a few of these dates.

Besides working for Lena Rupe, I did a lot of other gut-bucket blues sessions, too. These were usually bootleg sessions outside union rules, cut in Victor Augustine's studio in the Godchaux Building using real prehistoric equipment. We recorded cats like Elton Anderson, Little Eddie Lang, and Riff Ruffin. I remember also going down into the country with Leonard James to cut a session for somebody like Lonesome Sundown or Slim Harpo and getting paid eight dollars a tune (and each tune took hours). It was a kick, but needless to say we never did it again for that kind of funny money.

It was a strange and amazing time to work as a musician in New Orleans. I remember doing a session with Irma Thomas in which we cut a Dorothy La Bostrie tune, "You Can Have My Husband, but Please Don't Mess with My Man." Dorothy La Bostrie was a real presence on the scene. She was kind of an unpaid talent scout, who brought in Little Richard to do "Tutti Frutti," which she wrote. She also wrote Johnny Adams's "I Won't Cry" and "Mickey Mouse Boarding House" for Big Boy Myles—real hip tunes. She was especially good at bringing about first records; she not only wrote them, but got them recorded, and got the records heard.

And other people came from other directions: Joe Scott, from Don Robey's Peacock label, would blow in from Houston to record Miss Lavelle and Junior Parker. I first met Joe when I worked a session with Miss Lavelle and put down a nice little guitar riff on her song "Teen-Age Love," and from that point on Joe hired me regularly; ten years later Junior Walker picked up the riff in his song "Cleo's Back." Junior Parker was one of my favorite "sweet" blues singers; he had a string of hits, starting with "Mystery Train," which became a hit later for Elvis. I have people like Joe Scott to thank for crossing my path with a few of those great ones.

During the late fifties New Orleans music began to change, and a lot of the change came first from the drummers. Earl Palmer had been considered the main funk drummer for a while; after Earl left to do session work in LA, Charles "Hungry" Williams took over for a bit. All of a sudden, though, a bunch of new drummers popped up—cats like Smokey Joe Johnson, John Boudreaux, and finally James Black, who had been a trumpet player with Roy Montrell's band.

John Boudreaux played one kind of funk, June Gardner and Smokey Joe another. Their style was similar, but with nice subtle differences, and both of them were real hip. Then James Black got wind of Elvin Jones when John Coltrane came through New Orleans, and James added the Elvin Jones element to his drumming.

Every break I got from working in the joints in the Quarter, I used to go to Vernon's to hear John Coltrane when he was in town. Every night I used to sit up behind McCoy Tyner, because I wanted to learn how he played piano. But Trane's music would get so intense—and my head was getting so narcotized—that I'd nod out every time they started, coming out of it only when they finished the set. I never saw a thing McCoy was putting down.

A lot of this new rhythmic experimentation was going down

over at AFO Records, which was the breeding ground for the new sound. AFO—"All For One"—was put together formally by Harold Battiste, John Boudreaux, Red Tyler, Roy Montrell, Chuck Badie, and Melvin Lastie as a record company in 1961, but as a group of musicians who were trying on new things, it had been around for a couple of years before that. Not only were these musicians searching for a new sound; they were trying to create a way for black musicians to hold on to their own music, instead of giving up control to unscrupulous white producers and record company execs.

I feel real blessed to have been around AFO, because they were putting down so much of the new and fascinating music that was coming out of New Orleans at the time. Since I hung with Roy Montrell anyway, I was on the inside with this new funk style from the beginning. Playing gigs on Bourbon Street and in the studio, I got to know a lot of the AFO cats.

AFO's first record, an R&B tune by Papoose's brother Lawrence Nelson, who called himself Prince La La, was called "She Put the Hurt on Me." That very first AFO disc went Top 40 on the R&B charts. The second, "I Know" by Barbara George, was number one on the R&B charts and even hit the top of the pop charts, too. This was the kind of immediate roll AFO found themselves on. It was awesome.

The arrangements on these and other tunes changed the way music was being played in the United States. Those first two songs, along with others by AFO, opened up the door wide for Motown and influenced Herb Alpert, who cleaned up the style on Melvin Lastie's cornet solo on "I Know" (no funky-butt for Herb) and turned it around into his monster instrumental hits of the mid-sixties. The kind of phrasing the AFO horn section laid down influenced R&B and rock and roll horn charts; twenty years later, you could still hear echoes of the sounds Lastie and the others had put down on "I Know." What John Boudreaux was doing with the drums on a record like "She Put the Hurt on Me" deserves a special look, too. Instead of playing a back beat on the snare drums, he played all four beats on the snare, a little New Orleans funk cha-

cha. Suddenly, the Supremes' "Baby Love" and other Motown hits had John's groove stamped on them; they didn't know how to play as fonky as Boudreaux, but you could hear it all the same.

It was an exciting time; things was happening and blossoming different. A buzz was in the air. Even Dave Bartholomew, who represented the older sound of, say, Fats Domino, tried to hire cats who could do the new sound—but the problem was, it was unclear for a time who had the sound and who didn't.

This is how the sound would be passed around: On the bass, Richard Payne was coming up with a funk groove that matched some of the new drum rhythms. Chuck Badie, another bassist, picked up on it, and because he did more recording sessions, he became known for that sound, though really Richard was the innovator—he just got lost in the shuffle. From Chuck Badie, the sound wafted over to Sam Jones, who was Cannonball Adderley's bassist, and seeped into more mainstream jazz. (Cannonball and Nat Adderley came to New Orleans a lot. They hung with the cats from AFO, and recorded with Nat Perrilliat, a talented New Orleans tenor player, as well as Ellis Marsalis and James Black.)

In the meantime, the funk fungus kept growing; a cat called Willie Tee (Wilson Turbington) put together a funk/R&B/jazz group, Willie and the Gators, that was an absolute killer outfit. He had George Davis on guitar (George was the epitome of the New Orleans jazz guitar player who also could play funk); George French on funk-a-sized electric bass; Earl Turbington, Willie's brother, on alto or soprano sax; and David Lee, an up-and-coming funkster, on drums. They mixed it up both ways, one moment playing complete funky-butt and the next turning the music to real out jazz—avantgarde stuff, but always grounded in the funk.

This approach proved influential. When Joe Zawinul, a keyboard player with Cannonball Adderley who later founded Weather Report, heard this sound, he kind of slid around the side and put it on "Mercy, Mercy, Mercy," which was a big hit for Cannonball's quintet. AFO also inspired Cannonball to cut "Jive Samba," "Tengo, Tango," and other tunes like that. The saddest thing was that at right about that time, Cannonball was fixing to put out a record with a lot of these cats. They cut this great album on Riverside Records with Melvin Lastie and Nat Adderley playing cornets; Red Tyler, Nat Perrilliat, Alvin Batiste, Harold Battiste, and Cannonball playing saxes; Ellis Marsalis on piano; Sam Jones on bass; James Black on drums; and a New Orleans singer named lzzycoo (who recorded the original version of "Blow, Wind Blow" for Ace) on vocals. Right after that, Riverside went under and left all these people, who had been so hopeful of busting out of the pack, in the can. I think in some way that led to the AFO band packing up, with some of them heading out to LA.

During the last year or so of the AFO scene, in the early sixties, my former guitar teacher Roy Montrell tried to get me to cut a couple of guitar duets with him. He also hired me to play organ on a few songs—I guess to help me out, because he knew I was grinding away at my scene down on Bourbon Street. He had a tune called "One Naughty Flat" on which I played organ, although it was written for two guitars. Out of this grew two new projects, an album I cut for AFO where I played organ and piano, and a duet act I worked out with Ronnie Barron called Drits and Dravy. Both "One Naughty Flat" and the Drits and Dravy records were beginning to get airplay, when, next thing you know, the AFO musicians left New Orleans for the greener pastures of LA, ending my recording future with them. They didn't last long as AFO out there, although a few of their members became active producers and session players; it was a premature end to a creative force.

I was also still in close touch with Shank, my ripping and running partner, and I kept getting caught up sideways in his trickerations; Shank never changed his ways. Obviously, he had it in his power to get me pissed at him, but I could never stay mad at him for too long. One night, after he had pulled some bad issue on me, I tore over to his house, ready to stab him. I came in there with my knife out, and he croaked, "Is that all you got to use on me?"

I said, "What you mean, is this all I got? This is enough to put you away."

"You better get a gun, motherfucker." He pulled this huge revolver out from somewhere, didn't even point it at me, but he got me backpedaling fast. Later, I found out his gun not only wasn't loaded; it didn't even have a firing pin. It was some antique from the Wild West days.

There was so many times when I was sure I'd never talk to him again, but he'd call me up from Philadelphia or Las Vegas and tell me he was flying into New Orleans the next day, and every time I'd meet him, anyway. Despite it all, I just plain loved the cat.

Shank used to run with a little clique of cons and dope fiends, among whom were two guys named Wimpy and Herbert. Around 1960 or 1961, the police in New Orleans set up a sting operation to catch wanted felons, one of the first of its kind to come down. They mailed out an invitation in the name of a new-in-town fence who was paying long dollars for any and everything for a party, and Wimpy and Herbert showed up and got busted. Shank was merciless with these guys. "I told you not to go to no fucking party," he said. "What are you, stupid? You think a real fence is going to fucking give you more money than he needs to? They gonna give you as little as they can, you stupid bas-tards. . . ." These were guys who were fixing to do seven, fifteen years, and he's putting them down—and even they couldn't stay mad at him, he was so outrageous and cheeky. I felt blessed Shank told me not to make that party.

Once, he conned one of my old ladies out of her watch; all he said was, "Let me see your watch," and he had it off her hand, on his hand, and he was gone. Last she ever saw of that watch. It didn't take but two seconds. Shank was like a shark, never resting for a con, because he had an oil-burning dope habit. All those old dope fiends were like that: steady on the hustle for their habit and always thinking ahead.

* * *

During the early sixties, the racial scene in the clubs began to change. Dick Johnson, a New Orleans drummer, opened up an integrated club on the corner of St. Ann and North Rampart. That was an instant success, where all kinds of musicians could jam—until the vice and narcotics squad came and shut it down. But other venues sprouted up to take its place.

All kinds of people were filtering down to New Orleans at that time. There was a saxophone player from Cincinnati named Rufus Go, alias Nose, who used to work down the block from us at the Showboat with Sugar Boy and the Cane Cutters. Every now and again, I brought Nose in to play solos on sessions. What was nice was that Nose had been doing sessions up north for Sid Nathan's King and Federal labels; he brought something new to the music—and those different little flavors here and there made New Orleans music exciting all over again.

Ike Turner was also showing up in town a lot to do recording dates, and Ike was aware of the New Orleans thing, too. Everybody in the record industry in those days leaned over to listen to what was coming down here. Recognition of the new New Orleans sound started with Barbara George and "I Know"; then Lee Dorsey followed it up with "Ya Ya." We all knew Lee was going to get across: His sound was fresh and funky. I had produced "Rock" Lee's first record for Cosimo's Rex label, and I still remember how he knocked me out with a song that became "Lotti-Mo" (which Cos didn't like but was later produced by Allen Toussaint and became a great regional record). You just knew the guy was a national hit waiting to happen, because he had that little funky thing going. He was Allen's perfect vocal vehicle.

One of the secret elements of New Orleans music was that so much of it had a family feel. A lot of good music in New Orleans had come out of families who played together—the Nevilles are just the best-known example. Besides them, we've had the Carbos (Chuck and Chick), the Lasties (David, Popee, Melvin), and the Adamses (Gerald, Placiden, and Justin). Everything was feeling good. The old-timers was still working, and so were the newer folks.

There was plenty enough work for everybody. I'd be working twelve hours on my gig on Bourbon Street, then six hours in the studio, and on top of that guys would call me to make another gig somewhere else. There just wasn't time to do it all. If for some reason you didn't have a gig and needed one, all you had to do was drop by Leroy's Steakhouse, which was just next to the Dew Drop Inn, and you could find yourself a gig fast. All the cats were making a little money and feeling fine—until the day came down when the unions announced that Cosimo's studio was off limits.

The two musicians' unions in New Orleans, the ofay union, Local 174, and the black union, Local 496, didn't understand anything from day one. They was on each other over turf wars, and on the musicians because we was mixing races in our sessions. The main thing they seemed to hate was going through changes with the paperwork, but each was also angling to pack local gigs with just their musicians. The only difference between them was that Local 496 was much more lenient about letting me pick up my checks at their union hall than Local 174 was about blacks picking up their checks there.

At one point, Local 174 called me before its trial board again on the charge of hiring black musicians for what they called a "white" session. I asked them, "What's a white session?"; they couldn't answer that one. They were pissed off because I would hire guys for their playing ability, which always ended up in racially mixed sessions. Local 174 wanted all white musicians in their sessions, period.

Sometime around 1963, I believe, Cosimo Matassa began using more advanced equipment to overdub takes at his studio, which kicked up an even bigger fuss than the race wars between the unions; the fear was that the new gadgets would allow producers like Cos to hire fewer players and run shorter sessions. Both unions immediately put a ban on Cos's studio, which we musicians ignored. Well, when the unions said they were going to fine us if we kept working at Cos's, most of us said, Fuck the union. What the hell do they think they're talking about? So after maybe a day or two I was over at Cosimo's doing a session with Wardell, Smokey, and some others, when Nick Tadin, the white musicians' union representative, shows up. "Mac, there's no contract for this session. You and these motherfuckers are going to get fined."

I said, "Well, okay, but let's just deal with it after the session." Tadin hung around a little bit and wrote up notes. They brought me up before the trial board and asked me who the guys were I was playing with. I said they were Harold Battiste and the AFO band, who at that time were out in California; I didn't want to jeopardize the fellas at the session, and I knew I couldn't cause Harold any trouble 'cause he and his cats were out of town. When the union found out it wasn't Harold, they brought me back before the trial board and doubled my fine.

I said, "You can't double my fine. It's against the Taft-Hartley Act." I didn't know this myself; my lawyer had given me the lowdown on it. Well, they threw my lawyer out of the trial board, and then they *really* broke the Taft-Hartley Act—they tripled my fine.

Around that time, I began cutting sessions for Joe Ruffino at his little studio, which was okay for what it was. But the union was beginning to throw a chill over the recording industry—and, as a result, the whole musical scene—in New Orleans just when it was about to take off big. Acts like Ike Turner, Otis Redding, Bobby Bland, and Junior Parker, who had been coming to New Orleans to cut their records, suddenly began to cut elsewhere—especially in Memphis (which led fast to the whole Memphis Stax soul sound that was so big in the mid- to late sixties). The union managed to burn down the music scene in New Orleans. It was a shame and a waste.

During my hassles with the union, I occasionally ran into Papoose Nelson, my old guitar teacher. Papoose had fallen quite a ways since the early days, when I was studying with him; he was a garbage head, a cat who would drink cheap pluck, smoke a bag of reefer, pop all the pills he could pop, then chase it all down with a shot of dope. Whatever he could get his hands on, he did it—real strange behavior.

Papoose wasn't the kind of hustler my partner Shank was. If he had the money, he'd do the dope. If not, he'd make out with whatever was available. Plus, Pops was a lonely little cat. He was sweet as can be, but it always seemed like everybody fucked him over royally, even though he never fucked over anybody else. He was just a good-hearted cat who happened to be strung out.

I used to pick Pops up sometimes over on Claiborne Avenue behind Local 496. He'd be sitting on the side step behind the union after finishing a rehearsal with Fats Domino's band. The rest of the band would all be gone and it would be just Pops by himself out there, sitting with a bottle of pluck in one hand and a joint in the other.

I'd say to him, "You want me to take you by your pad?"

He'd say, "No, I can't go home."

I'd say, "You want me to take you to your cousin's pad?"

"Can't go there either."

He had no place to go because all the people he knew would kick him out. He didn't have a real friend in the world, yet everybody dug him even as everybody used him. Both Papoose and his brother Lawrence had tough lives, and both ended up dying fairly young and under strange circumstances. Rumor had it that one or both of them had been knocked off, but no one could ever prove anything. (Even Shank died under unusual circumstances, overdosing in a city far from New Orleans. What was weird about Shank's death was that he never screwed up with dope; he had shown me how to test its strength, and always, always did it right. When it came to tragic magic, Shank was a scholar.)

One of the nice things I remember about Papoose was that when he played a guitar, he was in another world. If you ever see one of them old rock and roll movies with Fats Domino's band, you'll see Papoose sitting there smiling and playing, his head bobbing and weaving, rocking on the stool. Pops came out of a family of killer musicians, not only good guitar players but fine singers in the spiritual church tradition. I remember that before Fats came out, Papoose would warm up the audience with his renditions of great blues pieces. He and his brother La La had a soulful down style all the way. I used to study everything Papoose did onstage. I even dug the way he held his cigarette in his pick hand between his last two fingers and how after his last drag he didn't even look at it, he just dropped it, kept playing like nothing happened. I miss them cats, both Papoose and Shank, because life around them was one series of adventures.

All in all, the city was in for big changes, mostly for the bad. Besides the bad union business, the other side of this sad story was what came down from the law, especially our wonderful district attorney at the time, Big Jim Garrison, a side-winding, double-dealing, two-faced, supposed Mr. Clean who was playing both sides against the middle for the good of nobody. But more of that later.

Before the darkness, there had been good music all over the city: on LaSalle Street uptown there was the Robin Hood, the Dew Drop Inn; on Louisiana Avenue, Vernon's, Holiday House; out in Jefferson Parish you had the Cotton Club, the Beverley Country Club, the Club Forest, New Orleans East, Natal's Safari Room, and plenty of others. Almost every big-time, nationally known act I've talked about was working these joints. Bands would pack up from one gig, say, in Jefferson Parish, then go hit a gig in St. Bernard Parish, then end up the evening at an after-hours set in the French Quarter.

In a few years, new freeways and so-called urban renewal would cut up neighborhoods, creating a no-man's-land where before there had been places full of clubs and streets where people looked after each and other. Canal Street, which had been thriving, died. Where you could have walked in the Texas Lounge, the Brass Rail, or the Monkey Bar any night of the week and seen great music, now there are just cut-rate drugstores, burger-chain joints—ho-hum crap.

But before all this came down, I had my own private freeways to travel. The streets was my home; for a while, they was good to me, kept me from harm while I went about my own brand of tragic magic.

UNDER A BAD SIGN

You better keep the laws of the great commandments
In this jungle we call the streets.
We're always stone defenseless;
This is not the land of milk and honey.
This is a place where people sell their souls out for money.
The sign of the times;
This is the time of the signs.

—"Glowing,"
Mac Rebennack

I was about sixteen and a year out of Jesuit High when I met Lydia Crow. High school seemed a million miles away by then; our band was beginning to break into the scene, but we were still scuffling at that point. At the time, Lydia was married to my bass player, Earl Stanley. Our whole band was real close. I can't remember exactly how it came down, but somehow Lydia and I got together and hit it off solid. Then, when Stanley saw how we were digging each other, he got pissed.

As Lydia and I got to see more and more of each other, Stanley got more and more upset. Finally, one weekend, the band and a bunch of the women who used to hang around us—including Lydia—went to Mobile, Alabama, to play a gig. We were all laying low in the motel when Stanley decided to go out drinking. I think the idea was that he was going to hit the honky-tonks and pick up a chick. He was trying to make Lydia jealous, but really he just pissed her off, and she stayed at the motel with me. Anyway, turns out that after a few drinks he broke into a tackle shop and tried to steal a handful of fishing rods and a radio.

In short order the cops tagged him, and his scent led them straight back to us. It was a stupid bust. Lydia and I and the rest of the band were knocked out back at the motel; suddenly, someone looked out the window and saw that the place was being surrounded by police. The bed was decorated with narcotics—hashish, goofballs, you name it—but someone threw the covers over the whole menagerie, and the cops went right by it. They looked and searched for whatever it was they thought we had, and missed the one thing there was. But it didn't matter, because they took the whole band down to jail anyway, and let the girls go. Lydia worked to get us bonded out; one by one, they let everybody go but me, because I was the bandleader.

This bust bonded Lydia and me even more, and after a while we were more or less living together. At first, there was a bit of friction among Lydia and Stanley and me on account of my being with Lydia, but by and by Stanley let it go. He had developed other interests by then, and he came to see it was all history between him and Lydia.

One night after a gig where I was playing drums, Lydia and I decided to get married. The band was playing a New Year's Eve holiday gig down in Jefferson Parish; after the gig, we rolled our stoned selves into a car and headed out farther into the sticks to find a justice of the peace who would marry us. By the time we made it to the JP's house, we were both nodding off so bad that other members of the wedding party had to hold us up and jab us on the shoulders to tell us when to give our "I do's."

We ran with a whole set of people who used their street smarts to get by. One of Lydia's best friends was a woman we called Opium Rose; another was known on the streets as Betty Boobs. Opium Rose was this real skinny Filipino chick. She made her living however she could, as long as she didn't have to go downtown and work a straight job. She turned dates, boosted stuff from stores, hung paper (forged checks), whatever she could. The kick we all got from her was her skill as a booster. She walked into a store looking like she weighed 98 pounds and walked out looking like 180. I can remember being in stores with her where she would just clean up. She'd come in with an overcoat and start packing stuff away. She lifted heavy things, stuff she could hardly pick up—TV sets, radios—put it all between her legs, under her arms, or however she could carry it, and walked out with it all under her coat.

Opium Rose's pad was a stop-off point where our band hung out a lot. Late at night, when it was too late to go home or you were too tired to go somewhere else or you didn't have the money to get a room somewhere, you'd go up to Rose's to nod out. Her little brother, Opium Al, was a dancer with our band at the time, so a lot of times he'd take us back there. It was a natural. All of the girls were boosters and hustlers of various types, and most of them, like Lydia, were real stand-up people. One of them was a cousin of Rose's who was around a lot, a drag queen named Anna Mae Wong. Anna Mae was a trip to behold—that guy looked more like a bitch than a bitch did.

There was a lot of characters like that around that set, which kept things interesting. One of them was this cat named Esquerita, another sometime drag queen, who was also a musician. Esquerita set up the original style that Little Richard copped later on— high, wavy, piled-up hair, women's sunglasses and lipstick and shit. We were supposed to go on tour once with S.Q. (Esquerita's nickname), until Earl King told me, "Man, I don't know if I would take that gig. Mac, S.Q. is big and strong; he'll try to turn you out." As much as I might have dug S.Q. when he was around Rose's, I took Earl's advice and stayed off of that tour.

Most of the girls who hung around our band had a lifestyle similar to Opium Rose's. All of us fucking musicians had the fantasy that we wasn't supposed to do nothing but play music, and our women were supposed to support us in the lifestyle to which we was never accustomed. That was the philosophy.

We were always a tight-knit little group, and Lydia felt better knowing that she could call and find me at Rose's or one of her friends' than not find me at all. If I wasn't around to be found, she'd start thinking, The son of a bitch is with some other bitch, and that was when the shit got bad (often as not, she was right). But when it was among our clique of people, everything stayed cool.

From the jump, Lydia didn't like a lot of the things I'd fallen into. But then her life got narcotic-crazy, to a point where she not only went along with everything, but got caught up in all the chunks of things herself.

Lydia started her drug trip doing goofballs; somewhere along the line, she got into the rest. At first we both hid parts of our respective habits from each other, and it caused a lot of trouble between us: She'd accuse me of holding a taste and in turn I'd accuse her of the same thing, as if either of us much cared whether we were holding or not. Later we turned the corner, and our arguments centered not on whether the other was *doing* dope but on how much dope each one was hiding or stealing from the other. We had some bad fights over this, yet the bond between us was strong enough that whatever we fought about, when the shit hit the fan, we was together on everything.

But no matter how caught up we were, she was the one who was always trying to think of ways to get us off narcotics, out of the shit. She got so crazy about it, she turned violent: She chocked me, she stabbed me, and she ended up shooting me, out of pure frustration. She knew we were so chained to this lifestyle that we were bound to go to the penitentiary sooner or later, and there didn't seem to be any way we could pull ourselves away.

There was a code in the streets back then that allowed as how you could do anything behind your woman's back, but you weren't supposed to let her know it up front. But I not only would let her know it; I'd throw it up in her face. I didn't know what the hell I thought I was going to prove, but I actually thought it would turn out cool—even though at some point things came down so far that even I knew they needed cleaning up.

At the same time, I was trying to be this half-ass pimp and

hustler. I was messing around with this skanky bitch I picked up who didn't mean nothing to me; I was just using her to try to prove some macho issue to myself. This jive action hurt Lydia a lot, and she put up with me until she had it coming out of her ears. In the end, though, she always went after me when she couldn't take any more.

One of the worst scenes was with this one goofy nymphomaniac who had fucked my band, other bands—she'd made it with everybody. One time, when Lydia was out of town, I got a scheme going to clean up with this girl by getting her into porno movies. When Lydia got back, we had a set-to. She said, "You *had* to do this. Everybody in town's telling me about it. What's wrong with you? Don't you know this bitch's excess baggage? She's useless!" "No," I said. "I'm going to make some money off her." How Lydia put up with this, I don't know; she had to have the constitution of Fort Knox.

During my time with Lydia I tried all the hustles, but I was never good at most of them. Turned out the only scam I was good at was forging prescriptions; I was never good at hanging paper. You need a good attitude to pull that off. I had a partner who was great at hanging paper; this boy was a master of disaster at that game. He got girls to turn tricks with merchant marine sailors, and while the whore had the guy occupied, he rolled the guy. He always rolled the tricks without their discovering it. As soon as he had his hands on their paychecks, he ran out and tried busting the checks while they was still turning the trick. He liked to line up a bunch of lames at the same time, which meant that for an hour or so he was running from one spot to another, rolling some lames, then busting their checks. The idea was to make a lot of money real fast that way, then lay low for a while. Still, no matter how good he was—and he was good—this guy got nailed and shipped several times.

We tried every kinda whicha way to make some money. As far as our music, for little in-between gigs we might make eight to ten dollars a night; for good regular gigs, it'd be thirty to forty bucks. Usually on those I'd be making leader-double money, maybe sixty to eighty dollars a night, but this didn't happen all the time. Because an awful lot of the gigs were for chump change, the money didn't add up to much compared with what some of the girls could make boosting or tricking—which could amount to hundreds of dollars for a night's work. They'd be making ten times what we'd be making or more. The percentages were verily in their favor. Of course, there'd be times when the girl would go out on a date and get busted. Then you'd have to come up with bail—go kiss some club owner's ass, run all over to put money together to make bond, and that's not easy. The women made more, but they got busted more often; then again, if we got nailed for possession or fraud to obtain narcotics illegally, they had to raise a bigger bond for us. It was a real trap.

One of the things that made the New Orleans scene so weird was the corrupt vice and narcotics operation. One cop in particular lived in my aunt and uncle's house. He was a certified dope fiend and a friend of my Cousin Snake; he was also a real rat. Well, somehow this guy had become a narc—a full member of the police narcotics squad with all privileges attached thereto— but he never stopped shooting dope, smoking weed, popping pills, nothing. This guy in particular would harass the hell out of us, because he knew everybody. He'd come to me and he'd say, "You're a fucking Lower-Slobbovian and your wife's a fucking Korean refugee. I'm gonna bust your asses today." He was the guy who tried to plant some shit on me on Decatur Street, but he made a lot of other stabs at framing me, including one time when he tried to put some weed on me. When his partner told him to lay off, the guy lit up some of the stuff himself and blew it in my face as he got in the car to leave. He'd say, "Don't worry, we'll get you tomorrow. You can bet on it. I'm gonna bust y'all by Thanksgiving." To show you what a cocksucker he was, he didn't even wait till Thanksgiving—he busted us on Halloween.

I ran into another vice guy when I was trying to put together some whores during my lightweight, try-to-be-a-pimp period. I found this girl in a bar who was willing to work for me; I had her head screwed on upside down, ready to make me a little money, no big issue. One day, this vice cop grabbed me and started to slap the shit out of me. "What you mean, turning my girlfriend out?" He backhanded me, but not too hard at first—he was really waiting to get me outside so he can stomp the piss outta me. "She came all the way from Germany to be with me. You got her all fucked up out there turning tricks. Who do you think you are?" So finally he pulled me outside. He and his partner kicked my ass all the way down Bourbon Street. His last words to me as I'm lying on the ground all busted up: "I want her back tomorrow."

(When I had my bullshit pimping operation, I tried an abortion business on the side with this doctor, whom I'll call Joe. Joe once told me he used to do abortions for women in a concentration camp in Europe. After the war, he had skipped to the States and ended up in New Orleans, where he stuck with the hustle he knew best. It was part of my job to get rid of the bodies of the little babies. Joe would give me a package with a baby inside, and I'd take it to the Seventeenth Street drainage canal and throw it in. For years, I used to have nightmares about the bodies of these little babies floating around in the water.)

Not surprisingly, we were in and out of jail on a basis that was abnormal even for street characters. By and by, I had moved up from chump-change gigs to regular studio work and good-paying gigs at Papa Joe's, Trader John's, and Madame Francine's in the Quarter. There was enough money between Lydia and me that we didn't have to be going through these changes. Yet we were still locked in a battle royal with each other; Lydia stole my narcotics to try to keep me from developing a bigger habit, and I would beat the shit out of her by way of retaliation (the kick of it was, sometimes she'd beat me—she was born to kick ass).

Some of her uncles used to stop me on the streets and would tell me, "Look here, Mac. If you don't let Lydia slide, we're going to stomp your ass." But it was her grandmother I really used to be scared of. She was like my grandmother, she had that gris-gris spirit in her blood. One day when we was over at her house, she pulled me aside and told me I wasn't treating Lydia right and showed me the candles she was goin' to burn on me. Later, I tried to make an excuse to get back inside her house to steal the stuff she had working on me, but I was in a narcotic haze and forgot all about it. I still believe I should have done it, because in the end things came down wrong.

One day I was hanging out with Opium Rose and out of nowhere she hit me upside the head with her belt, popped me with the buckle. I asked her, "What's going on? Why'd you do that for?" She said, "I'm just trying to get your attention. If you really want to stay together with Lydia, you oughta know she's staying at my place. She's ready to kill you."

"What?"

"Man, you been messing with this other bitch, and Lydia wants to put you out."

I got to say this about Rose: She was stand-up people, 100 percent in my book. She wasn't a bullshitter. Sure she might jive the police, but she was square goods with me and the people we hung with.

One night while I was hanging at Rose's, I saw her giving birth to her daughter, a strange and beautiful scene. We were all sitting in her pad, which she had done up with wall-to-wall mattresses. It was a real hip upstairs pad. We were all loaded and Rose was screaming and the doctor was doing his ministrations and it looked like the child was just about to come out when the doctor turned to us, real annoyed, and said, "Man, y'all can't be smoking and doing all that shit in here. Get out!" It was a real disappointment because I was hoping I'd get to help wipe the kid off or something.

I was older than Lydia, but she had a sense of being street-wise, plus a sense of integrity; I've known only a few women in my life that was close to being as stand-up as Lydia. She had more balls than most guys I knew.

Once, when she was pregnant, she found out I was fucking around with another woman. This particular one was bigger than Lydia, and I mean not only bigger but imposing-big for a chick. She was about seven or eight inches taller than Lydia, weighed about seventy pounds more. Didn't faze Lydia a bit. She walked into Papa Joe's club on Bourbon Street, where we were playing, and took her on mano a mano. It was about nine in the morning. The band had been playing since eight or nine the night before. Lydia walked into the joint, grabbed the bitch's hair, pulled her off the bar stool, and smashed her face into the floor. Bartender jumped over the counter and I yelled, "Hey, man, let her be. It's Lydia." He said, "We know. We just going to get rid of this other one here." These guys who ran Papa Joe's put the girl out, but Lydia wasn't satisfied. She ran out of there, went after her target (who's running down the street for her life by now), pulled a gun out of her purse, and popped a cap to scare her.

When the police had her, Lydia took more of a beating than I took, because she not only stood up to them, she'd tell them off. One day the police took in four of us—me, Lydia, a partner of mine named Stalebread Charlie, and his old lady, Mickie. While they were booking us, Mickie hit one of the matrons in the face with a powder puff, which set the police off against Charlie and me. The scene was comical, but we was getting whacked so hard the humor passed us by for the moment. As we were getting whacked, Lydia jumped up and screamed: "Look, you motherfucker, let Mac go. Mickie's the one who powdered the matron, not Mac." They gave her a whack for opening her mouth. But she didn't care; she kept on them. She didn't say, "Let me go"; she said, "Leave him alone." You don't see that in people in this day and age.

But to make a long Lydia story short, I never took the hint, and I paid for it. I came home one night to tuck in for a little shut-eye; suddenly, I woke up to find her kneeling on my chest, putting a pillow over my face. I was wheezing, but I managed to throw her off. Lying there on the floor looking at me with burning-hot eyes she said, "You get the message, you fucking rank asshole?" I said, "What you talking 'bout?" She says, "I saw you with that bitch in the car . . . acting like a chump."

She kicked me out of the pad, as she had time and again before. During these periods, unbeknownst to anybody, I would take up residence at the recording studio. Every night when we closed down, I would have to jimmy the lock in a funny way before Cosimo locked it, so I could slip in behind his back and sleep on the floor of the studio. During the day, when I wasn't working, I'd spend my time on the streets.

Besides Opium Rose and her clique, the streets were crawling with other characters, and most of these went by their street names: Tuffa Lip Tommy, Buckethead Billy, Marblehead, Pinhead, Fat Lester, Wimpy, Mr. Oaks and Herbs, Wop and Tex. Stalebread Charlie and Mickie were two of these characters; they ran a whorehouse not too far from the Quarter, near St. Roch Park. Charlie's front was working as a doorman at the Silver Frolics Club on Bourbon. Charlie was the funniest doorman I ever knew. I worked right down the block from him and soon I began to get a read on his game. His thing was to shift the expressions on people's faces as they walked by: He'd tell the *turistas*, "Hey, wanna get some good pussy? You got it here." Just stuff people normally didn't say in the fifties. "Fuck inside? Sure you can." He'd say anything to get them in the door. Other barkers had a little more class. Charlie just didn't give care; he was into Buddhism, Zen, all kinds of things you don't expect someone in his racket to dig. He was a real Beat character.

Around this time, I used to have a chauffeur by the name of Cubano George. When he drove me around, we'd run with all these Caribbean cats he was tight with, and one was a guy named Prince who was an artist from Haiti. Prince used to paint these strange murals on the walls inside and outside of buildings. These murals decorated the sites of different gris-gris and sanctified churches for various reverend mothers. In one place, he'd painted a nativity scene that at first glance looked regulation-issue, until you noticed certain strange qualities the more you looked at it. Take Prince's three wise men: One wore a general's hat, the second a cowboy hat, the third a porkpie. Also, one of the shepherds in this scene was lying on a sofa in the middle of a field of sheep. I don't think the old reverend mothers ever noticed.

He painted another that used to fry me because it was both so realistic and so skewed. It showed Jesus carrying the cross around the Stations in Jerusalem, and it went the whole way around the room; if you looked close, Jesus never once touched the ground. In the end, when He's falling down with the cross, not only is He not touching the ground, but there's somebody kneeling over Him who's not touching the ground, either. Later, you see the Romans nailing Jesus to the cross and the cross is just floating in the air.

Cubano George and Prince ran with this whole little clique of dudes who used to hang around the Dew Drop—people like Joe Hinton, whose dad was the doorman, and a musician whose street name was Porky Pig. Another cat hanging out with George was a smuggler who worked on the Havana–New Orleans boat. Wherever those smugglers shipped out to, they made it a point to bring back some stuff from those parts: hash from a run to Turkey, gangee from Africa, whatever was grade-A pure. He also collected hash and opium pipes from all over, and he'd sell them in sets. At one time I had a whole set, beginning with a mother and a father pipe, each about as long as my forearm; then they'd go to grandmother/grandfather pipes, great-grandmother/grandfather pipes, and great-great-grandmother/grandfather pipes, which got to be about six feet long. I'd decorate these pipes with tassels and froufrou. I also bought shrunken heads he brought in from South America, which he'd sell in these fancy little balsa coffins. Over the years I lost or sold them all, except for one—a guy with real red hair I nicknamed Eric the Red the Viking.

A lot of the musicians connected with this Caribbean scene would later pop up in my life in unexpected ways. One of the most significant of these cats was Richard "Didimus" Washington, who hung around with Prince and Cubano George, and gigged at G's club on congas, bongos, timbales, dombekis, and unique percussion instruments of his own creation. Didimus had spent the first years of his life in Ethiopia, then moved with his family to Cuba. As a kid, he'd studied for a time with Chano Pozo, the great conguero. So he was drawing on music from all directions—not only Ethiopia but Cuba and, later on, New Orleans.

When I first saw Didimus, he was playing with a group called the Crescents, which featured Elouard Burt on flute; Edward Blackwell, later Ornette Coleman's drummer, on a handmade drum kit; Didimus on handmade congas; Edward Franks on piano; Otis Deverney on bass; and, sometimes, a few others. Later, they changed their name to the Afro-Caribbean Sextet, Septet, Octet, whatever fit the gig. They put on Afro-Caribbean shows at dances all over the place, and they were really tough.

Didimus was the greatest conguero I ever heard, and the only one I ever worked with who played five conga drums—not one, not three, but five. Not only that, he had two bongos between his legs, and on a stand next to him two dombekis—a battery of nine percussion instruments. He played Haitian finger-style rhythm, and African-style, and mixed that up with his own Cuban jazz. I was lucky as hell to get him to join my first Dr. John band when we met up again in LA in the late 1960s.

On Christmas Eve 1961, my little band and I took a gig at a joint in Jacksonville, Florida. We was getting ready to go to the gig when we realized that Ronnie Barron, who always took forever to do hisself up for gigs, had disappeared. I went to look for him—and found him being pistol-whipped by the motel owner, who'd caught Ronnie with his old lady.

I went to get the gun out of the guy's hand. We wrestled for it; I thought my left hand was over the handle, but I was actually grabbing the barrel. We started in Ronnie's room and ended up outside in a brick garden. I beat the guy's hand against the bricks trying to get the gun away from him, and the gun went off.

I looked down and saw the ring finger of my left hand, my fretting hand, hanging by a thread.

I went berserk. I started hitting the guy in the face with a brick; I stuck my finger behind his eyes to try to pop his eyeballs out. Paul Staehle came up, and I took one of his drum cymbals and cut up the guy's face. Some time after that the police came and took me to the hospital in Jacksonville. The doctors there managed to reattach my finger, and later in New Orleans I underwent further surgery and began therapy to regain the use of my finger.

In the months after this incident, I went from anger to anguish to numbness. At the moment I was shot I saw not just my life, but my career, pass before my eyes. Everything I had been working for seemed like it might have been over. To get through it all, I tried to make myself as null and void as possible—a state I achieved through a heightened habit.

Now I was caught up in a trick bag. I needed to work, but playing guitar was out of the question with that lame finger. I began gigging as a bass player at the Famous Door Lounge with a Dixieland band.

I settled into the bass slot, playing stand-up with the four usable fingers of my left hand, with Murphy Campo, a local Dixieland band. It was all right for a while, but my finger was healing while I was doing this gig, and by the end of the evening— every evening—the wound opened up and I bled all over the bass I was using. This wasn't my ax, and I tried to keep it clean by rubbing it off real carefully after each gig. Still, I was rotting out the guy's strings, and since strings for a stand-up bass were real expensive I had to quit using it. Instead, I began using Earl Stanley's electric bass. Murphy didn't go for the electric bass at all; he kept calling it a guitar. Things went from bad to worse after that.

Finally the gig just was killing me, murdering my soul. The club owner, Hyp Ginley, used to try to keep me going; "Son," he'd say, "if you just can get your head screwed on straight, you can play here for the rest of your life." And all the while I was thinking, Oh my God, Mr. Ginley, I don't even know if I can play here another week. I liked playing New Orleans second-line, but the Campo band was into more of a Kansas City–style Dixieland, which didn't move me at all. Good players would come and go on this gig—killer piano players like Roy Zimmerman and Johnny Sansone, drummers like Monk Hazel and Dick Johnson— but as a scene the Famous Door wasn't making it. One day, James

Booker came up to me and said, "Mac, I know you're miserable. Listen, I'll teach you how to play organ. All you gotta do is whatever I tell you."

Booker had been staying with me and Lydia, but he'd never mentioned that he'd been playing for the Conforto family, who ran some popular Vieux Carré clubs. Somehow, he had conned the Confortos into buying a couple of organs, and he knew he was onto something. So one day Booker says to me, "Look, come over to Werlein's music store and I'll teach you how to play organ." A few days later, Bobby Blanchette, who ran Madam Francine's and Trader John's clubs in the Quarter, went over to Werlein's music store with us and paid cash money for these three organs and six Leslie speakers for a new club they were setting up. Threw a lunch bag full of bills at the guy, and next thing you know I'm at the club—and they're still building it. Blanchette said, "Yeah, we're gonna open in three days." I looked around. The place wasn't close to ready. Even the night of the gig, they were still putting the joint together. Blanchette said, "Don't worry. It'll be ready by the time you're set to hit." And, no shit, it was.

Booker and I worked strip joints like Madam Francine's, Trader John's, and Papa Joe's. We'd work four hours at Madam Francine's playing behind strippers. Then we'd work four more hours at Poodle's Patio playing a dance set. Then we'd go four more at Papa Joe's in a jam session. We'd start at nine at night and play till morning. All these places were within one or two blocks of one another. Madam Francine's and Papa Joe's were catercorner across the street in the French Quarter.

We'd start off the night playing behind the strip shows, in between comedians and magic acts. There'd be two different sets of bands, me and my band—the white act—and Booker's band, the black act. The only good thing about the segregationist issue was that it gave us a little work. The night would begin on a Jim Crow note, Booker's trio working out at one club, mine at another. But pretty soon law and order broke down. What would happen was that after an hour, the bands would take a break and begin switching gigs. Bit by bit, his band would move over to where we had been playing; me and my guys moved over to where they'd been. The kick was that we'd change only one person at a time. The Confortos and others wanted the music at the clubs to be nonstop, and I mean literally, so we'd work it out that after the first hour, the drummers for both bands would take a long solo; meanwhile, Booker and I might hit the head for a little relief, and trot over to switch places. We'd slide in, pick up the end of the song with a flourish after the drum solo, and carry it on, jamming with the other guy's band. After another hour, the tenors might switch, after the third the drummers would go. Never a moment lost.

The people we worked for—the Conforto family, Bobby Blanchette, and the rest—liked it when we had fun; they figured if we was getting our kicks, the audience would be too. And they liked throwing the crowd a curve or two when the changeover went down. Little disturbances like that helped to keep their joint happening all the time. People would drift in, watch the strippers for a while, talk to B-drinkers, then loosen up to play cards, which is what really kept the clubs in change. If the guys in the band ever got into trouble with the police, the owners would help bail them out. There was an unwritten law that we had to stay clear of narcotics—which, of course, was a problem with some of us. But they was real good to us.

The club owners kept their places open twenty-four hours a day, seven nights a week, and we played all seven. What the owners did was rotate the customers so that at least one club was always packed with some kind of action. The nature of the action was dictated by the time of day.

The audiences in the Quarter back then were easy to please, but we weren't really playing for them. Back then, you were really playing for the club owners. If the club owner liked the band, after all, you were in, you had a gig. There were a few basic rules: Play a loud, fast song, for instance, if a free-for-all broke out in the club. Otherwise, we all did just what we wanted to do. As long as the audience didn't throw rocks at us, the club owners were happy.

Papa Joe Conforto used to fracture me. He was a sweetheart. Every night, we'd play this old song "Down at Papa Joe's," and he thought it was a song we wrote for him. He would love it. We made up so many offhand songs at the time, he must have figured that was another one, special for him. "Down at Papa Joe's" or "Indian Love Call," another of his favorites, would put him in heaven.

Sometimes the muscle in these places could get carried away with their job. I'm talking about guys who was so crazy, they'd carry their pieces around in brown paper bags—guys who would go out around noon with lunch bags and come back in the afternoon after they shot somebody or scared somebody to death.

One night, we was working a gig at Madam Francine's backing up strippers, exotic dancers, a magician and comedian. The comedian was a little dude who had played Vegas for a while; somehow he'd wound up in Madam Francine's for a month or so. The first thing that happened when any guy—musician, comedian, or whatever—got booked into the club was that the ownership warned the newcomer that any girls who worked there belonged to pimps who either operated in this joint or were bouncers there.

This little comedian must have thought he was a wise guy, because before long he began making it with one of the girls working this spot. After a while, the girl got pissed at him over something, and ratted him off to the management. One night, our little trio was playing; it was just before our break and the comedian was supposed to go on next. Just as we were playing our last song, these two heavies grabbed the comedian. One of them said, "Bring that little motherfucker up here. I'm gonna fuck him up." The comedian turned white, and they started to pistol-whip him, kicked the shit out of him on the street corner. Because all the doors of the club were wide open, we caught it all out of the corners of our eyes just as we were winding up. Then the bouncers shoved him into the club and onto the stand, yelling, "Now go be funny, funnyman. Make us laugh now, motherfucker." The little dude's nose was bleeding and his shirt was all ripped and bloodstained, but he made it through his act. Needless to say, the comedian wanted to beat it out of town right then and there, but the club owner wouldn't let him go. He had to finish his contract. Them last days was real cold—by the end, even the club owner was ranking this guy's ass during his act.

Working at these places, I first got hipped to how lottery slang had spilled over to the music biz. A *gig*, for instance, was originally the mob term for a lottery bet—you'd place a dime gig, a nickel gig. Musicians turned this around to mean a date to play music. The word *ax* was another: To a musician, your ax was your instrument. Years ago, they told me, if they wanted to fuck up another lottery company they'd bring actual axes in and tear the place up. Later, to keep what they were doing sounding cool, they called the tools of their trade—rifles, shotguns, machine guns—their axes. That's the way musicians borrowed the word. If something was "in the bag," it meant that money from a bet or gambling operation had been collected. Musicians borrowed this term to signify a musical bag or groove we were in. There were so many words like that, it blew me away.

After our nine-to-midnight gig (for the *turistas*), things began to get a bit more interesting. From midnight to four, you had a different crowd, hip but not street characters. After four in the morning, you got the real low-down crowd, when the hustlers, pimps, whores, con artists, high rollers, and all the other characters put in their appearance. By about four, these folks had finished up with their hustle and wanted to spend their money or make up what they'd lost by jackin' or jeffin' somebody.

The jam sessions after hours at Papa Joe's were great. People showed up from all over town. Besides the hustlers and characters, a slew of out-of-town bands—whatever act happened to be working at Al Hirt's club, Lionel Hampton's band, Cab Calloway's band, Boots Randolph, Don Jacoby—would drop by. The music got way down during this stretch. We played your real serious New Orleans junko blues, and the racial barrier on performing (and anything else) tumbled because of the absence of *turistas*. These sessions were for the diggers and those who dug the lifestyle of the hip and crazy. The police knew that, and by and large they left us alone.

Those sessions were the first times I had to sing and work a house. When the regular singer got too hoarse to do it, I'd take over and handle the lyrics. By popular demand, I'd get up and sing long-ago-and-far-away standards like "How Much Pussy Do You Eat" or "Dope Fiend Blues." Along with the regulation standards like "Junko Partner" and "Lush Life," this was the stuff this crowd liked to hear. No watered-down material for them: It was lyrics like "I'll sit right down, roll myself a reefer . . ." that went over. "Turning tricks, sucking dicks, making bread, giving head . . ."—they spoke to their audience. That crowd also loved it when we'd mess with the popular songs of the time. You'd take something like "Got My Mojo Working" and rewire it so it came out "Got my little kilo Bella hustling and my junky partner won't 'turn on' you . . ."—things like that. These lines had nothing to do with the song, but they applied to the crowd.

They was the best-tipping audience of the night. Take your high rollers: They'd tip way more than they could afford, just to outtip someone else. None of them wanted to say he'd been outclassed by some cash-flashing character. The kitty was out in the open on the bar or the organ; one cat would take it and stuff in a hundred bucks. Some other guy might say, "Yeah? So-and-So just tipped two hundred," so the next guy'd have to match him.

You'd see some screaming action during those wee hours. I had a friend back then named Chang-Chang; he played organ in one of those joints and ran a slick scam. He had a little monkey on a chain that sat on his back while he was playing. Late at night, Chang-Chang would do his little bit. If some poor customer was passing out and the joint was half empty, he'd send the little monkey out to roll him. The monkey would dance out and lift the guy's billfold, then bring it back to Chang-Chang, who would take what he needed out of it, give it back to the monkey, and send the monkey back to the drunk to put the billfold in his coat pocket or leave it on the drunk's table. Even the animals were getting into the act.

* * *

In 1962 or 1963, Jim Garrison, the New Orleans district attorney, got a political hair up his ass about the so-called corruption that existed in New Orleans. What was ironic about this action was that Jim Garrison was backed when he ran for DA by a lot of the club owners, who threw together a considerable amount of cash to help in his campaign. I used to see Garrison around Stalebread Charlie and Mickie's whorehouse, and at other places, too. I thought he must have been cool—and then all of a sudden, when he got in office, out of the middle of nowhere, he turns Mr. Jive-Ass Morality.

The first sign on the wall came when he began setting up sting operations. An out-of-town fence threw a party at a local joint, and invited a lot of dope dealers and hot-goods merchants. People was sitting around cutting dirty deals of every conceivable variety, in front of a two-way mirror, when in walked the police and took them all off to jail. A lot of those folks caught a fair amount of jail time—seven years, fifteen years, and the like. This sting made a splash, but at the time no one thought it was anything more than a one-of-a-kind grab for media attention. But that wasn't how Big Jim wanted to run things.

Next, Garrison came in and started padlocking everything—gambling joints, whorehouses, the works. Real quick, the whorehouses was busted, starting with Stalebread Charlie and Mickie's place. Garrison did it to keep these clubs and whorehouses shut—which was a totally different approach from the other DAs, who'd just shut a place down for a day or two in order to show they were on the side of Louisiana law and order—while letting everybody get a little bribe taste and keeping business popping as usual.

And Garrison didn't hit just a few joints; he went after them all. One night during a gig I went outside for a break and looked down the street, and half the doors up and down the block were padlocked. People were wandering around in the street looking lost and dazed because only a few joints were open. For one thing, these joints were the reason all the *turistas* came to New

Orleans. Without them, New Orleans turned into just another Hoosier or Bozier City. The action wasn't closed down just on Bourbon Street; it was all over the place—St. Charles Avenue, LaSalle Street, music strips up and down Canal Street and out in Jefferson and St. Bernard parishes.

This spasm of righteousness had its costs. New Orleans underwent a new crime wave, because all the bouncers and heavy-action types who had previously been employed now had to find other ways of making cake. You had some guys pulling armed robberies; some girls who had been B-drinkers turned out into the street as street whores. Girls who had been whores in the whorehouses became boosters. Before, the club owners in the Quarter had run their turf like dukes; they had a system for everything. They had their own muscle working in the clubs or out in the streets. If there was trouble in Bourbon Street, their guys would deal with it, whatever it was, before the police ever got there. People from out of town wouldn't see much trouble before it was taken care of—and fast. There was a coolness about it. Jim Garrison's political reign of terror dismantled this structure. When he was through, we had a real law-and-order problem on our hands.

Unfortunately for the musicians, live gigs and vice went hand in hand, and with all the joints being closed down, suddenly jobs began to get tougher to find. A few years after Garrison started his work, the whole guts of New Orleans had been ripped out. As a result, guys I had been working with, fine musicians, had scattered all over the place—to New York, Chicago, Memphis, and LA. The scene was dead, and there would be no getting it back to the way it had been.

As New Orleans caved in on itself, so did my relationship with Lydia. Finally, one day Lydia said she'd had enough: Either I'd move out or she would. We got in a fight over that; I knew I was being an asshole to her, but I just couldn't let her go. Somehow, I thought I could live four lives at once. In the end, though, you can't do it. You got to choose one and go with it. So at last, we split. It was a real shame, because she had a deep understanding of things. Later, so many hard blows befell her, not the least of which was the San Gabriel Penitentiary, where she did time that really might have been mine: We were set up for a drug bust, and Lydia got the case. They brought her up on a count of possession. She wound up going to San Gabriel, the state pen for women.

Soon enough, I got shipped, too, from one last bust that put me off the bricks solid. I tried to be cool about it, but what I couldn't understand then was that it wasn't just my way of life that was ending—thanks to Jim Garrison, it was also the city of New Orleans that we'd loved.

TIME CHANGES

> *I sit in the cell;*
> *I suffered like hell,*
> *All for the want*
> *Of a shot of dope.*
>
> *I rant and I rave*
> *For the drugs that I crave.*
> *To ease my raggedy nerves*
> *I pray without hope*
> *To the goddess of dope*
> *Of whom every whim I would serve.*
>
> *See these tracks all in my arms,*
> *Tell me do you know what they mean;*
> *They were left by the finger of death,*
> *My training nurse, my sister morphine.*
>
> —*"Tragic Magic,"*
> Mac Rebennack

I remember the bust that did me in: The narcs picked me up with two bundles of heroin wrapped in gum wrappers. Each package contained thirty caps of heroin. There were two cops sitting in a Cadillac on the other side of Elysian Fields. We had just picked up a stash near a house there, and the narcs were sitting down the street waiting for us. I threw the packages into

115

a ditch as soon as I spotted them, while the narcs were still a ways from us. I knew right away that somebody had ratted us off, because I heard one narc say to the other, "Look for them Juicy Fruit gum wrappers." They knew what they was looking for.

They busted us and that was that. This was long before any official form of plea bargaining. We're talking strictly about back-door lawyers dealing with back-door judges dealing with back-door cops, making back-door deals. What it came down to was that I had been busted so many times that I found myself staring at some dismal time.

I was locked down for a while on that beef. I still get a lot of 'plexes about those times and I hate remembering back on it. Some of the people who was involved with me are now doing fine and I don't want to put their business in the streets. The only ones I'll mention have either passed or are doing so much time they may never see the bricks again.

When it hit the fan for me, they wheeled me off to parish prison; then, after a while, I wound up in a program for dope fiends that was going down in the Fort Worth federal prison. When I finally got to Fort Worth it was a relief: Coming out from a gig that was a stone 365-by-24-by-7, it seemed almost like being on vacation. Three hots and a cot always appealed to me. I had no responsibility, and I could always connive myself to work in a music room some kind of way.

I began my rehabilitation on the garbage crew. I got a janitor's diploma out of this revolting development, and I picked up a high school–equivalency certificate, a GED, with the help of a soulful brother named Joe.

Joe was one of my roomies. He was a cat with learning, who was doing a bit for murder and a few federal crimes. He was a Muslim and he was into bettering hisself, more so than most of my homeys there. Most of these cats didn't give a shit about anything, but Joe did. He had honed his English during his time, and he schooled me the same way. He used to make me learn new words all the time. I probably don't remember half the words he taught me, but back then I knew a hell of a lot of them and how to use them.

Joe was really good people; he encouraged me, helped me get my GED. He made learning fun for me—that was the difference between him and all the other teachers I ever had. He made me want to show him I could do things. Joe was the sweetest cat you'd ever want to meet. He was dead into the Koran, and got a charge out of showing me quotes in the Koran that applied to Christianity. He also helped me a lot because other cats were scared of him. He'd landed on the inside because he had strangled someone trying to steal a necklace to support a drug habit; he'd also wasted a cat on the inside, just defending himself. So he got a lot of respect in the joint—he was a good guy to know.

By the time I was transferred to Fort Worth, not only was I studying, I also had managed to work my way up to a job in the band room, and started gigging with some of the other cats. A lot of them were doing time on violation of the Boggs Act and the Harrison Act (interstate and international transportation of narcotics, respectively). Some of them were really good players: Hampton Hawes was there, Don Wilkerson, Boogie Daniels—a lot of good musicians from all over the Southwest. So we had real good bands.

And, of course, we all had to deal with the cure. The system had it in mind they were going to try to find a cure for your most chronic dope fiends. Now, I knew for a fact that they didn't have but a 1 percent cure rate, because I was one of the guys who got the gig of rifling the shrink's office to let the cats in group therapy know what the shrink was thinking. From all this, I knew who was listed in what condition. My sheet had me on some smoking charges—namely, I was psychotic, had delusions of grandeur, was a borderline dipsomaniac (I didn't even drink), and who knows what else. The kick to me was that the shrink was a young-punk navy doctor who was scared to get shipped to Korea, even though the war there had been over for years. The therapists in the pen had this claim that they'd cured Bela Lugosi, even though it was a certifiable fact that Bela died a dope fiend. No matter, the man had pictures of Bela on the wall, along with a Hall of Fame of other narcotics abusers.

Inmates came and went without much of a habit change, but the croakers thought they were doing the right thing. They put people into different categories depending on their condition. I was what they called a winder, a person who was on a volunteer commitment (to get my ass out of a much worse place) not too voluntarily.

Throughout my tour of better dens and dungeons, I got hip to a few facts of prison life. In every joint, there was a few cats who was very aware of what was coming up. For instance, there was this one fella who used to tell me, "Man, Mac, the money ain't gonna be in narcotics in the future; it's going to be in rehabilitating dope fiends." This was a long time ago, way before most of your self-help groups. "Tell you something," he said. "I'm going to leave up out of here and I'm going to make one score. And you're going to know I made it, because I'm going to make it with a judge. And I'll tell you how I'm going to do it. I'll make this judge embezzle a fortune out of this business. When it looks like my cut is right, then I'm going to leave the U.S.A., and the judge will take the beef. But they won't give him no hard time. He'll just end up in one of your country-club sets. And you'll never hear about me no more."

Well, I read about this story in the papers not long after that, and years later, on one of my trips to Europe, I ran into this same cat. He was doing fine, had himself a nice car, the works. He'd been in Europe this whole time.

There were all kinds of guys on the inside; when you get to know them, you discover a different kind of world that you don't hear much about in the papers. You had your big-time cats serving time with TVs, outside-world issues coming to their cells just like Scorsese had it in *GoodFellas*. They'd be in there having a good time, smoking Cuban cigars you couldn't even get on the street.

You'd find big-time racism inside, too, coming from Aryan

Nation types (though they didn't use that name much back then). I wasn't too well thought of by this aggregation of lames. I was with my own little clique of cats, my homeys from New Orleans, many of whom were black and members of the Nation of Islam. A few of the old-timers looked out for my front and my back; they taught me how to sleep with a straight razor under my pillow in case one of those sick motherfuckers tried to attack me in my sleep. They taught me to sleep real light, resting on my back so I could open my eyes and look up real fast, with one hand propped behind my head and my fingers around a straight razor. They also taught me that you had to keep the razor between the cheeks of your ass during the day so you could get to it fast if you needed it. That way, the guards shaking you down might not find it.

For all the square-goods dudes I met like Joe, there were ten who'd gone wrong. One thing that surprised me right off was the flak I caught from cats from home in New Orleans, guys I thought were going to be my friends. The first guy who tried to fuck me was a cat I used to run with, a partner called Cheeky. After I got him off my ass, I began to understand how he'd gotten his nickname.

After a while, some of the Crescent City cats gave me a punk, just some youngster who worked in the kitchen, for my satisfaction. I knew I wasn't fucking this kid, so we just looked out for each other; he kept me tightened up with zuzus [sweets] from the kitchen—which was like a sweet-tooth addiction to me, I liked them so much. But my partners had already turned this kid out, 'cause he looked pretty to them. He was a good kid, but there was nothing I could do about it; that's how it was then.

See, in the system—federal, state, or local, it don't matter — they got this whole fixation about turning pretty young things out, making them someone's personal whore. That atmosphere is so heavy that youngsters who won't be turned out can wind up dead; the ones who let themselves be turned out can get themselves fucked to death just as easy.

Cliques like the Aryan Nation dudes was always trying to

mess with people's heads. There didn't seem to be any heavy organization behind them, like there is today. These chumps would scribble their swastikas around the joint, and minority cats would have to be fearing for their lives. If they ever got a black dude or a Jew off by himself against eight or nine of them, they'd terrorize the shit out of him. But if you ever got them one-on-one, you'd see terror in that motherfucker's face.

The first thing to understand in the joint is that no free man (no warden) runs nothing at all. They run it in name only—the big chingodas are the cats with cash; they and the kites to the bricks (the links to the outside) have clout.

A few types stood out as special victims in this jailhouse order. First was your snitches, your stool pigeons, rats, and other vermin. Usually, if you was labeled a snitch, you was pretty surely dead—the only question was the time and the place. Short-eyes—child molesters—was targets for death, too. Fucking up some child's life didn't go down well with old-timers, many of whom had seen their own life fucked up by an adult once. One way they'd dispatch a short-eye was to put a mop wringer through his head like a busted watermelon, which branded them six-by-six; then they'd set the body on fire with gasoline or whatever they could scrounge. You could smell that shit for days after, but that was a warning to other short-eyes.

Later, I recorded a song passed on to me by an inmate at Angola Penitentiary in Louisiana, called "Angola Anthem":

Life is cheap in Angola. . . .

They give a convict a gun
to shoot another one if he run
They don't give a damn
if you're old or young
in the ponderosa
they'll shoot you just for fun
In Angola. . . .

The cane grows far as the eye can see
A man you truly have to be

When your back is aching and your hands are bleeding
A free man hollers . . .
"Cut that cane, you sorry thing!
Or I'll put you in the hole until next spring."

If somebody starve a animule
just cause it was mad
And the SPCA find out
he stone wish he never had
But over in where we at, boy
that stuff goes on every day

You know I was bum-rap'd
just t'other day
You know this is how
Angola'll make you pay
The kangaroo court—hah!—the kangaroo court
that's where the free man send you to
That's no kind of justice
for what you ever do
You get sentenced there
you'll never believe it's real
You just don't know
how it feels
to miss a many a meal
in Angola. . . .

I'm gonna tell y'all a little story
When I first came here, I committed a crime
I knew I did wrong and figured I'd just serve my time
My fall partner and two other guys rode here shackled to
    me
One o' them committed a worse crime than the other three
Judge said, "Hard labor"; Angola man said,
"This shotgun in my hands for you—
Just shoot them convicts if they try to run."

Cut that cane, you sorry old thing
I'll put you in the hole 'til next spring

Swing 'em high, cut 'em low
I'll put you in the hole 'til Hell snow

There's an underground system of communication between all of the dungeons. They send what they call "kites" between one and the other; the kites float, transfer messages, keep everyone up to date about the latest news. Drugs move just as easily; you get your narcotics smuggled in on a regular basis. Guys come to these places clean, and leave with a habit. Narcotics are cheaper than on the streets. How does it happen? How do these kites get back and forth? It's all built into a seriously corrupt system; it's all part of the plan.

Being inside for a while turned my head around a lot, and made me bitter to this day about government bullshit. As far as I'm concerned, our so-called constitutional democracy is no less corrupt than the setups they've got going in Central America or the Third World. And from what I've heard lately, nothing much has changed on the inside. Maybe the cats don't kill snitches and short-eyes so often anymore, but that's about all that's changed. Everything else remains the same.

In Fort Worth, they had a place called the Barefoot Ward, which was a part of the tunnels set aside for medical experiments. They would tell the young cats, "Volunteer for this, and you're going to get loaded." Me and my fall partner, the guy I was busted with, both signed up. They took me in and gave me a shot of something that made me dope-sick; they gave me some other kind of heart medicine that made me feel like my heart was going to explode. Then, as I was lying there freaking out, the croaker put this device on my head and gave me some kind of electric-shock therapy. The next thing I remember I was back to my own ward and all the cats were laughing at me, calling me a guinea-pig asshole for signing up for the pharmacological fun and games.

There were inmates who didn't make it out of the Barefoot Ward. One thing I'll never forget is seeing the body of one of my partners one night after he had disappeared into the Barefoot Ward. They had me working on janitorial detail at the time, and the spot where we removed the garbage was right by the morgue. In the tunnel I was working, I saw this cat's body on the table; he was stone dead, but his body was still trembling like a leaf. The guy had been dead for hours, and there he was, still shaking. Seeing him like that fucked my head up but good; I had to cop some extra Dilaudids from one of the crew that night just to chill myself out. I was shaking as hard as my partner on the table. For years, that vision gave me nightmares.

All of this was very traumatical for me. I've seen friends' throats slit, my partner on the morgue table, kids getting turned out—it's all very heavy, and a lot of it was stuff I'd forgotten until just recently, when I went through rehab. I asked my buddy, "Am I going to have to keep seeing this shit?" He laughed and said, "Yeah, you are." He's an old-timer who's made the route I was on; he's writing a book right now about his time in Lexington.

Guys like us who went through Fort Worth and Lexington and the like *were* guinea pigs; you had to sign a form that in the event of your death, nobody could claim your corpse. Your body and soul belonged to the man, to do as he pleased. None of us read those things. This shit don't exist no more because the cover has been blown off the croakers' scene. But back then, if you went inside with your eyes closed, they opened up real fast. They had to—or you wouldn't make it out of there alive.

HOLLYWOOD BE THY NAME

Our Father who art in Heaven
Hollywood be Thy name
Thy kingdom come,
Thy will be done,
on Earth
as it is in Hollywood . . .

—"Hollywood Be Thy Name,"
Mac Rebennack

In 1965, after I got sprung, I packed my threads and headed in a straight line for Los Angeles. The scene in New Orleans was dead, and a few of my old partners from New Orleans were already out on the coast, doing all right.

In 1962, when AFO Records had hit a wall in New Orleans, they'd decided to move to Los Angeles. They had just lost their number-one hit singer, Barbara George, to another record company, and the time seemed right for a move to the bigger and better. AFO members Melvin Lastie, Chuck Badie, Harold Battiste, Red Tyler, Roy Montrell, and John Boudreaux had just made an album with Tami Lynn as vocalist, and they took the album with them out to California, hoping to bust it open.

Before long, though, the group had split up because nothing as big as they had hoped had happened. Montrell joined Jimmy

124

Smith or Lou Donaldson's trio and began to tour; Red Tyler came back to New Orleans; others went their separate ways. Soon Harold Battiste began calling me, saying, "Hey, man, come on out here and work on this record with Sam Cooke," that sort of thing. I kept telling him I'd come; I'd get all choked up and emotional talking to them, and I'd mean what I said at that moment, but really I didn't want to leave New Orleans. I had my own little scene wired; I wasn't ready to move yet—it would take the law to convince me otherwise.

Back in New Orleans, before I was put off the bricks, I'd started hearing these records coming out of LA—stuff like Bob B. Soxx and the Blue Jeans, produced by Phil Spector—that sounded like a bad rip-off of the sounds AFO had been laying down a year or so before. What I didn't learn until later was that the band behind these vocal acts actually was AFO, or what remained of them, only they were distorted beyond belief by the Mickey Mouse mix. AFO had also done stuff on which I *could* hear them more directly—records like "Shake" with Sam Cooke, and cuts Bobby Womack and his brother were putting out under the name of the Valentinos.

When I finally got out to California in 1965, my in was with Harold Battiste, which was both fortunate and unfortunate. Harold had slotted into a groove out there in LA where he had a lot of work, and the bright side was that he could give me quite a bit of it. On the dark side, it's still painful to think about some of the lames that I ended up working with to survive.

Things started out okay. For a time, Harold was working with J. W. Alexander, who'd been Sam Cooke's manager. Cooke was dead by then, and J.W. was scuffling to keep Sam's label, publishing company, and songs happening, trying to do things the way Sam would have wanted. J.W. had been with Sam in the gospel scene with the Soul Stirrers; he was a singer and songwriter hisself. Everybody in the industry who knew J. W. Alexander loved him. He was just a sweetheart of a cat, a real rare dude.

Right up front, J.W. gave me a little job writing some lead sheets because he knew I had no money and needed a job. I couldn't even do lead sheets worth a shit, but J.W. and Harold Battiste helped me out. They let me write songs for them when they didn't even need no songs—Sam Cooke had left behind more than enough great material. They used me on sessions whether they needed me or not. At first, we did stuff with jazz and soul acts like Johnny Morrisetti, the Sims Twins, and the O'Jays; I worked on what I think was the first record the O'Jays ever cut. I also did a lot of other sessions where I and a few other musicians would lay down overdub tracks on top of some bubble-gum group or other. I played on some Monkees records, for instance, even though I never even met the Monkees. I worked for different contractors in LA, but especially for Ben Barrett, who hooked up musicians for a lot of Columbia and Motown recording sessions.

Barrett had a stranglehold over cats, which I didn't dig. One day I overheard him talking to someone in the studio, pointing out the various musicians. "That's my boy," he said, pointing around the room, "and that's my boy," and when he called my name, I said in what I thought was out of his hearing, "I ain't one of your fucking *booyys*." But he heard me and that iced me out of a lot of work with his clique, which was probably just as well. They had a little game set up where they'd invite you to some cocktail party—contractors, producers, musicians, they'd all go—and you was expected to invite them all to one of these dos in return. Well, I was staying in this little dope-fiend fleabag motel on Melrose and Van Ness, which was running me $17.50 a week, and I had no interest in having Ben Barrett and his clique down there.

I used to rent two apartments in this place, and in one of them I stored boosted clothes that these Mexican girls used to bring me. These girls went by the name of the Hot Tamales—one of them I called Rita Burrito, the other Gloria Hot Tamale. The place had a bad rep; nobody lived there but whores, boosters, dope fiends, and second-story men. It was a great place; I loved it, but I'm not sure some of your more uptown contractor types would have exactly felt at home there.

Pretty soon, I hooked into Harold Battiste's long-running ho-hum groove with Sonny Bono and Phil Spector. Harold was Sonny's producer, even if he didn't get the credit, and he worked a lot with Phil as a sideman and arranger. Harold quickly touted me to Sonny and Phil as a keyboard and guitar player.

Sonny Bono was trying desperately to copy Phil Spector's hit sound at this time. I'd show up for the sessions and find all these guitar players—Barney Kessel, Howard Roberts, Donald Peaks, and David Cohn—on the session, plus killer keyboard players like Mike Rabini, Don Randi, and Mike Melvoin; all these tough musicians, and all we'd be doing—all of us—was ka-ding, ka-ding, ka-dang, broken arpeggios for nobody knows. It was a monument to waste with echo all over the place.

What Harold did, as far as I could see, was to take Sonny's songs and make them musically well constructed. He did some great arrangements for them, considering what he had to work with: Sonny seemed to know only two chords on the piano, so every song he wrote used the same two chords over and over. And Harold took these songs and heroically made them sound like real music (mostly by throwing more chords in and mixing it up into a progression that made some musical sense).

One of the songs that Harold really did up right was Cher's "Bang Bang." I was at Sonny's garage one night, and he was hammering out his usual two chords; you could hear the essence of a song in there somewhere, but it took Harold to make it happen. He did this all the time with their records. When Harold first took me out on the road with Sonny and Cher, I was straw-bossing the rhythm section while he acted as straw boss for horns and strings. It was such a musical nightmare, my concern was just to get the fuck away where I could write and play.

The Spector gigs were interesting because he would pack a studio with thirty violins, ten horns, a battery of keyboards, basses, guitars, drums, which, mixed with much echo, became his famous "wall of sound." I thought to myself, What's all this? because in New Orleans we put out just as much sound with only six guys. We'd have a rhythm section and a couple of horns and make it sound fat; these guys would take huge amounts of people and make it sound little and reverb strange. I couldn't make anything out of it. It was just padding the payroll, as far as I could see.

But Spector, at least, was more musical than Sonny. He played guitar and his stuff had some musical value. And he was a very funny cat: He cracked jokes nonstop between takes. I liked him, but I never could see the sense behind his recording style. I always felt so stupid recording with him; it wasn't about music to me. His musicians used to become so alienated from what they were doing, in between takes you'd hear them hurry up and play something hip just to keep from going to sleep or going nuts. But I was glad for the work, because at the time I had been put on a sort of probation period with Local 47 of the musicians' union and couldn't play live gigs in LA. I could work out in Orange and Ventura counties, but for two years I didn't play live gigs in Los Angeles.

After a bit, I threw in the towel with Sonny and Cher and copped a job playing piano for Frank Zappa. Zappa had just put together his Mothers of Invention band, and I was supposed to be the piano player. I'd always go there to rehearsals with Elliot Ingber, who was a guitar player and a weed gourmet; I'd show up with a joint in my mouth, signifying I wasn't no dope fiend, just a weed head. Elliot would be signaling me behind Frank's back to get rid of the joint. I didn't know what the hell he was talking about, because I was looking at Frank Zappa, thinking this character must have been spaced on God-knows-what. What I didn't know then was that Frank was stone straight—he took no drugs of any kind.

I did a couple of sessions for him, though; everybody in the studio but Frank was wandering around high on acid. Frank had written me this part to play, five or six notes on the piano over and over—not much different than Sonny and Cher. In the background, a twenty-voice choir croaked out monster sound effects, something like "Gggrrrrrrhhhhrrr!" When I had had about all I could take, Les McCann walked in and I asked him to hold down my chair, telling him I had to go to the bathroom. I walked out of there and never came back.

This marked the beginning of a whole mess of "acid rock" sessions where I worked as a sideman. At the time, all these little acid groups were springing up like mutant fungus after a chemical spill. One of these was the group I call Iron Butterfingers (Iron Butterfly), who Jessie Hill and I worked with on a cover of an Allen Toussaint song that Lee Dorsey had cut called "Get Out of My Life Woman."

We went in there intent on helping them get over, but that didn't last long. First, this one guy says, "Listen, Mac, would you mind? Stop playing the piano." I stopped playing. Then he says, "Would you mind leaving the studio?" They had a guard escort me out of the building. Jessie was playing tambourine on the date. At some point later they told him just to stand there and "play smiles." They shipped him next, and we were the only two New Orleans players on the date. This coming from the motherfuckers who made "In the Garden of Eden, Baby" but couldn't even make it sound like what they were saying—truly a bunch of lames.

Later, I played another date with Buffalo Springfield to do some of their stuff. They had made noises about how they wanted a real New Orleans piano sound on the recording, so along with me they also hired Marcel Richards, another New Orleans piano man who worked with Lee Dorsey on "Ya Ya." In spite of what they told us, this session turned out to be another Phil Spector ho-hum-type engagement. Only Marcel wasn't going for this shit. He was a piano player and he wanted to play for real on the date. He was brand-new to the LA session scene, so I told him, "Hey, look, you want to make this date, just play this shit." He kept saying, "This shit don't feel like music." Next thing, Marcel was gone, and I was stuck doing all the same old crap I'd been doing out there all along.

There was so many sessions like that, it was beyond belief. I could never have imagined all of this session jive going down in New Orleans. Back home, whether we was working a three-hour, six-tune session or a six-hour, twelve-tune session, we went in there and nailed the music. There was no fucking around, no ego-tripping and no wasted time, and we had fun doing it. It was the kind of music you got a kick out of recording. That's why it was a real treat for me to do the occasional Motown session in LA or to record with Johnny "Guitar" Watson, Larry Williams, or even Little Richard—with that kind of cat, sessions had that old New Orleans flavor. Everybody could be funky and have some fun. All in all, though, this was a bad time for me, because if I ain't having fun with music, my life ain't fun.

The whole time I was in LA, I was more or less a fugitive from various issues, so I had to keep one eye over my shoulder at all times, watching for heat. A good bit of this time, I was living in Hollywood at a dope-fiend motel with the snappy-sounding name of Hollywood Executive Apartments. There was four musicians and four or five girls staying in this one room.

Joy, the lady who ran the building, was so kindhearted. She fed us when we didn't have no money. She was like a little angel to all these derelicts. She cooked great Italian food. Her place was under a constant bust—police in and out for this or that. She just put up with it. She was one of them rare people who had a heart for this.

One day, the deskman called me up and told me, "Mac, there's some guys looking for you. I don't know if they're feds or what." I booked out of there, out the back and down the fire escape, and over to this other pad around San Vicente and La Cienega, where I chilled until things was safe again.

From almost the beginning of my stay in LA I belonged to a little clique of New Orleans musicians in exile. This group consisted of Didimus, my percussionist partner from New Orleans; Jessie Hill; Dave Dixon; Al Frazier; Morris Bachamin; and Alvin "Shine" Robinson. We all hung out together and helped each other get session gigs, and kept our ears open for chances to do our own recording, too. With all the cats we had, we put together a strong New Orleans rhythm section. Harold Battiste formed a group out there called the New Orleans Musicians Association, and bit by bit they were easing our guys into various recording sessons. What we eventually wanted to do was to infiltrate a label and put our stamp on the music, to re-create and update in LA what we had going in New Orleans before everything fell apart. Basically, we wanted to do what Berry Gordy was doing with Motown and what was happening in Memphis with Stax.

Jessie Hill and I tried starting a publishing company called I Found It Music and our own little label, called Free Records, but I'll say one thing, it was a big mistake to call a record company "Free"—that's what everybody expected, a free record. The concept backfired. But the three of us who ran it—Jessie and I and Dave Dixon—were especially tight. We were all staying at the same place on Melrose and Van Ness, and we had offices in the hotel where we hung out a lot, writing songs and scheming and conspiring. People were in and out all the time, cats like Steve "Lemon" Mann, a guitar player who turned us on to Blind Lemon Jefferson's records and loads of old stuff we'd never heard before.

Dave Dixon opened a strange little office where he ran his label, Spade Productions. If you walked into the control room, the first thing you saw was a huge painting of Adam and Eve and the apple tree: Eve had a snake coming out of her pussy, a human tongue stuck out of the serpent's mouth, and Adam was jacking off. In the hallway, Dave had pictures he had painted of flying saucers, and photographs he claimed were of aliens. There was also a nine-foot-high painting of an alien that my old whorehouse partner Stalebread Charlie had donated. It was quite a scene.

Dave Dixon had a pad with his wife, Bernice, but he would hang with me, Jessie Hill, and the others for alarming rates of time—five or six days a week sometimes. In the early days, Dave used to bring me to this joint called the Ash Grove, which booked all these blues and folk acts. Dave liked to go down there and shuck as a blues man; he could play a little guitar and get away with it, with Lemon playing all the hot bottleneck licks while Dave was bullshitting. That was really a fun gig because Dave, even though he was shucking, could really sing the blues. Dave always made a gig like this in a disguise; two or three weeks later, he'd turn up and pass himself off as somebody else, and get himself another gig under a different alias.

The next dubious break that came my way was a regular-paying gig as a producer for Mercury Records, which was run by a sweet guy named Irving Green. When I went to work for Mercury, I told Green, "I won't take the job if Harold Battiste isn't part of the team. Whatever we do, we do together." So Harold and I began to produce stuff for Mercury, most of which was as lame as everything else we had done in LA. There were a few good sessions we did with King Floyd, Junior Parker, and my running partners Alvin Robinson and Jessie Hill, but I remember my stint with Mercury not so much for the music as for the truly strange way the company was run.

One day another Mercury exec put on a tape for me to hear. "We're thinking about signing them," he said. "They're called the Fool."

"That's not a very good name for a group, is it?" I said. It was an awful, unlawful shock to the ears.

"Man, don't knock it. They're the Beatles' tailors." This was the kind of thing we was continually dealing with at Mercury.

The next thing they did was fuck over a project I had to do with Junior Parker. They knew I was all on fire about doing a record with Junior; they called me about four in the morning one time and said, "You got to leave in an hour to go to Chicago to produce Junior." They sent these two lames over to where I was to snatch me for a 6:00 A.M. flight. We got to the studio early, got our tunes written and our chord sheets ready. Then Junior Parker called, about an hour late, and says: "Man, I can't make it to Illinois today. I'm in Texas. I can't get there." Two days later they fly me up to Frisco, supposedly for the same gig. Again nothing happens. Even though nobody ever copped to what was going down, I'm sure Irving Green knew this project with Junior was unlikely to happen. They were just using me as bait in case something did.

Jessie Hill, Shine, and Dave Dixon, and I wrote a lot of songs together. If, for instance, we had an album to do for Mercury, we would sit down the week before and start writing songs, all night and day, for four or five days; on the sixth day, we'd take the songs to Harold Battiste to write the charts up for us. On the seventh day we'd catch a few zees, then go ahead with a rehearsal. Finally, we'd do the date. This was how we operated for a whole mess of acts—Junior Parker (finally); Jessie's records for Mercury; Ben E. King, Wilson Pickett, Aretha Franklin, Delaney and Bonnie for Atlantic; and so on. We really knocked material out fast as a team.

Most songwriters don't sit up writing song after song after song until they get one that fits; usually, people write songs if they get an inspiration. We used to call ourselves Shit on Me Productions, because we was always left with the shit jobs— either the quick productions or the skanky acts. At least we got half of the publishing royalties, even though for most of these acts that didn't usually amount to much. And if we were writing tunes for a Mercury act, we would be lucky ever to see any of the royalties. During the whole time we were working for Mercury, turns out we was nothing but a tax write-off for them. We was bustin' our ass trying to make hit records for these people, and they didn't even care what happened to the acts they recorded. King Floyd's a good example: If you listen to his Chimneyville records, which he made just after he split with Mercury in about 1967, you can hear that he had the same great stuff when he was at Mercury, only Mercury didn't try with him; it almost seemed like they did everything they could to make sure he never had a hit. I know the way Mercury treated him took a chunk of heart out of the game for Floyd; it also killed our spirit, too—the way project after project amounted to nothing.

I didn't have a show-biz attorney to hip me to the hints of the fine print back then. I had attorneys of the criminal variety— the kind who were working to keep me out on the streets. Looking back on it, I'm sure that's why the management at Mercury dug me: They knew I was working from behind the eight ball, that all the while I was running nickel-and-dime hustles off them—stealing chump change here and there, hustling masters to other record companies, scamming free records—it was understood that they'd come through with bail money when I needed it, in return for my keeping my hands off real money I should have been earning through proper channels. I was nickel-and-diming them, and they were ripping me off; it added up for somebody, but not for me, though I couldn't see that at the time.

I was aware that we hadn't received no statements for nothing—no songwriting royalties, no producer fees or royalties, no arranger's fees or royalties. We were just being paid get-along money weekly, nothing else. I had asked Harold if he'd got any statements, and he said no; I talked to the rest of the guys—again, ixnay. All of a sudden, somebody wised up to how we were checking things out; next thing I know, this so-called bodyguard pops up, muscles flexed like a bodybuilder on steroids, and suddenly the intimidation machine was working overtime.

In spite of all of this, I really dig Irving Green, and Ahmet Ertegun and Jerry Wexler of Atlantic. The reason I liked them from the beginning was that, underneath it all, they loved the music. That was their redeeming merit, no matter what other kinds of skanky shit they pulled over on you.

Next, Irving Green sicked his pal Irving Garr over my head. Garr had been a vice president at ABC-Paramount; he was about ready to retire when Irving Green, his old friend, talked him into leaving ABC (giving up his retirement money) and coming to Mercury to start his own little imprint. The guy got stuck with us.

Now, Garr was one bitter guy. Real quick, he figured out that Irving Green had him into a tax-write-off label that was never going to happen. I didn't even know what Irving Garr did at Mercury's (Pulsar) label and Irving Green didn't explain; his sole job seemed to be to keep us thrown off guard as much as possible. I was so caught up in trying to make music that I couldn't see for myself what was going on. I was already iced out of the picture when I finally got to see what was happening.

The way Green always worked was never to allow anyone

who worked for him to see the forest for the trees, the trees for the leaves, the leaves for the nightmares that woke you up screaming in the middle of the night. To this day, I think he pulled me into the deal not so much for what I could do but because he knew I knew the whereabouts of these guys in Louisiana who had once been on the Mercury label. Green wanted to find these people; I wouldn't give them up, so they busted my balls in return, and stuck me with mostly shit projects. Their figuring, it seems to me, was that if they drove me crazy enough with this bad stuff, eventually I'd come back to them begging for mercy and they could get the lowdown on the acts they were looking for.

Plus, people at Mercury got used up, squeezed dry, then spit out. They had a great engineer named Abe Voco-Kesh in my time at Mercury and later; I saw Mercury literally work that guy to death. This poor guy was set up in this one little studio on Cumpston Street in the Valley. I remember weeks passed by when I would come and go doing sessions there, but this guy never left. I'd leave, come back a week later, and he'd still be there. He began to get skinnier and paler; he'd get high and not pay no attention to his condition, and no one cared. Sure enough, one day they had to take him out of there in a pine box. I'm sure it wasn't that anyone had it in mind to kill him; they just wanted to use him forever, and they used him up.

All of this time, I was getting heat on a fairly regular basis—fed, state, and city heat. The whole time I was working for Mercury, Irving Green talked these deep mystical parables to me ("You're the Jack of Diamonds, I'm the King of Diamonds," and so on). He knew I was into magic, and he was playing me, unscrewing my head. The whole place had an aura of fear for me. They had me so scared, I didn't know who to fear more—the feds, the narcs, or the industry. At least with the police, I knew they had badges to identify themselves and played by their own rules. With Mercury, you didn't know how far who was willing to go. The problem was, they seemed likely to go all the way if they saw you as a serious problem.

One day, Irving Garr told me, "You got to make a record

with a guy named Graham Bond." I had never heard of the cat, but I was ready to roll with it.

The Graham Bond job marked the start of a long-running saga. First off, Bond couldn't get into the country. He was stranded for weeks in Jamaica. But at last he showed up, looking real pale and creepy, saying he's Aleister Crowley's bastard son. He turned up on the doorstep of my apartment with pentacles, upside-down crucifixes—the original Merlin the Magician. He'd brought his old lady with him, a sweet chick named Diana who played the congas, and he began talking about making a record in which he figured on playing the organ and saxophone at the same time. I already had a doubt about him, but the organ-and-sax scene really made me wonder what I was getting into. At a convenient moment I asked Irving Garr if he was sure he wanted me to do this project, which was one of the big mistakes I made at Mercury. Asking that question, which Garr took to mean that I was questioning his authority, marked the start of hellfire on earth for me.

Garr looked at me as though I were his slightly retarded, long-lost pet slug. "Don't worry about it," he said, a phony grin plastered across his face.

The next day, Garr came into the studio and hit me again: "Remember Wayne Talbot?" I nodded my head; Wayne was an old buddy of mine from Houston I hadn't seen in some time.

"We just got him out of Huntsville," Garr said. "He's gonna help you out on the record."

I got all excited; Wayne was a cool cat, and I was glad he was finally hitting the bricks. The next day, Wayne showed up, and we were talking about the record when Wayne asked, "Say, my man, where am I going to stay?"

Garr turned on him like a mad dog: "Go get yourself busted. That's where you're used to staying, in a jail cell. Stay in the fucking jail tonight. Don't talk to me about money now."

Wayne, real cool, ignored this garbage and said, "Well, speaking about money, can I get me an advance on the record? Then I can go get me a room."

"You get no money till the record's finished," Garr snapped.

I opened my big mouth: "Well, I'll put him up." Me, who didn't even have a pad (by now I was living in a shooting gallery with a hustling broad named Darlene). I'm going to offer this sucker a pad. None of us had a dollar to our names, and I'm offering to be a charity organization. This is how the whole thing started. Irving Garr set up this predicament to show me I shouldn't fuck with him.

We started working on the record, and Wayne told me, "I can't work no more like this. I'm dope-sick. I need some serious money."

I said, "Okay, see what you can do."

We started walking down the street, and before I knew it, Wayne pulled a shank on a guy, jacked him up against a wall, and took him off. In the middle of the day—he couldn't even wait till the sun went down!

Darlene, poor thing, found out about it. She'd been turning tricks trying to support us (she couldn't even support herself too well), and suddenly she got the charity syndrome, too. She started turning tricks overtime and scamming off dope dealers. Which makes us all hot as a firecracker in Venice, California; they already got our names and photographs on the wall of the Venice police station. We got into a close scrape with the police down there; Darlene managed to get us out of there by running our car over a concrete highway barrier and losing the police. Real Bonnie and Clyde stuff.

But then Wayne started feeling bad about our circumstances; the charity flu had come full circle, and one day he came to me: "Mac, I picked up this royalty check laying on a desk over at Mercury. Maybe if we bust this paper, we can cop some weight."

The check turned out to be for many thousands of dollars, and we managed to bust it all right. Nobody at Mercury said a word, but they had an inside straight about who was doing what. Not too long after, Irving Garr invited us all to a party. Sometime after we got there, Irving motioned for me to come over to where he was standing, next to this fish tank. I was overloaded, over the edge. Out of nowhere, Irving grabbed my hand and held it near the tank. "See those fish?" He pointed to two suckers with big, nasty-looking mouths. "They're piranhas. They can take your hand off like a meat grinder. How do you like that, you fuck?" That ranked the party for me.

In retaliation, Graham Bond decided we were going to work a little hoodoo ritual to nail Irving Garr. We set up the whole load on top of the studio: black candles, incense, baron samedi (spirits of the graveyard in gris-gris) psalms to recite, gris-gris bundles. Graham did his whole Aleister Crowley routine; I did my gris-gris shit; Wayne did nothing; the smoke poured forth. The next day . . . nothing happened to Irving Garr. All our mysterious manipulations had been misdirected; the whole thing had lamed out. So now we went over the edge. Fuck the hoodoo; we'd get Garr through the direct method. We decided we'd shoot him, then run over him with a car till he was dead. In the middle of this conspiracy of dummies, Graham Bond said, "I'm walking. This just isn't the method Aleister Crowley would want me to use."

We shot back, "Fuck you and fuck Crowley! We'll do this without you. Darlene will help us. She's got a car." Before we could get her in on the plans, though, she got busted in the car. Suddenly, no Darlene, no car. We turned to another cat named Ruben to help us out with his car. We went to see him, and Ruben got busted for possession of the gun he had. Now we were really through: no car, no gun, no Darlene, no Ruben. The plan was flushed down the pipes for good, bad, or worse.

Soon after this, I found out through Irving Green that my buddy Harold Battiste, who had been my guru and business partner since I was a youngster, had begun to have his doubts about me. He had approached Green, complaining that I was a hopeless dope fiend, that I couldn't handle the work anymore. He was going to bring Melvin Lastie in to replace me.

Now this was enough to get me upset, but then Green added to the twist: "See, I told you not to bring in Harold," he said.

"Jesus, I didn't want both of you in the first place. You brought him in, and now he wants to get rid of you. You better deal with it."

"What am I supposed to do?" I ask.

"You gotta talk to Irving Garr about it," Green said. "He's in charge of you."

Now I knew I was buried. My own partner was crucifying me, and to save myself I had to kiss the ass of a man I've just been plotting to kill. I knew I couldn't handle it on my own, so I asked Melvin Lastie to help out; Melvin popped into town early for a little gig, and called a meeting of our little clique, Shine, Jessie, Dave, Morris, and a few more. Melvin said, "You thought Harold was your friend, but he's going to fuck all of y'all. He's fucking Mac over right now. That's why I'm here—to take Mac's place. That's why I called this meeting."

Melvin stirred up a red-ant nest then. All kinds of resentments and grievances busted open and that meeting pretty much closed my career with Mercury. I had been betrayed by Harold, and even though we worked on projects together after that, we drifted apart and went our separate ways. But things was breaking fast in LA, and other opportunities were glimmering on the horizon. An old New Orleans character named Dr. John was about to be reborn like a phoenix from the ashes.

PEOPLE CHANGE STRANGE

When all the clouds in the sky
Disappear in front of your eyes,
And you hear a lullabye
You once knew but you can't recognize:
Ornette Coleman singing tenderly;
You can hear the tune,
But you can't find the key.
You're in the Twilight Zone.

—*"Twilight Zone,"*
Mac Rebennack

In the 1840s and 1850s, one New Orleans root doctor was preeminent in the city for the awe in which he was held by the poor, and the fear and notoriety he inspired among the rich. Known variously as John Montaigne, Bayou John, and most often Dr. John, he was a figure larger than life, a medicine man who claimed to have been a prince in Senegal before he was abducted and taken to Cuba. In Cuba he had gained freedom and shipped out around the world as a sailor, eventually settling in New Orleans.

For many years, I had nurtured my little idea of forming a musical group around the personality of Dr. John. Through my contacts with gris-gris and spiritual-church people and by reading

New Orleans history that my sister and others had turned me on to, I had begun to dig the importance of Dr. John as an early spiritual leader of the New Orleans community. But it was when I read a piece by the nineteenth-century writer Lafcadio Hearn that my head really got turned seriously around. In Hearn's story, I found that Dr. John and one Pauline Rebennack were busted in the 1840s for having a voodoo operation and possibly a whorehouse. I don't know for sure, but there's a strong chance that Pauline Rebennack was one of my relatives, so I feel more than an incidental sympathy for the man whose name I took as a stage name in 1967.

At a certain point, our little group of New Orleans exiles in LA managed to grab some open studio time through our Sonny and Cher connection. Harold Battiste arranged for us to slip in and cut a few tunes on free studio time, and through Sonny and Cher he sweet-talked a deal for us with Atlantic for a new album, though neither Ahmet Ertegun nor Jerry Wexler, the heads of Atlantic, were aware at that time of what we were cooking up.

During these stolen hours, Alvin "Shine" Robinson, Didimus, John Boudreaux, Jessie Hill, Dave Dixon, Plas Johnson, Morris Bachamin, Harold Battiste, Steve Mann, Ron Johnson, Joanie Jones, Tami Lynn, Shirley Goodman, Sonny Raye, and Ronnie Barron joined me to lay down the tracks that turned into the *Gris-Gris* album.

Ironically, I had been shopping the Dr. John concept around for a long time by this point—but always with Ronnie Barron in mind for the character of Dr. John. But when the time came to cut the songs, Ronnie wasn't available; his manager, Don Costa, didn't want him to do it because he wanted to slot Ronnie and his band into a Curtis Mayfield and the Impressions or the Staple Singers kind of direction. When Ronnie nixed the idea, I decided I would wing it and fill in the Dr. John slot.

It was a big kick to cut *Gris-Gris*. While we were doing it, Hugh Masakela was cutting his first album here in the States; suddenly, in Gold Star Studios, where Sonny and Cher and Phil Spector cut their stuff, there were Hugh Masakela and his South

GRIS-GRIS

In 1967, after a couple of years of studio and other kinds of sidetripping in LA, me and my New Orleans partners-in-exile finally fell into a situation where we could cut an LP on an idea I'd had since before I left New Orleans.

I had always thought we could work up an interesting New Orleans–based concept behind the persona of the legendary conjureman Dr. John. This would not only allow for a dash of gris-gris in the lyrics and a view of an untapped side of New Orleans, but would also let us musicians get into a stretched-out New Orleans groove.

With the help of Harold Battiste, we recorded at Gold Star Studios between sessions Sonny and Cher were doing there for Atlantic Records. The album we created, *Gris-Gris*, was heavy on rhythm, percussion, and guitar, and light on keyboards. I did play some organ, as on the songs "Mama Roux" and "Danse Kalinda," but stuck mostly to guitar. Steve Mann and Ernest McLean also played guitar on the session. On some songs we used two basses (Harold Battiste and Bob West), and our percussionist, Didimus, also doubled up on a bunch more instruments with the rest of the cats.

We were looking for an unusual, textured sound, and the cats nailed it. Naturally, we wanted the album to sell, but we weren't into bending our music to fit somebody's idea of what the market was about. First and foremost, we were into it for the music.

This attitude isn't often appreciated by record companies. To give you a for instance, at one point later on, I was doing a session for Bobby Darin when Ahmet Ertegun walked into the studio looking for me. He was pissed off, wanting to know what this *Gris-Gris* album was all about. He was walking around the studio yelling at me: "Why did you give me this shit? How can we market this boogaloo crap?" He was stuck with a record that was done on the sly, and he was acting as if he wouldn't release it.

But we was of the mind that a hip record might sell if it was pitched the right way. The way we was looking at music-making was that it was circular in its groove, with no corners. That was what the old-time hipsters had meant by *hip*—something that hadn't been squared off to fit into some kind of computerized, market-ized nightmare.

In any event, Ahmet must have sensed something happening. We made five more albums for Atlantic before the deal fell through. Our theme song of that time, the first cut on the album, was "Gris-Gris Gumbo Ya-Ya." It framed a mental picture of an imaginary New Orleans and put our main character, Dr. John, out front and center:

Gris-Gris Gumbo Ya-Ya

They call me Doctor John
Known as the Night Tripper
Got my satchel of gris-gris in my hand
Tripping up, back down the bayou
I'm the last of the best
I'm known as a gris-gris man

Got many clients come from miles around
Running down my prescription
Got medicine cure all y'all's ills
Got remedies of every description

Got gris-gris gumbo ya-ya
Hey, now, gumbo yeah-yeah

If you got love troubles
Got a bad woman you can't control
I got just the thing for ya
Something called Controlling Oil and Get Together drops
If you work too hard and need a little rest
Try my Easy Life rub
Or put my Boss Fix jam in your breakfast

Got gris-gris gumbo ya-ya
Hey, now, gumbo yeah-yeah

They call me Doctor John
Known as the Night Tripper
Got my satchel of gris-gris in my hand
Day tripping up, back down the bayou
I'm the last of the best
I'm known as the gris-gris man

(continued)

> *Some War Water*
> *If your neighbors give you trouble*
> *And put your business in the street*
> *Try my dragon's blood, drawin' powder,*
> *And my sacred sand, try a little Black Cat oil*
> *If your woman got another man*
>
> *Got gris-gris gumbo ya-ya*
> *Hey, now, gumbo yeah-yeah . . .*

African band, with Stuart Levine producing. His band, and my funky gang, were another world compared to the acts the engineers had been used to; I remember their actually being scared of us. And my group weren't just oddball New Orleans characters—every now and then the police would put in an appearance, looking for those of us who were still fugitives. We made ourselves remembered.

Even though he hadn't been expecting it—to put it mildly—after scoping it out for a minute Ahmet Ertegun decided to release the album. I had no idea until I got a call one day to show up someplace for an album photo shoot. I was totally amazed at this move; none of us imagined the material would ever be released.

It turned out that *Gris-Gris*, without any hand-hustle on our part, fell right into the hippie groove of the moment, and became a kind of underground hit. Atlantic didn't promote the record too much; its rep spread strictly by word of mouth, and it became a cult phenom by being played on what were at the time called "free-form" radio stations. Harold Battiste, who had a slick ear for a gimmick, tried to get me and the band to wire ourselves up with electronic gizmos à la Jimi Hendrix and go totally psychedelic, but I didn't go for that. At that point, we had barely even begun to think of ourselves as a band; our eyes were still set on trying to infiltrate ourselves into Mercury and Atlantic as a studio unit.

Then one day, Dave Dixon, Stalebread Charlie, Didimus, and I went with most of the rest of the people who became members of the first Dr. John band to Topanga Canyon to hang out. We had been gigging loosely together as a band for a while—playing here and there around LA, nothing full-time. We were down by this stream in the canyon and Charlie Maduell broke out his flute and started playing, and frogs started chirping to it. Didimus picked up some rocks and began playing a groove; Dave Dixon had found some kind of animal bones and began playing those. Stalebread Charlie had a tape recorder and taped our little nature jam. We called this the "Symphony of the Frogs." Before too long, all these naked people came down the creek bed, attracted by the music and the chirping, and started dancing. We were getting into the people dancing, and they were getting into our music. It all got very intense. When it died down some, Didimus said, "Hey, we should take this to the people." That's how the Dr. John road show began.

Even after *Gris-Gris* was released, we were still pulling together the elements of a stage act. We had a groove we was into then: riding around LA with candles and incense burning in the car. It wasn't a hippie thing so much as a mixture of our own New Orleans mystical jive and the trappings of the old Beat scene. See, Stalebread Charlie, even when he was a pimp back in New Orleans, was considered a beatnik, as was Dave Dixon, who was an outnik and Beat schizophrenic.

We came out of Topanga Canyon with the "Symphony of the Frogs" still laying heavy on us; we began talking, and Didimus said, "Let's cut down hustling sessions, and start gigging steady. Let's just play; fuck the money." That's how we got involved with the Be-Ins and the Love-Ins, the In-Ins and the Out-Ins; we took every gig we could. We weren't in it just to play; we wanted to put on a show. And we were going to show these people New Orleans style.

I knew enough about the old minstrel shows that when I put together the original Dr. John act, I used a lot of the shtick they did. My entrance onstage with a puff of smoke was inspired by the minstrel magicians; I lifted their snake-handling routine by having one of the dancers, Kalinda, come out dancing with a snake wrapped around her body. Didimus choreographed the dance, but I came up with the snake idea from what I had heard from my grandfather and all the other old-timers. I also had Kalinda do a limbo under a limbo stick that was set afire, another old spectacle reborn. What I wanted was entertainment for the eyes as well as the ears, and I knew the minstrels were the best there was at laying down a show. It was a kick to bring back that idea of showmanship to the rock and roll era, where at the time there was little old-style show biz happening.

Along with minstrels, I had my other sources. When I did my first gigs with the Dr. John band, I looked up some of the older Indian cats in New Orleans and bought some of the stuff they didn't use no more. Smiling George of the Wild Squatoolas and a few other cats from the Creole Wild West sold me some Indian suits. One woman, Sadie Hayes, made me a suit of alligator, snake, and lizard skin with chamois in between to hook it all up. When I put on that uniform, I looked like Frankenstein coming down the street. When this stuff started coming apart in pieces, I had to start hanging around taxidermy shops big time, scavenging new material to help put things back together.

The original Dr. John band, the Night Trippers, was made up of John Boudreaux on drums; Al Frazier on bass; Jessie Hill as singer and percussionist; Alvin "Shine" Robinson on guitar; Didimus on percussion; myself on piano and guitar; Morris Bachamin on tenor; Steve "Lemon" Mann on guitar; Ronnie Barron on organ; Shirley Goodman, Tami Lynn, and Joanie Jones singing background; and Kalinda dancing.

My partner Didimus was a key reason why things happened the way they did. Even before we had our band, when we was doing studio work in LA, his vibe made something different happen that was real special. As a percussionist, Didimus not only had the fieriness of the Afro-Caribbean rhythm, he also was into bebop, off-the-wall stuff, mixing Ornette Coleman, Chano Pozo, and Sun Ra. With him driving us on, and with Harold

Battiste's productions, we were making music in time signatures that were totally out of connection with other things happening in rock, mixing up out-jazz with R&B and New Orleans roots music.

Unfortunately, Didimus was undependable on the road. As soon as we hit the highway, he'd develop abscesses in his arms, or come down with some illness, or just not show up for gigs; he was a dope fiend, like the rest of us. He'd start falling apart on the road, and I had to fire him as often as I had to fire James Booker. He was especially good at missing key gigs with an audience full of record people. You'd walk into the dressing room and there he'd be, nodding off, standing up but bent over half in two, with his head sucking his toes and his butt sticking up in the air. Later, we'd find out he'd been standing there for hours.

On the positive side, when he was with it, he'd bring up-and-coming percussionists to play during our gigs, in the tradition of bringing up and teaching younger players. At the time, I didn't appreciate his taking on strangers; it just seemed he was avoiding having to play something like "Walk on Guilded Splinters" to death, taking a bow to a cat who wasn't anywhere near as good. Now I understand it better, and I know what kind of good he was about—he gave a lot of young cats a break. He was a strong part of the band from the beginning to about 1973 and the *Right Place* album. Just after that, he hooked up with a woman who put him on a cabbage-juice diet to heal his ulcers; the diet killed him.

Alvin "Shine" Robinson was our guitar player, and one of the best singers in the band. His was the voice that was always between me and the girl singers. My voice was low and froggy; Shine had a husky voice, too, but was a real singer, not a shucker like me. By taking the difference between where I sang and where the girls sang, he laid a middle ground that rounded out our harmony. He had one of them rare voices that showed him to be a singer's singer in his own gut-bucket bluesy way; he could take it à la Ray Charles or à la Big Maybelle, but no matter how he took it he liked it ratty. He played a strong rhythm guitar, too, not as sophisticated as Roy Montrell or Papoose, but powerful. He pushed the band all the time. He was pretty much a regular member of the band until he fell sick in 1989.

There was a lot of other characters and interesting musicians I met during that time of maximum strangeness in LA. Every now and again I'd bump into Jim Morrison at gigs at the Whiskey à Go-Go in Hollywood. He had eyes for our dancer Kalinda. And I'd run into Jimi Hendrix, who I got to know a little earlier when he was playing guitar under the name of Jimmy James in Little Richard's band at a place called the Red Velvet. I worked there myself occasionally with our little New Orleans clique.

In a lot of ways hanging with Richard's band was like old home week for me; because of his New Orleans connection, he had a lot of New Orleans cats in his band—Eddie Tillman on bass, Wade Jackson on the drums, Tank Jernigan on tenor, and a Texan, Billy Preston, on organ. Jimi and Billy were two of the few non-New Orleans cats in the band, but I dug their style. Sometimes Jimi'd open Richard's set with a solo on the Freddie King song "Hideaway," which he played real tough.

Later, after Jimi'd become a star, we did gigs with him at rock festivals, and his music would hurt my ears, he'd play so loud. I didn't pay a lot of attention to his stuff, especially all the experimentation he was doing with the wah-wah pedals and other gizmos. I thought he was a killer guitar player, but I wished he wouldn't have played so fucking loud.

I knew the loudness, as well as other things going on, must have fucked with him in some kind of way. He'd come off his set in pain, his ears ringing, his head hurting. I'm sure all that shit took a toll on him. You just can't stand right in front of that kind of volume and not expect to get away without some damage. When he was playing, I'd make sure I was inside a dressing room or a trailer, which was usually way behind the stage—sometimes as far as a half mile—and still it hurt my ears. That wasn't my style; I liked to savor the music while I was playing, or listening.

I used to feel sorry for Jimi, especially the way he handicapped himself by working with just a trio. I don't want to knock the cats, but in the other circumstances I'd seen him—say, with Little Richard's band—he was single, free, and easy, and didn't have to hold up a show himself.

Another strange deranger who slid into LA during that time was my old New Orleans whorehouse partner, Stalebread Charlie. I was with Charlie, Wayne Talbot, and some other folks once when suddenly Charlie jumped up and said, "Come on, we gotta go to this really far-out place I found." Turns out the place is a big building on Los Feliz Boulevard with huge letters on the front: M.I.N.D., which turned out to stand for Mental Investigation of New Dimensions. Charlie pulled up in his old beat-up Packard and we walked in. The place, which on the outside looked like it could have been a private pad, became on the inside a kind of business operation. In the huge main room, someone was projecting what looked like a black-and-white home movie.

Charlie says, "That's what I want you to check out. Sit down, now."

The projectionist turned the film off as soon as he saw us and rewound it for our benefit. On the screen came a movie of a flying saucer landing in the desert. After it landed, these hippie-looking dudes got out; then some old folks came along to greet them, seeming to tell them they wanted to fly away on the saucer. (It's hard to say for sure, as it was a silent flick.)

Wayne and I looked at each other and said to Charlie, "Yeah, that's all right, Charlie. We'll see you later."

Our blasé attitude must have pissed Charlie off; he had reams of books, folders, and pamphlets in his car about flying saucers, and he was dying for converts. We all piled back in the Packard, but instead of taking us back to his pad, he brought us to Griffith Park Observatory. We walked off out into the woods, and he told us, "This is where I eat parsley, and communicate with the space brothers." As we got our skeptical bearings, he went on to say that this was where he came to take a course in which he was learning how to hone himself from a piece of rock to a shining diamond—that is, to be cool enough to go on a flying saucer with the aliens.

Later, he showed up at the house where my band was practicing and dragged everyone out to look at these little lights in the sky.

"They look like stars to me," I said.

He looked up. "Watch. Now they're going to do the falling leaf-type manuever," and the stars actually did a little flip-flop. It's not too convincing. We told him it was just an optical illusion, but Charlie ain't one to be sidetracked. Again: "Watch, they're going to do something now," and sure enough the lights started to move and groove. We were getting into the show by now—not necessarily sold, but digging it. "Make it do it again," we said. Charlie said no, but to watch closely because something else would happen, and it did. By the time he finished, the whole neighborhood had come out to watch his show.

This business of the flying saucers went on for months and more months. As time went on, he became more and more determined to have us witness something that was a kind of secret, deep, mystical gumbo (or that's how I thought of it; he never would tell us exactly what it was all about). Charlie finally persuaded me to go way out into the Simi Valley desert, where there was a guy who had what he called a "cloud buster." Turned out to be a bunch of pipes that looked like a telescope with old plumbing fixtures stuck on it. I was getting pretty aggravated with Charlie's heaven-on-earth carryings-on by now; the contraption didn't even look finished to me.

Charlie told the guy something and he pointed and wiggled some plumbing fixtures at the sky. These same two fucking lights that Charlie had conjured up back in town now came out of nowhere. I said, "Hey, Charlie, that's cool. That's real hip today. But I'd like to see the real thing—the real flying saucers come land on the desert like in that black-and-white movie."

But Charlie wanted to make a big issue out of the two lights. "Ask them where they're from," he says.

"Are you fucking nuts?" I said. "Ask two fucking lights where they're from?"

"Ask them where they're from. Go ahead. Ask them now."

So I asked them out loud. Charlie says, "No, ask them in your mind." I did that, too. Maybe it was too long-distance. I got no answer.

Many of the studios were paranoid about having any connection, no matter how obscure, with him. Once, Jessie and I got thrown out of a studio when we showed up to hustle a song of Charlie's about Martin Luther King called "His Body Is Gone, But His Spirit Lives On"; when he hustled a path-crossing he'd had with James Earl Ray into a big article about himself in *Life*—and told them he was a songwriter with I Found It Music, which became I Lost It as soon as the Feds came looking for us—I decided to cut out as much of this side-tripping as possible.

Dave Dixon, like Stalebread Charlie, was another guy whose forte in life was to be real *out*—that is, to push other people's buttons, and his own luck. For instance, when he traveled anywhere, he never used his real name. He'd always sign motel registers and the like with a funny name: Goncy O'Leary or Buck Black or Zeke Gloxxe. People would ask him, "Say, how do you pronounce that name?" and Dixon, very seriously, would consider this question for a moment before answering slowly, "Gloxxe, the name is pronounced Gloxxe, like *clocks*." It was a big issue with him; he got the whole band started on this kick. James Black signed as Vonzig Darke; James Booker inked in as Veldun Crokkstudd or O. D. Slycopp.

Dave loved to put people on. He used to sit up till late at night in his office after we got through working; we'd all want to crap out, except for Dave. He'd put a tape on and invent a radio show, making up the whole thing—all the voices, all the characters, the whole plot. He'd create great melodramas, really funny short stories for the radio; he'd have friends over and speak parts for his little show, with Dave writing just a step ahead of them all the way. It's a shame none of those shows ever made it to the air.

Another thing Dave did was write a piece of music with Earl King entitled "Focus on Sanity." Dave and Earl had a different way of marking musical notation: Some parts would be written in different colors; their notes would have wings, feet, and eyes. In short, nobody could have played it. Dave went into a studio where Wardell Quezerque was the arranger once and replaced the session music with "Focus on Sanity." When the musicians and Wardell came in, Dave said, "This ain't nothin' to sneeze at; this is what they're doing in New York." He threw Wardell's arrangements to the floor, picked them up again, rearranged them, and began counting it off: One, two . . . one, two, three, four . . ." And this one cat was actually going to try to play it. He blew out a long note and stopped dead—he couldn't do it. That was the kind of kicks Dave dug.

Another kicks character in the celestial realm during these days was Steve "Lemon" Mann, the guitarist I'd first met in the Sonny and Cher days. He knew all kinds of ancient folk licks, which he recycled in his session work and in his own music. He introduced me to Van Dyke Parks, Taj Mahal, Ruth Ann Friedman, and a lot of other people I really dig. Lemon was so spaced in some sessions that the whole guitar section would be facing one way and Lemon the other. You could just not believe the guy was actually going to pull it off and play. He was one of the first people I met who did LSD, heroin, and speed at the same time, but no matter what he was on Lemon could play the guitar to death. I'd used him on a number of sides with Mercury; he had been over the edge then, and got himself stuck in psych wards for long chunks of time. They'd only let him out to do sessions.

In the middle of a Jessie Hill and Shirley Goodman session, after being in there for seventy-two hours, I called Lemon up and said: "Man, Lemon, do you have any uppers? These guys are ready to fall on their faces." Lemon says, "Of course." He brought in a matchbox loaded with capsules and almost everybody came around for their ups. We proceeded to do a few takes, with me on guitar and Ronnie Barron on piano, when all of a sudden Ronnie crawled off the piano stool and started to lick one of the background singers' knees. I looked around the room and saw Dave Dixon standing by one of the conga drums, playing with them, feeling them up like they was a woman. I was looking at

John Boudreaux, and he was looking at his drumsticks with an expression that said, What are these? Al Frazier was lying on the floor with his bass, laughing. Most of the horn section had stopped playing and were looking at each other quizzically. Jessie Hill and Shirley Goodman, two people who hadn't taken this stuff, were still trying to sing the song! Then the bug hit me. I went over to Charlie Underwood, the engineer on the gig, and yelled, "This session's over. Fuck this shit! And fuck you!"

Turns out Lemon had given us all LSD, which was a brand-new drug to me. I had never even come near acid before. The date ended; everything went wrong. On top of getting in a fight with Charlie Underwood, I got pissed at Lemon for giving us this stuff, although I should have known better than to ask in the first place. Besides being a guitar player, Lemon was a chemist. He and his partner used to brew up stuff in his pad.

I jumped in a cab on Melrose and looked down on the floor of the cab and saw a used rubber, and for some reason that set me off. I went into hysterics. The driver threw me out the cab and didn't even ask for the fare. I walked to some friends' pad to get off the streets, because I knew I was out of control. I got these suckers laughing so much their landlady threatened to evict them—until I got thrown out of there instead. I was on a crazy laughing jag that lasted for about two days. After a while it got to be horrible. It wouldn't stop. I hated it.

But what happened to me wasn't the worst of it. Al Frazier had a very bad trip. He had to go home to New Orleans to attend his mother's wake the next day, and he was never the same again.

This kind of trip was all over the place in them days. I can remember getting dosed on speed one night in Frisco when I was playing a gig with the Sir Douglas Quintet; a guy came up to me and squirted me in the nose with some methedrine nose spray. I was vibrating way into the next morning. I never could handle any kind of upper, and I couldn't handle the acid/upper head vibe. I just didn't like the wired-up nervous energy, the blissed-out faces and burnt-out brain cells that came with the experience.

But I did like some of the acidhead characters, and some of

them even made it out of that time in one piece. Recently I saw Lemon's manager and partner in crime from the old days, the fella with whom he brewed up all those mind-bending concoctions, and man, was I surprised. They used to call him Dr. Electric. Now he's Mr. Square Goods, and he's doing all right for hisself.

By the time we actually began to do legit tours to promote the *Gris-Gris* album, the original band was breaking up. We'd cut a second album, *Babylon*; but John Boudreaux wouldn't fly with the band, so we had to get another drummer, and other guys began to come and go.

I'd thought that *Gris-Gris* would be our first and last album with Atlantic, but I guess Ahmet Ertegun or Jerry Wexler smelled something happening, because they asked us to do a second album. Harold Battiste and I got together and began writing songs, and Harold contributed some real hip meters to the arrangements. *Gris-Gris*, which a lot of people think is such a hip album, had nothing unusual on it meterwise. *Babylon* was a different story. We cut songs in 11/4 and 5/4 time, real odd-groove stuff. On top of that, a lot of the songs were about the end of the world—which, given where my head was at the time, were real easy to write.

Emmett Grogan and his Frisco tribe of urban hippies, who called themselves the Diggers, were hanging out with us; all the clothes we wore on the *Babylon* album cover came from the Diggers' free store in San Francisco. The Hell's Angels were there, too; very strange people were coming and going. The Diggers took care of us, feeding us and looking out for our welfare. But Didimus was very uncomfortable with the mime troupes, Merry Pranksters, and the rest of the freaks. He was about the music and the Nation of Islam; he wanted no part of the underground freak scene at all. He was another rock of support, though: I had doubts about the Dr. John concept—I still snatched studio work for other acts whenever I could—but Didimus kept my head in

BABYLON

Our second album was cut in late 1968—the year of the Tet offensive, and of the assassinations of Bobby Kennedy and Martin Luther King, Jr. It was a heavy time for me: Not only was the Vietnam War raging in all its insanity, but, as a semioutlaw, I was being pursued by various kinds of heat across LA.

In its lyrics and music, this album reflects these chaotic days. At times hard-driving, at other times following a deliberately spacy, disorienting groove, *Babylon* was the band's attempt to say something about the times—and to do it with a few unusual musical time signatures ("Barefoot Lady," for instance, was cut in 11/4, 5/4, and 4/4).

The lead song, "Babylon," sets the tone. To a 3/4 and 10/4 groove, it lays out my own sick-ass view of the world then—namely, that I felt our number was about up.

The album was based around New Orleans chants, tilted sideways by the odd meters we set them in. We were trying to get into something not unlike Dave Brubeck's *Time Out*, but with visions of the end of the world—as if Hieronymus Bosch had cut an album.

Didimus helped a lot on these sessions, especially by bringing in a guy we called the Mad Professor, John McAlister, this kid who played Indian tablas and was into electronic quarter-tone music. He had a device called a quarter-tone piano and huge miked-up gongs that rang out distorted waves of sound. Another of his devices, a Harry Partch creation, was this thing called a transceleste that was about twenty-eight feet of metal tuned in quarter-tones. He ran up and down this instrument playing all the chromatics, and even ran a pot of water over the notes to alter the pitch sharp or flat.

Didimus locked into John because he had an ear not only for Afro-Caribbean sounds but for avant-garde jazz, too. *Babylon* was a mix of these influences, and Harold Battiste's and my out-meter foot beater repeater grooves.

(continued)

Babylon

Babylon
Was represented in the Bible by a stone.
Babylon
Thrown in a river and lost in a storm.

Babylon
And never, ever again will anybody ever want to call you
*   their own.*

Babylon . . .

This is how you're going to sink now.
I don't care whatever you think now.
I'm going to bring my wrath down on you
So you'll feel the weight of truth now.
Going to drive you like the rock of ages into the sea.
Going to disappear like the pebble into eternity.

Nobody wants to say what's best left dead.
A tidal wave is going to dig your grave.
Never again will you hear the secret sound of no beautiful
*   singer's voice.*
No angels playing guitars or plucking on their harps.
No flute, no trumpet player will be left back of town.

Ain't going to be no ditch diggers, no construction workers,
No pimps, no hustlers, no jaw-jerkers.
No city lights, no pretty sights will shine on you again.
No actors, no Max Factors will smog your mind and leave
*   you blind.*
No politicians, no high religions to guide you from the
*   dark.*
No more love-ins, no more human be-in's will light up
*   Griffith Park.*

[Sound of atomic explosion]

Babylon . . .

On your hands is the blood of the prophets and all the holy
*   ones.*
Everyone you executed with your machine guns.
You're bringing about your own destruction, Babylon.

> *I'm putting you down, down, down where you can never*
>   *rise up again.*
> *Watch your ashes light up the midnight skies once again.*
> *After reading the words of this old scroll to you*
> *I hope y'all cap back on the message I just told to you*
> *About Babylon . . .*

the Dr. John game and now, looking back on it, I'm glad he did. For the longest time, gigging with the Dr. John band meant playing little dates, places with funny money. Nobody knew who we was; often as not they assumed we was a band of hippies and tried to lay acid and other kinds of wrong narcotics on us that weren't our drugs of choice.

San Francisco was one place where we always had to be on the lookout for this kind of psychedelic action. The chemist Owsley used to come around and hand out reefer to the band. He never hit us up with LSD because he knew how much I hated the stuff, but he usually left us marijuana. When we was doing a gig at the Avalon with the Grateful Dead, Jerry Garcia gave us a pad to stay at, and sometimes we'd get spooked as a result: What you had was a bunch of guys from New Orleans, paranoid from the jump, walking into someone else's pad and finding a big bowl of reefer. The scene looked like a setup to our sick-ass minds; our New Orleans ethic had it that you was in trouble if you ever had more drugs on you than you could eat. If you couldn't eat it fast, you didn't have it around. Charlie Maduell, my sax player from New Orleans, who had just gotten out of Angola, sat at the door of this place the whole night, never sleeping, guarding us with a 9mm Walther.

The feel of San Francisco at that time was so strange to us New Orleans cats. Charlie Maduell and Didimus were the first two to make me aware of it. We went to cop in the Fillmore district one day; Charlie sat in the back of the car, burning a black candle on the floor with a jack of clubs turned upside down and reading the Death Psalm to curse the police so they wouldn't see us. We had no idea where we'd find narcotics; we just knew they was out there somewhere. Suddenly, Charlie says, "Stop at that corner!"

Charlie jumped out and ran into this bar. We had no idea where we're at; we don't know this bar from Adam. In a moment Charlie came running back out saying, "Give me the money. It's gonna be good." When he came back with the goods, it was just as good as he said. He had a bloodhound's nose for narcotics.

Didimus, on the other hand, had a nose for people. Because he was part Ethiopian and part Cuban, he had a very acute, off-the-wall perspective on what was happening in the here-and-now of America. At one point, Didimus began to warn me about Charlie: "Mac, Charlie is fixing to go off."

The last night we were playing in the Bay Area, Charlie came on the gig dressed up like Count Dracula, with purple gloves, purple lipstick, purple kicks on his feet, and a purple bag over his elbow while he was playing the sax. He turned to me after the gig and said, "I'm wearing my funeral outfit because I'm dying with this band."

I said, "What's the matter, Charlie, the music ain't happening?"

He said, "No, it's this place. It's Babylon; it's Armageddon. I'm going home tomorrow."

I said, "Can't you give me a two-week notice?"

"You got your two-week notice," he said. "But find someone tomorrow. I'm gone."

He went to New Orleans for a pit stop, then down to Florida, where he got busted. He ended up in Raiford Penitentiary in Florida, which was the last place in the United States that had chain gangs. Shortly after he got busted, Charlie wrote me a letter and told me how much safer he felt there than he had out on the streets of Frisco. Now he's in Angola Penitentiary doing one to too-long-a-time.

CHAPTER NINE

THAT OLD HOODOO MOON

Every time you get next to me
You tell me that I really can be free
Living in eternity.
There can be miles and miles between us,
But we all living in the same moment.

—*"Black John the Conqueror,"*
Mac Rebennack

In order to understand a whole lot about the Dr. John scene,
you've got to know a little bit about what the hoodoo means.

In New Orleans, in religion, as in food or race or music,
you can't separate nothing from nothing. Everything mingles each
into the other—Catholic saint worship with gris-gris spirits, evangelical tent meetings with spiritual-church ceremonies—until
nothing is purely itself but becomes part of one fonky gumbo.
This is why it's so important to understand that in New Orleans
the idea of voodoo—or, as we call it, gris-gris—is less a distinct
religion than a way of life.

New Orleans is rich in religions of the people; standard-issue
affairs like the Roman Catholic church, the Southern Baptists, Meth-
odists, Presbyterians, and other organized groups have never really
taken hold in their purest forms. Instead, a number of homegrown
religions have arisen; they're all distinct from one another, yet they're

tangled up with each and other, too. These are the spiritual churches: Sang Christo, gris-gris, orisha, santería, and obeyah. Despite their many little differences, all have a main root that remains the same: You got love problems, health problems, job problems—even if you need a tip on the numbers—you go see your spiritual-church reverend mother, and she'll help you out.

There are some links between New Orleans gris-gris and the voodoo, santería, and macumba you find in Haiti, Cuba, and Brazil. Gris-gris is especially tied into voodoo in Haiti, because many of the people in New Orleans who practice gris-gris are descendants of people who were brought from Haiti in the early nineteenth century, after Haiti's war of independence against the French. Yet no matter the links, the groups in New Orleans have developed their own particular stamp that sets them apart from the religions of Latin America.

I first picked up some knowledge about gris-gris from my sister, Bobbie, who was into it from a distance—she had an expert's library on the subject—and from David Lastie who worked at the Bop Shop Record Store. When I was thirteen or fourteen, David would put me in his pickup truck and ride me around town. By hanging around his family, especially with his mother, I copped a lot of understanding about the gris-gris and the spiritual church.

About the fourth or fifth time I met Mr. Lastie, he laid a piece of red cloth on me and wrote one of those spiritual sayings on it, followed by the initials MCS. I asked him what the MCS stood for, and he enlightened me right away: Mother Catherine Seals, probably the greatest reverend mother in New Orleans during this century.

From Mr. Lastie I learned that Mother Catherine Seals performed miracles. I also found out that her Temple of the Innocent Blood, a home for run-down whores who were ill or could no longer make a living, was at the same time one of the earliest spiritual churches in New Orleans. Along with prostitutes, Mother Catherine also took in women who had had coat-hanger abortions and were turned away by Charity Hospital; she saved their asses, then put them to work for the church. She called the children of these women her angels; all the older women (and some men) she called her saints.

Mother Seals's approach was interesting because she combined gris-gris with all kinds of other practices: She was half evangelical Christian, half New Orleans Indian (the Mardi Gras Indians' saint is the Native American figure Black Hawk), and of course she mixed a lot of Catholic saint worship in there, too. Mother Seals healed people in her church through the laying on of hands, and by a mystical extraction of objects from people's bodies. This healing aspect is what makes the spiritual church akin to gris-gris, which stresses healing with folk medicines made from roots and herbs gathered in the swamps and woods around New Orleans. Yet, even though there is an overlap, the gris-gris people and spiritual-church people don't have much to do with each other. Their ceremonies and their beliefs are different, even if their roots are the same.

Mother Catherine was so powerful in her time that pieces of cloth from her altar used to be snipped off and inscribed with prayers by other reverend mothers, who would pass them on to help people in need. Her name was also used to evoke help from God; you'll see her initials, MCS, appearing in cemeteries and on walls around New Orleans.

One day I was visiting the Lasties and met a neighborhood woman in the backyard; she sat me down, took my hands, looked me straight in the eye, and said:

> *You going to go on a long journey.*
> *You going to travel across the pond*
> *and have plenty of children.*
> *And everything you think about today*
> *is not going to end up being*
> *the way you think of it.*
> *The cross you bear*
> *is the cross you choose to bear.*

Then she looked me even deeper in the eye and began telling me parables:

You're not in season.
You're out of order.
You got to be in order . . .
all in order.
You got to be in season
in order to catch
the right season when it come.
You got to be in order . . .
all in order . . .
to find your way in this world.

It was my first encounter with a reverend mother, though I didn't know it at the time. Much later in my life I met her again, though this time I recognized her for what she was. She was an old, old lady by then, and she'd moved from the Ninth Ward church to her daughter Mary Ann's. She told me all kind of things—stories about my children, for instance—that seemed like nonsense when I was a kid, but later came to pass. Many people in her family stutter; some are tangle-eyed; some are very deep, like her husband Deacon Frank; and some prophesy in parables.

Other reverend mothers were just as heavy. For instance, when the daughter of Mother Cansanero was kidnapped by a pimp, it's said she made a pilgrimage on her knees carrying a cross all the way to Florida and back. Even when she got her daughter back, she didn't lighten up; she worked herself to death for her children—which included all the children in her neighborhood.

Later, when I was around twenty and was deep into the action on the streets, I used to go up into the bell tower of the St. Roch cemetery to steal grease from the bells to make goofer dust with. Goofer dust is a combination of dirt from a graveyard, gunpowder, and grease from them bells; if you throw it into somebody's eyes it'll blind them, and throwing it behind them while they're walking away can put a curse on them.

St. Roch Park also used to be New Orleans's narcotics-dealing park extraordinaire, so making a run over there was convenient for me in several ways, even though such a combination of drugs and gris-gris is not what the reverend mothers were about. I used the goofer dust and other gris-gris ceremonies to curse my enemies and bring me good luck with the police when I was out doing my business.

In the early sixties, when I was doing a lot of sessions at Cosimo Matassa's studio, I hooked up musically with another kind of spiritual-church faith healer named Prophet Greene, who wasn't anything like the real article; I always got a kick out of that old jive-hound's name—he made *profit green*, all right. He billed himself as "Prophet Greene from New Orleans"—he wasn't from New Orleans, and that was your first tip-off right there—and he had himself a little revue that was somewhere between a minstrel show, a snake-oil hustle, and a revival. He used to fascinate the shit out of me, because he was one of the first cats I ever met who sported big-time diamonds—I mean the kind you might see on Liberace, except most of Prophet Greene's were real; all his clothes were tailor-made, and he was one of the first cats I saw driving a flashy foreign car, a Jaguar I think it was. Prophet Greene paid us well and as soon as the gig had finished, so everybody dug him. He always used to send out for a case of Taylor's Tawny Port and Cream Sherry and a big batch of oyster po'boys for everybody when the gig had ended. Prophet Greene had figured a way to mingle the sacred and the profane into a finely wrought thing, and I dug that about him, too.

But no matter how you cut it, Prophet Greene wasn't the genuine spiritual article; what he did represent was a hustling offshoot of the real thing. Only later, when it came to me a little bit unexpectedly, did I seriously begin to get into the real thing.

One of the first of my serious contacts with the reverend mothers happened a bit before I did the *Gris-Gris* album. I ran into Mother Shannon, a well-known reverend mother, and told her I wanted to cut some voodoo songs. She said, "Oh, no, you can't do that." Then I said, "Well, how about if I just used the tune but changed the words?" and she gave me her okay to that.

In the early 1970s, my friend Boots Toups and his wife Oneida, and Jack Richardson, who ran a santería botanica in New Orleans, got together with two reverend mothers and they asked me to front a temple, which we ended up calling Dr. John's Temple of Voodoo.

Boots Toups, whom I'd met in the late sixties, was a character and high spiritual soul floating around New Orleans. He was from the lower Ninth Ward, had been shot a number of times (he had bullet holes all over his head, neck, and body), and was considered retarded by his family and a lot of people over there; in fact, he was an aware person, a high-degree Mason, high in voodoo and witchcraft. But the thing about Boots was that he was also a character. If he decided the time was right to go off on a spree, he'd disappear and be drunk for a week.

I remember Boots showed up one night after I hadn't seen him for a while, his head all swathed in bandages. I said, "What happened?" He said, "Oh, this guy shot me in the back of the head. I put some straw in the wound, drank some whiskey, and fell asleep in the back of a truck. The next day I went over and got it fixed." He'd been shot so many times, it was getting to be second nature to him.

For a guy who many claimed was retarded, Boots wrote an eloquent and correct charter for the temple; one of our reverend mothers got on the phone with the Louisiana secretary of state, Wade Martin, and got the charter filed properly so that our temple and others would have official state recognition. A state charter protects the reverend mothers from getting busted by the vice squad for their healing practices and fortune-telling, as well as protecting their right to predict lottery and racehorse numbers, which the vice cops would otherwise claim aided and abetted gambling.

The Dr. John Temple of Voodoo was run out of a gris-gris shop on St. Phillips Street, and over the years I hung out there quite a bit. In the comings and goings, a couple of the reverend mothers managed to catch me on the side and pull my coat about the real doings of gris-gris; they'd tell me, "Mac, we got you fronting this thing, but you got to know the real deal; we got to school you about gris-gris."

Every time I was in town, I got a call from the reverend mothers, and my schooling continued; eventually I met them all. Now, unfortunately, many of these women have been forced to scatter around the country as things have changed in New Orleans. One of my favorite mothers is now in Miami. Her house in New Orleans had been broken into so many times and she had been beaten up so often—terrible things for an old lady to have to suffer through—that she packed up and left.

I had known only a little about the tradition before the reverend mothers began to school me, and most of what I knew concerned Mother Catherine Seals and her Temple of the Innocent Blood. I knew that spiritual-church music was solid. If you ever heard Deacon Frank Lastie or Reverend Hill play drums, you was hearing some of the beats of New Orleans in their original forms—styles related to African ritual drumming as it came down to New Orleans—just like if you ever heard Paul Barbarin play drums you'd be hearing the original second-line drumming. This drumming really turned me out, and led me to check out not just spiritual-church music but a lot of other things connected with the hoodoo church.

I dug the spiritual- and hoodoo-church people because their bag wasn't like organized religion. They were organized, in that they would help their local community, but besides that they were loose and free, just looking to help. In 1960, when I had got shanked in my back, Mrs. Lastie treated me by passing a tomahawk over my back and mixing up a formula to help me heal. She laid a spiderweb over the wound to encourage coagulation and on top of this burned some leaves; not only did I heal very fast, but the treatment didn't leave no scar.

That kind of medical treatment was one of the things they provided for the New Orleans community. They never pretended that they could heal everything, either. They'd look at what was wrong with you, and if they could heal you they'd do it; if not, they'd tell you to go see a doctor.

When I was being schooled by the reverend mothers, I had not yet gotten any kind of hold on my narcotics problem, and they knew it. None of them came right out and called me on it, but I knew that a few of them were more than a little skeptical of me. I didn't apply myself to learning what they had to teach with anything like the attention they expected.

Now, I got to admit I wasn't the easiest student to win over. One of these reverend mothers used to make me swear I would do right by them, repeating a series of oaths: "If you betray this trust, may devils rip out your tongue to the tenth generation." When I took these oaths, I thought some of them was kind of funny; to me, they sounded more like welcome-to-the-family Mafia rituals than spiritual promises. But I don't want to push my luck, so the parts I learned under oath I won't reveal.

One of the tough things about my spiritual education was that when they were teaching me these things, most of the time I had just come in off the road, dead tired and constantly nodding off. The reverend mothers kept pumping me full of coffee and kola nuts to keep me awake; they propped me up, shook me awake—some of them were pretty mean, and got their kicks from slapping me, yelling at me, and telling me off. They would long-windedly rap me to sleep and I would long-sleepingly try to wake up for them; I let them down a lot of times.

But they didn't give up easily, and I've got a lot to thank them for. Once, when we were driving to a gig in Lafayette, Louisiana, we found ourselves in the path of an oncoming hurricane. When the weather began to get really bad, I stopped by the side of the road and called this mother. Reverend, she said, "Don't worry, we'll pray, we'll burn candles for you. The hurricane won't bother you." Sure enough, the hurricane veered off in another direction. Now you can say that maybe it was going to do that anyway, but I'm not so sure. These women had some power.

I remember when I cut the song "Hollywood Be Thy Name," with its lyrics riffing off the Lord's Prayer, I caught a lot of flak from the mothers. Boots came by my pad in the middle of the night and dragged me off to one of the mothers' houses. "Mac," he said, "you truly messed up. You really did it. This is the lowest form of blasphemy. We didn't think you'd ever do something like this."

I said, "That's why I did it."

One of the reverend mothers looked at Boots and said, "I told you that's why he did it!"

But they forgave me eventually, and kept at my education. The mothers taught me that everything in nature is part of God, and everything of God is spiritual. My schooling continued with Jack Richardson and Noel Guillot, who used to take me along with these santería and orisha people out in the woods near Mississippi to collect large amounts of Dr. John the Conqueror and Adam and Eve roots, two kinds of herbs used in healing and gris-gris rituals. Boots Toups, meanwhile, taught me how to write Aramaic, Hebrew, and Arabic; he had the reverend mothers teaching me the right names for all the trees and plants. I forget a lot of this now, but back then I knew which roots were under which tree and which were used for mystical high magic, low magic, hoodoo, orisha, and obeyah.

I also learned more about ceremonies. Your typical hoodoo ceremony went down when a reverend mother was called upon to heal someone. Friends and relatives of the person being healed would show up at the reverend mother's pad; often there would be several reverend mothers in attendance. A litany would start the ceremony. The four corners of the room, which represented the *quatre parishes* of the universe—earth, wind, fire, and water— would be cleansed by sprinkling water and burning incense. Sometime during the litany, someone would begin to chant and play sacred rhythm on broomsticks nailed with bottle tops, Coke bottles, pots and pans—anything available. A person or two might bring congas and start to build the rhythm. All of these voices, congas, bottles, and pans would work together until a mesmerizing chant was laid down to help the healing. The music was a way of getting into the spirit to heal the meat.

A little later, during the time my album *In the Right Place* was on the charts, I stumbled onto a prop that I became especially fond of: Prince, a mummified head that I bought from a trapper in the backwoods of Georgia who sold pelts and snakeskin and the like. Recently, I've seen several photos of me with Jerry Wexler at Carnegie Hall in which I'm holding Prince casually under my arm. I used to bring Prince on gigs, set him atop a mike stand, and mount a hanger with clothes underneath him; situated proudly behind some keyboards, he looked just like a very heavy, very still member of the band. Nobody ever asked, "Is there something wrong with that guy?" He just looked like an extra musician.

Prince ended up getting me and some gris-gris people in trouble when a santería church was busted and the head was confiscated by the police. Jack, who ran the Santería Temple of Baal, got his ass busted smuggling guns to Latin America in boxes marked ARTICULOS RELIGIOSOS; when the police came down on him, they busted Prince too. Prince ended up in the hands of Dr. Minyard, the New Orleans coroner, who was able to supply me with some of the story behind the head atop the man. The police had suspected the head belonged to someone who had been snuffed, but Dr. Minyard traced Prince's fancy dental work and discovered he had been used as a practice patient in a dental school in the 1800s. A century and many adventures later, Prince now resides in Charity Hospital, along with a host of other medical oddities.

A round 1971 or 1972, the band did a gig called the Mardi Gras Mambo out in Leander Perez Hall in St. Bernard Parish. This was one of many corrupt parishes in Louisiana; I remember narcotics squad undercover agents offering me and Professor Longhair marijuana during the gig—pot that had just been confiscated from members of the audience earlier in that same gig.

Boots had put out a lot of publicity for these gigs, including a pamphlet promising that I'd be tossing Dr. John the Conquerer roots out free during the gig (you'd have to pay for them if you came for them later at the shop). During the show, I got spooked by my own song—"Jump Sturdy"—in which I'd mentioned Julia Jackson, a well-known gris-gris herb doctor, and said she had killed Jump Sturdy, the song's central figure. After the concert, a strange-looking old woman came up to me; she looked like she was in Mardi Gras costume, though later I realized she was probably wearing her regular root-doctor clothes. She said, "Dr. John, I got to talk to you." I could tell she was real pissed off, and I thought, Uh-oh. She took me aside and said, "Do you know who I am?"

I said, tongue-in-cheek, "No, but you look familiar." That was the wrong thing to say.

She said, "You don't know me from Adam. I'm Queen Julia Jackson. What you said about me in your song was a goddamned lie."

I said, "I think I im-marble-ized you." I meant it, but I was coming off half-ironically, too.

This pissed her off even more. "You're never going to be *im-mortal* 'til you're dead. Do I look dead to you?" And she walked off. I never saw her again.

As the neighborhoods got more and more fractured and a lot of the reverend mothers got older, they were able to do less and less for the city and the citizens. They were not of the meek; still, many of them suffered, especially my friends the Lasties. Melvin Lastie, one of the guiding lights behind AFO Records and a great cornet player, was stricken with cancer around 1970, when he was just in his early forties. The doctor told him they could operate to remove the cancer, but that he wouldn't be able to play after the surgery. He said he'd rather die than lose the ability to play. So he refused treatment, and became something like a Christ figure amongst the spiritual-church people. I've seen pictures of him, thin and pale, looking like Christ. His suffering was terrifying and inspirational.

Boots Toups also suffered. His first wife, Oneida, got poisoned by a witch in New Orleans and died. After that, Boots got shot a couple more times, *and* got poisoned! At last I heard he had died, although I never knew for sure if this was true. A number of times, I've seen old-time gris-gris people around New Orleans, and they'll still tell me, "Hey, I just saw Boots." I want to ask them, "Did you see him in the spirit or the meat?" but I can't; that's the one question you can't ask. Because even though I've got a feeling he's dead, it might be that he's just laying low.

It's so painful for me to think of the reverend mothers—who once were the spiritual backbone of this city and held communities together in a respectful way—now that most of them are gone. It used to be that people who couldn't afford doctors and hospitals would go to see a reverend mother or hoodoo doctor in their neighborhood for medical advice and spiritual comfort; the people of gris-gris and the spiritual church kept a sense of togetherness alive by being the trusted servants of the community. That's to some degree missing now.

They was so believing in their thing and I loved them for that. That's what I consider spiritual people.

RIGHT PLACE, WRONG TIME

I'm a digger, a hippie,
An acid head and a saint,
A daughter of the revolution,
A minute man with war paint.

I belong to the KKK and the NAACP;
A Berkeley student in the John Birch
  Society;
A missile erector, a propaganda collector;
A medical dissector, a states' rights protector;
A Hell's Angel member of the Black Panther
  party;
Been a Communist member since the early
  1940s.

Wear a ten-gallon hat, carry a baseball bat;
I sing "My Country 'Tis of Thee"
on the corner of Sixth and Main Street . . .

—"Patriotic Flag Waver,"
  Mac Rebennack

In the late sixties I was touring with my band on our Gris-Gris show when the inevitable happened again—we got busted, this time in St. Louis, Missouri. The cops shook the band down and found us loaded with just what they were looking for: drugs

171

in the bottoms of traveling bags, tucked away in sax and guitar cases, a veritable pharmaceutical horn of plenty. In order to avoid having the whole band thrown in jail and our amps and instruments impounded, I took the heat for the bust. I was the bandleader, and taking the heat came with the territory.

When the cops hauled me downtown and gave me my one phone call, I decided to run down the side-windingest operator I knew, Irving Garr, my boss man at Mercury. As much as I despised him, I figured Garr would be able to get me on the bricks pronto. Before he could say a word, I told him, "Look, I'm here in St. Louis and I'm busted. I need you to bail me out."

On the LA end of the line, other than Garr's usual raspy breath, I heard absolute dead silence, followed by a three-beat pause and the click of the phone being hung up. Irving had lived up to his reputation all right, but not exactly in the way I had hoped.

After Irving back-handed me, I had one of the musicians in the band get hold of Brian Stone and Charlie Green, who at the time were managing Sonny and Cher and Buffalo Springfield and whom I knew through my work at Mercury. Barry Holt, a lawyer hired by Irving Greene, sprung me through a bail bondsman in St. Louis and fixed up a deal where Charlie Green was supposed to cover my bail. What I didn't know until later—and this had nothing to do with Barry—was that Charlie on his own decided to stiff the bail bondsman, so that within days there was a fugitive warrant out for my arrest.

But the implications of this bit of double-dealing wouldn't step up and slap me in the face right away. The first piece of business I had to attend to was finishing our tour. Charlie and Brian managed to bond me out of the St. Louis lock-up fairly quickly, and the Gris-Gris show continued to Detroit, Cleveland, and other cities in the Midwest. By the time I got back to LA for a little layover time, Charlie and Brian had worked up a proposition that was difficult for me to refuse, defuse, or confuse.

Charlie, who was the hustler and front man of the two, put it to me with the subtlety of a fistful of brass knuckles to the mouth. "We got you out of jail," he said. "Now we get a piece of your action." I wasn't in no kind of position to argue with them. Not only was I totally out of it, feeling bugged and crazy, but I was dope-sick, too, and sinking like a lead ship in a hurricane. So it was a clean setup for Green and Stone. "All we want to do is manage you," Brian added, as though he were trying to reassure me of his good intentions. Because I couldn't see clear to any alternative, I gave them my okay.

My relationship with them remained all right for about four bars in. Brian seemed basically cool about things. He was the quiet one, the numbers man, and he was trying to keep the books straight and maintain an open line to me. But Charlie was one bent character. He thought of himself as the star and me as the roadie of his operation. Even though I wasn't on no kind of star trip, I didn't want my manager hanging around, running down some kind of Jumpin' Jack Flash number and trying to upstage me. Beyond all that was the basic problem: A drugged-out band hooked up with a starry-eyed manager results in a chemically unbalanced situation and, in general, a fearsome sight to behold.

In late 1969, the band and I began recording an album called *Remedies* for Atlantic, the third album of our bargain with them. In the middle of the sessions, Charlie and Brian said to me, "Listen, Mac, you're getting way out over the edge. We think we gotta put you in the psych ward and get you cleaned up and detoxed." Even though Charlie himself could have used detox as much or more than me, I had to admit there was a lot of truth in what they were saying, so I agreed to have myself committed to the UCLA Neuropsychiatric Center. While I was in there, a friend came to visit me one day and hit me with some bad news. "Hey, dope," she said, "these guys are about to have you declared incompetent to handle your funds. They're going to chalk you up and wipe you out."

To get out of there, I conspired with my girlfriend at the time to book an escape from the nuthouse. One night she slipped me out of there, ran us out to the airport, and got us on a plane to Miami, where we chilled out and lay low for a while. After the events of the previous six months, Miami was some sort of relief. I didn't have no gigs, but at least I was free. In the meantime, *Remedies* had come out and was doing pretty well; down south, at least, it got a fair amount of airplay. But as I listened to *Remedies* on the radio and later, after I got my hands on a copy of the album, I noticed some peculiar cuts on the disc.

After Green and Stone put me in the psych ward, they had finished the record without me. One side of the album was basically finished before I was booked downtown, although I probably would have added a few last touches here and there. The other side, though—which was taken up by the longest song on the album, "Angola Anthem"—was unfinished: I had only laid down a scratch vocal for it, and was supposed to cut a finished vocal later. Charlie and Brian simply left my scratch vocal and the scattering of background vocals as they had been before I was shipped to the psych ward.

One of my reasons for making this album was to get the word out about the horrible conditions in Angola Penitentiary, the state prison farm in Louisiana. A few weeks after the album was released, while I was cooling out down in Miami, I read a review in *Rolling Stone* and discovered that the reviewer thought I was talking about Angola the country—that's how far they missed the issue.

By now I was just lying around, feeling like homemade shit because the record sounded so raw and had been so misunderstood. I had heard through the wire that Mercury and Irving Garr were salty at me for this and that. But I didn't have to worry about them because I knew they weren't likely to find me anytime soon. The one person who knew my whereabouts was Jerry Wexler, whom I'd contacted to hustle some session work at Atlantic's studio in Miami. Jerry was glad to help me out, and for a while things went well.

At this point, in 1970, after they was done fucking up the *Remedies* album, Charlie and Brian approached me with an offer of reconciliation. Why not, Charlie said, set us up with a European tour that would follow up on *Remedies?* The charts showed *Babylon* doing well in Europe. It would be a good time for a tour. What the hell, I said; I needed the dough. A European tour would be nice (Charlie had booked us at a big festival in the Netherlands, a festival or two in England, and the Montreux Jazz Festival). Let bygones be bygones. Feelings of generosity and good vibrations were passed around like a shiny new red satin dress before a drag queen's ball. Things was going to be just right.

We hit Europe like fifteen different kinds of bats out of hell. My short-lived detox effort at UCLA had achieved absolutely nothing in the way of rearranged attitude about my habit. On top of that, for one reason or another, most of my band weren't able to get visas to go on the trip, so I had to scramble and hire backups. This really threw me sideways—especially the loss of my percussionist, Didimus, who was the heart and soul of the band.

Didimus came from a family of Coptic Ethiopians; he himself had grown up mostly in New Orleans, but his background apparently caused traffic jams in the State Department's visa office. The word finally came down that there was no way he was going to be given visas for half the countries we planned to visit, or even be guaranteed the right to return to the United States once he had left. Because of this, Didimus decided to remain in LA while we traveled to Europe.

I was able to take my regular drummer, Freddie Staehle, and our background singers. I hired a trombone and bass player who lamed out on me, and an organist who couldn't cut it on the keyboard but who could handle snakes, which was crucial to our show.

We got over there with this crew, and the tour stunk. Charlie Green naturally was everywhere all at once, hamming it up, playing the role of the shuck-time fool. One of our first stops was at a festival in Wales, one of those big Woodstock-like multiband shows popular at the time. It had rained that morning, and I remember there were little pools of water here and there on the stage.

While we were waiting for our turn, I watched a band called Stone the Crows go through their act. During the last song of their show, the guitar player took a solo just as he stepped into one of these puddles of water. The solo was a heavy feedback and distortion-extortion number, and he was near the peak of it when his foot hit the water. What happened next was strange and creepy. He began to do all sorts of body contortions, and the rain of distorted sound continued just like he was working out on his solo. He rolled around for what seemed like minutes, then finally fell down into the puddle in a grand closing finale of stoned "acid" picking. At last, the roar of his guitar dimmed to a hum; the song was over and the audience gave the band a big round of applause. As the rest of the band left the stage, the guitarist lay in the puddle. I remember thinking, "This guy's carrying the dramatics too far." It was only when a roadie tried to unplug the guy's guitar and got a jolt that anybody figured out what had happened. As soon as the crew realized he'd been electrocuted, they turned off the juice and rushed the guy to the hospital. He never made it; I heard later in the evening that he had died on the way there. That was my introduction to Europe, three summers after the summer of love.

Throughout all this, our play-as-you-pay bass player continued to give me trouble because he wanted to work out on trombone. Things finally came to a head at the Montreux Jazz Festival, which was a big deal for us and a major showcase for our act. In the middle of our set in Montreux, this motherfucker drops his bass, picks up a trombone he'd hidden in the wings somewhere, and starts dancing around the stage, playing Pied Piper to the audience's mountain villagers. I was playing the guitar and suddenly found our act switched from a fairly respectable guitar-organ-drums-bass sound to a bizarre guitar-organ-drums-bad trombone combo. I was so mad I wanted to kill the bastard then and there. Instead I fired him on the spot, and not long after I got rid of the organist and guitarist, too.

Toward the end of the tour, Charlie decided we should record an album I'd been kicking around for a while, which I wanted to call *The Sun, Moon and Herbs*. It would be a three-album conceptual set: The *Sun* was the record you put on when you woke up in the morning; later, in the afternoon, you'd put on the *Herbs*—the herbs you eat, the herbs you smoke, the herbs that heal you. And last would be the *Moon*—night music dedicated to the enchantment of the evening and the moon goddess. Real lunar-sea action.

All I had left of my regular band were the drummer and background singers/dancers. I was lucky to have picked up a talented player named Ray Draper on percussion and tuba during our stay in Amsterdam; I kept him close to me to use on the album when I got to London. To fill things out a bit, I began making a few calls around London in the hope of scrounging up some musicians to help me out. I hired Graham Bond, the crazy sax player whose album I had produced for Mercury a few years before, and through Graham I hooked up with a mess of horn players. I made a few more phone calls, and things seemed to be working out.

Somewhere along the way I met this guy at a gig in London who gave me a bunch of what he called "magic beans." These were strange, psychedelic-looking colored seeds, and the guy said I should plant them and they'd bring me good luck. Before I had a chance to do so, though, the London police nailed Ray Draper and me and booked us for holding suspicious-looking beans, which they thought were LSD tabs. On putting them through analysis, they found they turned up negative on all known drug charts, so the police had to cut us loose. When I got down to Trident Studios, I planted a bean in a patch of ground outside, just like the cat had suggested.

Trident Studios was a strange place, located down two flights of steps in a large, open sub-basement, with the control room perched up above like the control room of a nuclear reactor. When I walked down onto the main studio floor, I was stunned by the number of musicians sitting around waiting for me to show up.

Eric Clapton was there, sitting in on guitar, and with him

were Carl Radle, his bass player, and a couple of other players. Eric had only recently broken up with Blind Faith. I also hired Walter Davis, Jr., a partner I had met in New York, to play piano; when I showed up, I found not only Walter but his wife, Mamie, the kid they had just adopted in India, and another passel of musicians that included part of Stevie Wonder's group. Somehow the word of my session had spread by way of Ray Draper and Rocky Dimuratsi to the community of African and Caribbean percussionists, and off in one corner of the studio I found a whole battery of drummers, about thirty guys in all, from places like Nigeria, Gabon, Sierra Leone, Jamaica, Trinidad, and Tobago. Finally, to top things off and round them out, Mick Jagger and Doris Troy were down there in the hole, too, fooling around and waiting for the music to begin.

I had met a lot of these cats here and there long before this gig. I first ran into Mick and Keith, probably at some do of Jerry Wexler's, in LA in 1967 or 1968. Later I worked with Keith in New York and LA.

Eric I knew a little better. I had gotten to know him in LA around the time he hooked up with George Harrison's old lady Patti. Later I worked with him in Florida, when he produced a record I was sitting in on featuring Buddy Guy and Junior Wells. He was a sensitive player, an incredible guitarist, and I was touched he'd take the time to help me out on the session.

I knew Walter Davis by way of Ray Draper, whom I knew in turn from his playing with the band Red Beans and Rice in LA. Walter's wife Mamie was involved in the music biz, too— she was a songwriter who'd penned (with Joe Williams) the Count Basie hit "All Right, Okay, You Win," among other tunes. Walter and Ray were junko partners and coconspirators from way back in the game. They had themselves into the narcoticized *The Sun, Moon and Herbs* days. Together with a cat called Michael X from the English Black Panthers, Ray and Walter had cooked up some scam to put the touch on Mick Jagger. It was a jive deal that Mick didn't even care about, and it ended up being just another PR splash for everybody—except that Walter and Ray caught heat about it from British immigration, who kicked them out of the country.

Trident Studios was jammed; we had enough musicians to make six bands, though not exactly the right instrumentation for what I wanted to cut. But I decided it didn't matter, that we'd go ahead with the cutting anyway. Things started out magically on the *Sun* part of the album. Kenneth Terroade, who later ended up working with Bob Marley, kicked things off with a beautiful flute solo that put everyone in the right mood, and it went on and on from there. The session lasted nonstop for days. Everybody was sitting around smoking hash and opium, and things sort of dissolved into one big wall of smoking, toking, and no okey-doking.

I played mainly organ and piano, with a little guitar sprinkled in, depending on whether Walter Davis was sitting in on piano, and I also spent a lot of my time directing this sprawling band of musicians. We got hours of incredible, almost effortless tape in the can, wrapped it, and sent it via Charlie Green back to LA for mixing and other postproduction work.

A few weeks later I got back to the United States and took a call from Charlie, who said, "Listen, we're not going to give the record to Atlantic. You're going to sign up with Blue Thumb Records. I've got a deal all worked out. It'll be great for you. Don't worry. I've got everything in the bag."

This is when I started to get seriously worried about my relationship with Green and Stone. I reminded Charlie that I was under contract with Atlantic for three more years, that Atlantic had paid for the studio time, that they had already started a promotion campaign for the album in Europe and the United States. Besides that, I liked Atlantic. I had a good relationship with Jerry Wexler and I didn't want to fuck it up.

"Don't worry," Charlie said. "I'm your manager. I'll fix everything up for you."

This was when I knew some fonky shit was going down. Some people from Atlantic called, asking me with deep concern if I knew where the tapes of the London sessions were. It seemed they had asked Charlie, but he danced around the issue. Finally, I had to book a flight to LA to get the tapes myself directly from Charlie so that I could deliver them to Atlantic. I had to meet with him off and on for days before I finally persuaded him to give me what he claimed were the tapes of the London sessions.

Before he delivered the stuff to me, though, I had an up-close and personal run-in with the consequences of being busted in St. Louis a year and a half before. I was staying at a friend's apartment when one night the desk clerk called up and said, "Mac, there's two guys down here asking about you. You better get the hell out of there fast. They got big guns and they're coming up after you." I ducked down the fire escape and beat it out of there to a different apartment in another part of town.

I found out through the wire that the two gorillas were bounty hunters who had come to LA to collect a fee for bringing me back to St. Louis. This was the first I had heard about Charlie Green bouncing my bail—I'd been a fugitive for eighteen months, and I didn't know it. As soon as I realized what was happening, I put Barry Holt on the case to try to straighten the mess out. Bail was wired to the bondsman to set him right and make sure the tag men stayed on a leash. In the meantime, talks were begun to clean up the charges back in St. Louis; I left LA a free man, my tapes in hand.

When I finally got back to Miami, though, I discovered serious problems with those tapes. For starters, a lot of the songs had been tampered with. There was stuff on the tapes Green gave us that wasn't recorded in London, and there was stuff from the session that wasn't on the tapes. None of the *Sun* tapes were in the batch Green gave me; what we got consisted of only part of the *Moon* and *Herbs* sessions, and not necessarily even the best of that stuff.

My heart began to sink as I listened to the crap Charlie had laid on me, but there was nothing to do except work with what I had. I worked hard with Tommy Dowd and Albie Galutin and all the pro engineers working for Atlantic's Criteria Studio in Miami and tried to sort out the mess. We worked on the project for weeks, identifying the original takes, taking out the stuff Charlie had overdubbed, and adding touches we thought were needed where things were erased.

Jerry Wexler gave me a lot of help and support during this time. Once he had realized the depth of Stone and Green's insanity, Jerry urged me to get a new manager. "Try Albert Grossman," Jerry suggested. "He used to handle Janis Joplin and now he takes care of business for Bob Dylan, The Band, Paul Butterfield . . ." Then he added just that little twist I should have learned to watch for. "I can't stand the guy," he said, "but he's a good manager." Jerry didn't lay it on too heavy; he just put the thought in my mind and let me chew on it.

For the next couple of months I continued to lie low in Miami, working for Atlantic, but bit by bit I ventured out to test the waters. Finally, I began putting my band back together for the occasional gig. One night, after a lost date somewhere beyond the rainbow further on down the road, Albert showed up along with The Band and we all went out to grab a bite to eat. We were all sitting around the table, Albert doing his best to look like Benjamin Franklin, The Band (Robbie Robertson, Levon Helm, and the others) looking like the characters they are, and Albert said to me, " I like your stuff, Mac. I want to sign you up."

I was fairly impressed with Albert's action, if not with Albert himself. He certainly had The Band pointed in the right direction. These were cats I had known from my days on the chitlin' circuit way back when; back then, they'd been playing with Ronnie Hawkins and I was working funky little road dates in Arkansas, Louisiana, and Texas with my band.

I thought Albert's proposition over for a while, and finally I made a deal with him that I thought was cut and dried. The very first thing he did was hand me over to his hand-chosen flunky Bennett Glotzer, who informed me that Albert and company now owned one-third of my publishing rights. "The hell you do," I said, and I got out of his office fast. This was the beginning of a hate-hate relationship between me and Bennett Glotzer that turned into an ongoing saga.

Albert had set me up in Woodstock after I had signed with his agency. My old New Orleans partner Bobby Charles was up there (he had his own deal cooking with Albert) and The Band was up there and we all hung out together and jammed for a couple of weeks. They were good partners to hang with, and they did a lot to set my head straight. Still, the more I found out about what I had gotten myself into with Albert and Bennett, the more pissed I got. Here's how I made my feelings known: Every morning, I put a dead bird on Bennett's doorstep, lit some black candles in front of it, and sprinkled goofer dust in a circle around that. I wasn't even doing it as a ritual; it was just a little charade, intended to create disturbance in his mind. Later in LA I saw him in front of the Troubador Club on Santa Monica Boulevard. As we were talking, he reached into his coat as if he was going for a shank or a piece, and I busted the shit out of him. Real soon after that, the same thing happened between us at a gig I played with Etta James—he went for something inside his coat and I whacked him, this time with a bottle over the head. I was almost booked for assault and battery, but from then on Bennett kept out of my face.

In 1972, soon after my dustup with Bennett Glotzer, I got a call from Keith Richards. "We're gonna be coming to LA to cut an album," Keith said. "You want to play?" They needed all kinds of musicians, so I rounded up a crew that included the singers Shirley Goodman and Tami Lynn, my guitarist Shine Robinson, Didimus, and myself.

The sessions with the Stones, which turned into their album *Exile on Main Street*, came out all right. They weren't necessarily totally stand-up people, but I dug working with them, even though I wasn't a big fan of their music. I liked the rhythms their drummer, Charlie Watts, was putting down: His style clued me that he had listened to at least some jazz and fonk stuff. In general, I wasn't a big fan of British rock. I liked the Beatles because I thought Paul McCartney and John Lennon was good writers, but a lot of the English stuff, including the Stones' music, seemed to me like watered-down versions of what we had done over here.

During these sessions, I came up with the idea to write an

album of songs with Earl King for the Stones to wax. The album, to be called *Pornographic Blues*, was a takeoff on the raunchy blue versions of popular songs I remembered from the New Orleans clubs and whorehouses after hours, when the hustlers, cons, pimps, and whores came in to carouse at the end of their working evening. Earl King and I wrote handfuls of tunes for the project; later, I got pissed off at the Stones for their *Cocksucker Blues*, a rip-off of our album concept but with no compensation or credit to me or Earl for the ideas. At the same time, Didimus really got steamed at them because they didn't give him proper credit for playing on *Exile on Main Street*; they had put down the percussionist's name as Amyl Nitrate. The rest of us didn't care so much if we got a credit, but Didimus was serious about it; he wanted his name on everything that he had a hand in recording. He put the whole nine yards of curses down on them cats.

One day not long after that, after I had finished doing some other session work, Jerry Wexler came by the studio with Leon Russell. I was feeling loose and was messing around with a slew of Professor Longhair numbers like "Tipitina" and "Hey, Little Girl," Huey Smith items such as "High Blood Pressure," and even a song or two like "Stack-a-Lee" and maybe "She Scattered Everywhere" by Archibald, an old-style New Orleans pianist who worked the Poodle Patio on Bourbon Street for years.

Jerry pricked up his ears for a minute and jumped up all excited, saying, "Hey, I never knew you played the old New Orleans stuff." Now Jerry had only known me for about seven years by now, knew I was from New Orleans, that I hung out with my New Orleans partners during my exile in LA, worked a modified New Orleans style during my Gris-Gris tour, yet somehow he'd remained unhipped that I was a piano player, that I had what he called "that rhumba-boogie funk" in my blood. One thing led to another and we began to talk while I continued to play. Jerry was knowledgeable in his own right about New Orleans music: He and Ahmet Ertegun had recorded Professor Longhair and other New Orleans talent back at the beginning of the game.

While we were talking and I was playing, Jerry had the

engineer tape our conversation. Later, he made up his own little private Dr. John demo out of this evening, with commentary and all, which he gave to a lot of his friends. Of course, Jerry didn't mind billing me for the studio time—his company, his private tape, my bill. But it all led to a good outcome, because from that goof came the idea for my next album, a roundup of New Orleans standards called *Gumbo*.

Before *Gumbo* went down, I booked back to Woodstock to try to rearrange the chemistry between me and Albert. To get the meeting off to a businesslike start, I made my case about Bennett Glotzer. "You need to un-sic this fucking asshole off me," I said.

Albert gave me some noncommittal reply, so I shouted, "Albert, you know what I think about you?" and he came back with something very philosophical, which pissed me off. To let him know I meant business, I grabbed one of the little peyote buttons he'd been growing in a flowerpot next to his desk, chopped the head off, bit the tufts out, and ate it. I didn't even want to eat the damned peyote—I just wanted to aggravate him as much as he was doing me. He went berserk and screamed: "I've been growing that peyote button for years! That really meant something to me, and now you've destroyed it!" I didn't care about that; as far as I was concerned Albert was trying to screw me three ways to Christmas, and he'd earned his doom and destruction. But what I was asking myself at this point was why I'd eaten that peyote. I don't even like peyote, and I was starting to feel a little nauseated.

The argument, if you want to call it that, then really got out there. Albert implied, without ever coming right out and saying so, that he had the power to destroy my career and was thinking about doing just that. He was very hip about skirting around the edges of this threat (probably because he was afraid I might be taping the conversation). We raged around the room, screaming at each other for a good twenty minutes before he finally threw me out.

The only guys who were cool with me now were The Band. They were truly down characters and kept me from getting 'plexed out behind all the changes. Of course, they were suffering themselves from dealing with Grossman. To somehow get our heads out of all the garbage, we holed up for a while and played and finally taped some tunes they eventually recorded with Allen Toussaint under the title *Rock of Ages*, which in my mind, as nice as it was to cut, was affected by what was happening at the time.

In bits and pieces, the deal between Grossman, Glotzer, and me became clear: they weren't going to do anything *for* me; instead, they'd take money *from* me, on top of the percentage they were taking for handling me and their efforts to splinter up my band. As soon as I grasped this deal and all that it was about, I said "Fuck you" to Albert and I walked. They sued me, but it didn't matter. I wasn't going to be jived like that anymore.

In between all of this down-goings, Jerry Wexler and I put together a band to record *Gumbo*. I used most of my regular band—Freddie Staehle on drums, Didimus on congas, Ronnie Barron on organ, Shine Robinson on guitar, and Jimmy Calhoun on bass—along with a few members of my old New Orleans LA group: the Lastie brothers, Melvin and David, on cornet and sax respectively, and Harold Battiste, with whom I had patched up my disagreements, on clarinet and alto sax. Another nice touch on the album was the addition of one of my musical mentors, tenor player Lee Allen, who had been the heart and soul of Cosimo's J&M Studio back in New Orleans.

Cutting the album was a stone kick first to last. We did the high spots of New Orleans R&B—Earl King's version of "Let the Good Times Roll," Fess's "Tipitina," my own composition "Somebody Changed the Lock," "Iko, Iko" by Sugar Boy Crawford and the Cane Cutters, and other songs—that had defined the New Orleans sound from 1950 until DA Big Jim Garrison and the music unions shut the doors on the scene ten years before.

Once we had wrapped the album, though, I had to face the music out on the streets. Now I had two fiends claiming to be my manager—Albert Grossman and Charlie Green—both of whom had truly evil shit aimed at me. But as far as I was concerned, both were fired.

GUMBO

In 1972, I recorded *Gumbo*, an album that was both a tribute to and my interpretation of the music I had grown up with in New Orleans in the late 1940s and 1950s. I tried to keep a lot of little changes that were characteristic of New Orleans, while working my own funknology on piano and guitar.

One of the great kicks of this session was using Melvin Lastie on cornet and Lee Allen on tenor, two of the horn players who did so much to create the original New Orleans R&B sound. Lee is especially famous for the many, many smoking tenor solos he did on records that came out of New Orleans. I mean, his sound made hits out of a lot of records that might otherwise have been ho-hum. He put the fine on "Junko Partner" and "Little Liza Jane," and on the latter tune, Lee, Melvin, and Melvin's brother David Lastie end the song with a New Orleans–patented "ride" chorus, where all the horns jam and go for themselves.

On this album and a number of others, I used Freddie Staehle as drummer. Freddie has been the main drummer with the various bands I've put together over the years, and is the younger brother of one of my first drummers, Paul Staehle. In New Orleans roots music, the drummer is crucial, chronic to our thing because he lays down the foundation of what New Orleans music is all about: the funk.

Freddie has his own idiosyncratic thing, of course, but he basically follows a New Orleans style that leans heavily on the bass drum playing double-clutch rhythms (like two eighth notes rather than one quarter note as the basic pulse). Rather than play the one-bar patterns typical of most rock and even R&B drummers, the New Orleans–schooled drummer will break up the beat into two- and four-bar patterns (and sometimes even an eight-bar pattern). Two and four on the back beat is sometimes only implied; sometimes the groove is felt in cut time, which is one half the tempo, or double time, doubling up the groove.

There are many different styles of second-line drumming, and they are as extreme and different as "Zigaboo" Modeliste's drumming on the Meters' records, Vernell Fournier's samba-type groove on Ahmad Jamal's "Ponciana," Earl Palmer's fonky feel on Little Richard's "Slippin' and Slidin'," or Charles "Hongry" Williams's fonk on Huey Smith's "High Blood Pressure," or Junie Boy's second-line feel on Lee Dorsey's recording of "Working in a Coal Mine."

Of course, the source for this rhythm goes much further back than that. All the old marching bands (and most of the current ones, such as the Dirty Dozen Brass Band) have it. So do the spiritual-church cats, like Melvin and David Lastie's father, who was a spiritual-church drummer. This style was developed in the studio in the fifties by Earl Palmer and Charlie Williams. Later, in the late fifties and early sixties, Smokey Joe Johnson and John Boudreaux took it even further.

One of my old favorite songs on *Gumbo* is "Junko Partner," a New Orleans classic that was the anthem for the dopers, whores, pimps, and cons. This song was a standard, with all kinds of different verses, in Angola State Penitentiary.

Junko Partner

Down the road come junko partner
Lord, he was loaded as can be
Lord, he was knocked down, knocked down loaded
You know he wobbled all over the street

Singing six months ain't no sentence
Lord, you know one year ain't no time
They got boys on the Ponderosa
Serving nine to ninety-nine

If I had one million dollars
Just one million to call my own
I'd buy the land around the parish prison
and I'd grow me a big mootie [marijuana] farm

Once I had plenty of money
I had good friends all over town
Now I burnt up my last money
Even my jonky partners have put me down

(continued)

> *I gòt a woman in the parish*
> *and another in the house of D*
> *and another in St. Gabriel's*
> *Doin' a li'l time for me*
>
> *Give me a little whiskey*
> *When I get a little frisky*
> *It's a mighty good drink*
> *When you get a little dry*
> *Give me reefer*
> *When I get a little sickly*
> *But give me a little heaven [heroin]*
> *Before I die*
>
> *Down the road come junko partner*
> *Lord, he was loaded as can be*
> *Lord, he was knocked down, knocked out loaded*
> *And he sang this dope-fiend song to me*

So I was twixted and tweened and jacked up in the middle of all of this. On one side, my career was going good guns with *Gumbo*; on the other, all this business hoodoo messed it up. I was stuck somewhere in the middle, playing the role of the victim while I'd already staked out the image of the cool guy in front.

Around the time we recorded *Gumbo*, I was a methodonian—on a methadone-maintenance program to keep a lid on some of the old habitual rituals. But getting a grip on my habit was tough, and I ended up somewhere between semicool and semicrazy—probably mainly crazy, but with a cool streak and just trying to cope with the changes.

After we cut the new record, I decided I'd had enough of the mighty-coo-de-fiyo hoodoo show, so I dumped the Gris-Gris routine we had been touring with since 1967 and worked up a new act—a Mardi Gras revue featuring the New Orleans standards we had covered in *Gumbo*. I put a good little band together, and for the first time in memory Atlantic set up an actual promotional tour for us. We played all the high spots, Carnegie Hall and other joints like that, and wonder of wonders, our A-side forty-five, "Iko Iko," began to take off as a Top Forty record.

Around this time, Charlie Green and Brian Stone came slinking into the picture again. Somehow they and Charlie Underwood, a recording engineer I had worked with who owned Nashville West Studio in cahoots with an old timer named Huey Meaux, had managed to get their hands on a ragged bunch of demos I had done for various artists during my days as a producer, songwriter, and arranger; now that I'd hit the Top Forty, they wanted to put out a mess of rehashed Dr. John stuff. They called me to ask if I'd help them clean the tapes up; most of them were just me and the piano doing our thing all alone. I told them, "Man, I don't want no part of this, and I'm going to kill y'all if you do it." The two Charlies came back at me: "Well, that's cool, Mac. We know this stuff could be great, but you come back to us when you change your mind." Of course, real soon, I saw the stuff come out anyway.

Using those tracks and a couple of tapes they'd made of me playing the piano in their office, they began pumping out the "unofficial records." They even used a recording of "Mean Cheating Woman," a song by a graphic artist friend who designed some of my album covers, made as a favor for Stanley years before when he was breaking up with his girlfriend. They put out a whole series of albums using this stuff, which has been reissued over and over again under different titles with different covers; the most common ones are called *Anytime, Anyplace, Anywhere* and *The Best of Dr. John*. The funny thing is that one of the records, the one with the song "Just a Square from Delaware," sounds almost halfway like a legitimate record, because it features a backup track I'd done for some forgotten group lost in a psychedelic time warp.

Soon after that, another group of operators, whose identities I haven't yet uncovered, hired a band to lay down overdubs on yet another collection of jingle and jam session tapes I had recorded in the early and mid-sixties. This album, called *ZuZu Man*, hit the market on the Trip record label soon after Charlie and Brian's stuff. A singer who was supposed to be me was dubbed over this stuff; I don't know who the guy is, but he ain't a very good imitation.

Once the mystery characters had done their dirty work, the bootleg disease began to spread like the Hong Kong flu down to Texas, where Huey Meaux, who had his own tapes of me from the days I'd worked for him as a producer and arranger in Louisiana and Texas, pressed a couple of Dr. John albums all his own, a hustle I none too dearly appreciated.

About this time, Allen Toussaint and I reestablished contact with one another while he was doing work on The Band's *Rock of Ages* album. Allen was working closely with the Meters too; I'd known the Meters—Art and Cyril Neville, Joe "Zigaboo" Modeliste, George Porter, Jr., and Leo Nocentelli—from way back in the game. Allen suggested it might work out real nice if the Meters and I could figure out a plan to record together, since we were both coming out of more or less the same groove. The result of it was that in 1973 Allen and I and the Meters got together to work on my album *In the Right Place*.

In the Right Place turned into a fine collaboration. A lot of different artists pitched in to give me lyrics on the song "Right Place, Wrong Time," which became one of the A-side singles off the album. Bob Dylan started it off by laying a line on me—"I'm on the right trip, but in the wrong car." Then Bette Midler gave me one: "My head's in a bad place, I don't know what it's there for." Doug Sahm also pitched in: "I was in the right set, but it must have been the wrong sign." Everybody gave me a little something, which helped because I was way short of a finished song myself. They got me all inspired, and I came up with the old Ninth Ward slang "I'm just in need of a little brain salad surgery," which was a way of saying you're out looking for head. The brain salad surgery bit got caught up in pop slang through my record promoter, Mario Medious, whom we called the Big M. M was also working as a promoter for Emerson, Lake and

Palmer, and through Mario, who loved New Orleans slang, they heard the "brain salad surgery" rib and used it as the title of their next album.

I still caught lethal darts from my past managers. Not only were Charlie Green and Brian Stone running their hustles by me, but Bennett Glotzer had managed to split my band up. Glotzer had pried loose Ronnie Barron, my organist, by offering Ronnie a major role in Paul Butterfield's new band and various other kinds of glittering baubles and sweet lies.

Just before I recorded *In the Right Place*, I hooked up with yet another high-flying, low-balling manager I thought would kick me into the superstratosphere of rock and roll. This time the character was Phil Walden, who managed the Allman Brothers, the Meters, and a bunch of other people, and who everybody was beginning to steer clear of. But Phil has the Allmans and he had managed Otis Redding, I said to myself, so he can't be *all* bad.

Phil's hustle was that he wanted total control of his acts: He owned not only your management, but the booking agency that set up your gigs and the travel agency that sent you on your way— he had an angle on every piece of your business. Now, this setup was obvious; any idiot could see the hustle from a hundred miles away coming down Interstate 75 to Macon, Georgia, where Phil based his scam. He got away with it with most of his acts because they had been with him too long to argue about it. The Meters and I, we weren't going for it. But we also knew that Phil Walden could hook our record deal up crossways between Atlantic, my label, and Warner Brothers, for whom the Meters recorded. So we decided to stomach Phil Walden for as long as we could and hope for the best. For me, this was the beginning of another wrong-way connection that seemed to last an age.

In the beginning, like most left-field arrangements, everything looked just fine. The Meters and my band began to tour a lot with the Allman Brothers, who were definitely a hot property at the time. We worked as the opening acts at a lot of big gigs, and everything seemed to fit into one long, cool calculation—not only because it gave me and my band a lot of exposure, but also

IN THE RIGHT PLACE

In 1973, I got together with Allen Toussaint to do an album with the Meters, who were the fonkiest rhythm section anywhere. I had known Allen and the organist for the Meters, Art Neville, from the recording scene in the late fifties and early sixties. The other Meters—Leo Nocentelli on guitar, George Porter on bass, and "Zigaboo" Modeliste on drums—I got to know in the late sixties as they came onto the scene.

The album had more of a straight-ahead dance feel than ones I had done in the past, although it was still anchored solid in R&B. Atlantic pushed hard to promote it, and it yielded two hits—"Right Place, Wrong Time" and "Such a Night."

"Such a Night," which I wrote, is a ballad, a sweet, easy groove that Allen developed into something that sounds almost like an old music-hall softshoe tune. Allen has always been one of the keys to great New Orleans R&B as a writer, player, producer, and singer. I had written the song eight years before, but Allen convinced me that we needed it for the album and I'm glad he did; it became a hit, with that fonky Allen Toussaint touch to the production.

Such a Night

Such a night
It's such a night
Sweet confusion under the moonlight.

Such a night
Such a night
To steal away, the time is right.

Your eyes met mine
At a glance
You let me know
This was my chance.

You came here with my best friend Jim
And here I am
Trying to steal you away from him . . .

If I don't do it somebody else will
If I don't do it, you know somebody else will

And it's such a night
Such a night
Sweet confusion under the moonlight.

It's such a night
Such a night
To steal away, the time is right.
I couldn't believe my ears
And my heart just skipped a beat
When you told me to take you walking down the street.

You came here with my best friend Jim
And here I am
Stealing you away from him.

Oh, it's such a night . . .

because I really liked hanging with the Meters and the Allmans.
Duane Allman was another cat, like the members of The Band,
I'd met through Ronnie Hawkins way back. He had been playing
on a recording gig with Ronnie and me in Florida in the mid-
sixties, and at the time I thought, Man, this guy's a down-home
guitar-playin' monster. I like him. But then the bad juju began to
come up out of the ground: One day, after returning to Macon
from a gig, I found my house empty and all the furniture gone.
Later, a lot of this stuff showed up in Walden's studio in Macon;
this discovery confirmed my worst fears, and killed my relationship with Phil Walden.

Back in LA, I began to act as my own manager at last. It
was a decision that made everything about twice as hard, and
meant a whole lot more work on those nitty-gritty details I'd

never enjoyed much. I put together yet another band of New Orleans musicians, and began hustling dates.

Since moving from Macon I had kept in touch with the Meters, and we picked up our touring together with the welcome addition of Professor Longhair and his band. What we wanted to do was put together a New Orleans revue act to see if it would fly cross-country. We didn't cop a whole lot of interest in our angle at first; promoters loved the act when they saw it, but didn't think there was a market for it in their halls. In the meantime, Atlantic did what it could to help with promotion for me and the Meters, in support of *In the Right Place*.

Big M—Mario Medious—showed up to handle promotion. A Chicago hipster, he knew how to adjust the levers and wheels inside the music business to make a song a hit. Atlantic paid him to promote their records to deejays and program directors; during our tour promoting the album and the singles "Right Place, Wrong Time" and "Such a Night," Mario took care of the business he needed to in order to get record airplay.

Mario was very hip to the underground scene; he'd walk into a radio station and, right off, whatever the guy was down with, Mario had it covered. For him, it was all down to a fine science. Of course, this sort of promotion wasn't exactly unheard of in the record business, where it seemed like everybody knew what everybody else was into. I was shown how this old-boy setup worked later on the same year, 1973. That May, I had an appointment to meet Clive Davis, whom I got to know through my collaboration with Mike Bloomfield and John Hammond, Jr., on the album *Triumvirate*, which was released on the Columbia label.

Davis wanted to talk to me on a Monday about making a production deal with Columbia, but the Friday night before I was set to fly to New York to see him, Jerry Wexler called me and said, "Ain't no sense going to that meeting. Clive's going to be fired Monday." Since I didn't want to waste money on a trip with no purpose, I didn't go; sure enough, Clive was axed, just like Jerry had warned me.

In spite of M's dynamite work, Atlantic still managed to piss off both my band and the Meters, because the dates as my backup band were split between them, so that neither group felt they were getting enough work and exposure.

On top of this, poor Professor Longhair got more and more iced out of the picture as all this went down. Fess's story at this time was alternately hopeful and dismal: Atlantic put out a reissue of old Professor Longhair cuts they entitled *Professor Longhair: New Orleans Piano*; yet it seemed they only put the album out because they were bent out of shape after failing to acquire another set of Fess's sessions, recorded in Louisiana with Quint Davis and featuring guitarist Snooks Eaglin, the year before. In any event, the *New Orleans Piano* album could have been a classic if Atlantic had put Fess's great original version of "Tipitina" on it. Instead, they slapped down an unissued, alternate version, because they knew the original was worth more to them than just another album track.

As the New Orleans revue concept flopped, Atlantic reprogrammed its promo pitch and began to slot my band into a lot of TV rock concerts—"Rock Concert," "In Concert," "Midnight Special." With this and our other tours, and with M's magic touch and good promotion from Dicky Kline, Vince Ferraci, and my old partner Stanley Chaisson the record started happening. But in spite of all of this—my second hit record in a row and my second Top Forty single—I still hadn't made it clear to where I wanted to be. I found myself walking a legal tightrope: For one thing, I hadn't yet managed to get straight over the St. Louis bust all those years ago, which I thought had finally been cleared up in 1971; on top of that were piled all of the nightmare managers of the past four or five years, who had their fingers in me through their twisted deals and outstanding lawsuits.

To make matters worse, I came up with the brilliant idea to begin playing benefit concerts to help the Black Panthers, who were involved in raising money for their children's breakfast programs, and to do what we could to spring John Sinclair, a White Panther activist, from the pen. We began playing benefits all over the place—Detroit, Chicago, Los Angeles—which had the immediate effect of bringing serious federal heat down on our asses. For the first time, the band caught routine searches at airports; I got strip-searched, the band was pulled into rooms for once-overs—not just on international flights, but even on state-to-state hops. I discovered that we'd jumped into a whole new category of criminality. We weren't just garden-variety dope fiends anymore; now we had become political activists, the most fonky-knuckled lames of them all, which was something none of us was ready for.

After a few months of this action, the band began to flinch at hard travel time, and I got to feeling deeply blue. I went so far down that I began seriously to consider hanging up my rock and roll shoes. I thought about going back to producing, or out on the streets to a nice, steady job as an archaeologist or a court reporter—anything but the deal I was into then.

It was at about this time that I hooked up on a gig to do a little *Rock 'n' Roll* with John Lennon. My band was playing the Troubador in LA, and John showed up one night to sit in with us. These were the days of coke and booze in LA, and John was hitting both hard at the same time: He sat in on the organ, and was so fucked up he held three clashing notes while he slowly nodded off. Cher and Bonnie Bramlett were sitting in with us, too; Bobby Womack was there, and so was Elton John. But Lennon stole the show with his deep nod.

Shortly after he fell asleep, John decided he wanted Phil Spector to produce an album of rock standards for him, which would eventually be called *Rock 'n' Roll*. Because I had worked with Phil back in the game, I wasn't totally surprised when the word came down asking me if I was up for a date at John's session. A lot of the album had already been done by the time I showed up in December 1973 at the Record Plant West, where the sessions were being held.

The first people I ran into, Jesse Ed Davis and Danny Kortchmar, looked like two law victims. The night before, John had bitten Danny on the end of the nose and fractured Jesse Ed's wrist; now, here they were back to work. We killed quite a bit of time before John showed up. When he finally got there, he was in fairly good form. But for the rest of the evening, Phil Spector kept trying to keep hidden a bottle of lush John had brought with him, and when John finally got to the bottle, the session ended.

Later, Albert Goldman interviewed me, supposedly about my career, and sneakily brought up the topic of this session. I laid what I knew on him, which was bad enough but honest as I knew it; I never thought that Goldman would spin it into his twisted, mean-spirited hatchet-job *The Lives of John Lennon*. When I finally checked out the book, I was struck by how awfully jive Goldman's approach seemed. Even though John could be tough to deal with when he was lushing, there was another side of him—the sweet, vulnerable part—you could dig. The evidence of this other, less obvious side shows up in Danny and Jesse Ed's behavior; there must have been something about John that rang all sorts of good chords for them, given the amount of abuse they had to take from him on his bad days. In any event, this story came out twisted in the Goldman version; even worse, as far as I was concerned, was the fact that Goldman had jumped on someone who was six-by-six and couldn't defend himself.

After the Lennon session and lots of sessions with Ringo Starr, Harry Nilsson, and others, the band and I went back, with some hesitation, on the road. "Right Place, Wrong Time" was still Top Forty, but my life still wasn't happening. I wasn't getting no money, yet all around me I was seeing rich managers, rich record producers, rich songwriters, and all kinds of other rich rock acts. All around me the money flowed like wine, but the table must have been tilted the wrong way because none of it flowed to me. Lawyers was bogarting all my money; everybody seemed happy to keep me on the streets, rippin' and runnin', doing what I had to do to make that dollar so they could get rich. I saw creeps talking about buying third homes, and I didn't even have an apartment. I didn't have a place for my children to stay; sometimes I didn't even have money to feed them. I had ex-managers wearing mink coats. I didn't have a fur coat; I didn't even have a cloth coat. My manager had a Rolls-Royce; I didn't own a car. I didn't own a bicycle. I had nothing.

This state of affairs was enough to give me a major attitude. I got wired and weird, and I turned into a walking time bomb. My attitude affected all the cats in the band, my family, and everyone around me—the works. Every chance I got, I bent ears about the unfairness of the game, which didn't help my relationship with anyone. The general consensus about me was: *This motherfucker is getting to be a pain in the ass. He's not only irresponsible; he's out of his mind.*

Yet all I wanted to do was make some music, do something positive, and yes, goddamn it, keep a little taste for myself while I was at it. *Try to be solid as a rock, square goods,* I told myself, *nothin' beat a failure but a try, nothin' beat a don't but a do, keep on tryin', good things come to those who wait.* But I couldn't handle it. The whole scene was too tilted, and I had to hang on as tight as I could just to keep from flying off into the deep.

CHAPTER ELEVEN

BLUE MONDAYS

You may find me in a project slum
Hanging out with skid row bums.
I may look sick and I may act dumb,
But you don't know where I'm coming from.
All I got is a little common sense;
The best teacher is experience.
I'm qualified.

—*"Qualified,"*
Mac Rebennack

In the first half of the seventies, James Black and James Booker joined the Dr. John band—Black on drums and Booker switching off with me on piano and organ. Black was coming down from a big habit to a lesser one; most of the rest of the band had habits, too.

For a while, Booker was giving me more nervous breakdowns than I could handle. At some point when he was still very young, Booker had gone out on the road with Shirley and Lee, and a cat named Larry had turned him out; I don't know if the episode had traumatized him or what, but there'd been a definite change in him in the years since—among other things, he was trying to fuck some of the band. He started in on this one young bass player, and really messed up his head; the kid quit playing music. Booker thought he'd make him a better player. He really thought he was doing me a solid, thought he'd be making better singers and players of them. And he wasn't going to strong-arm anybody; he would do it by connivery.

I had more guys than I can tell you come to my room in the middle of the night wanting to change rooms to escape Booker's clutches. They'd get back to the room and Booker would have his habits on and tell them his name was Myrtle, or something else funny. Cats just couldn't handle it. Nobody wanted to room with him, myself included.

Because I was the bandleader, I was the person who assigned band members as roommates, and somehow it happened that Black and Booker ended up sharing the same room. One night about four in the morning, I woke up to find James Black banging on my door. He was frenzied. "I quit the band," he screamed.

I said, "What's the matter, James?"

"I get off the gig. I go out to eat and come back to my room, Booker's fucking a dude in his bed. I can't handle this, so I go to get some coffee; come back, and he's fucking the dude in *my* bed. I quit."

I said, "Oh, James, relax. We'll get you another room tomorrow."

The next morning, I went to Booker and Black's room. Booker answered the door. The guy he'd been fucking was still in there. I said, "Where's Black?" Booker said, "He packed up and left this morning." He was stone gone.

Other times, Booker would come into my room and keep me up all night talking about religion or arguing about politics. I'd be whipped for the gig the next day, but Booker just seemed to have been energized by our debate trials.

Shit like this happened all the time on the road, and if these happenings didn't come from inside my own band, they was emanating from other acts. In 1974, we were playing the Electric Ballroom once in Atlanta, with the Who and Toots and the Maytals. The promoter put on a big party for the acts and the press, and Keith Moon came in and dived into a table of liquor, cakes, and ice sculpture and pretty much busted the place up. Naturally, the hotel people didn't go for Keith's act, and they called the sheriff. As they were taking him to jail, Keith turned with a little flourish and yelled back, "Send the bill to Neil Sedaka."

Keith did the same thing at some guy's wedding in LA. He walked into the reception wearing a pilot suit and Nazi uniform and dived into the bar. He trashed the place. If I'd been the groom or the bride, I would have kicked his ass. But because of who he was, they were cool with it. Some friends dragged him out before he got into more trouble.

I have weird memories of all that shit. Harry Nilsson used to go for that stuff, too. I tried to stay the fuck away from the trashers. I didn't know where they were coming from. Keith seemed like a nice-enough cat when I talked to him here and there, but after I saw a couple of them maneuvers I really avoided him like the plague. That kind of carrying on didn't make no sense to me; I guess it's eccentric rich-guy fun or something, but it didn't ring my bells.

In the early 1970s, Walter Davis, Jr., Ray Draper, and I used to run in New York around Slug's Club on Third Street near Avenue B on the Lower East Side, and jazz legend Art Blakey had a pad that was nearby—around Sixth or Seventh Street. Walter and Ray knew a lot of stone jazz cats because they both came out of the East Coast jazz tradition. Walter had played with Charlie Parker, Max Roach, Dizzy Gillespie, Donald Byrd, Blakey, and others, and Ray had been a young up-and-coming jazz hotshot in New York before he ditched the city for LA in the sixties.

For a while Ray and Walter and I would cop at Slug's and meet this dope dealer in the band room, no matter whose band was playing. One day, we couldn't use that dressing room—a whole band was in there or something—and making our connection was getting complicated. Finally, Ray says, "Fuck meeting him. We'll go where he stays. Now look, we have to sneak through somebody else's pad to get there. When we go through, be real quiet. I don't want you waking this man up."

We slipped into this little pad; the walls were painted black, with one blue light in one room and one little dim red one in another. We couldn't see shit. Finally, we made it into somebody's bedroom; I could just barely make out a mirror on one side and one red light with a dark shade over it. Walter and Ray made it through, and I was coming through when all of a sudden I felt my foot tip a wastebasket over. It fell on the floor and up jumps this guy, yelling, "What the fuck are you doing? Who are you?" He flips on another light, and oh God—it's me and Walter and Art Blakey!

Walter says, real cool, "Oh, Mac, this is Art Blakey."

Art is half-asleep and all pissed off. Now, this was a true hero of mine; I wanted to crawl through the floor, it was so embarrassing. We had to go through the room where Art's son was, and he wasn't thrilled either. We finally made it all the way through the apartment, down the fire escape, and into the dealer's pad. She lived right across the backyard from Art. You couldn't just go through the front door of her building because the police had the place on permanent stakeout. Worst of all, we had to go back through Art's pad to get out!

I know a lot of people I never would have met in life who I met in embarrassing ways because of Ray Draper. In Europe, we met another guy who was some famous keyboard player. We came into this big, luxurious pad, where Ray had led us; we were in the bathroom with a woman dealer Ray had connected with, and I heard this great, classy piano sound coming through the walls. After a while, the music stopped, and there came a knock on the door: It's the piano player, trying to get into his own bathroom. Walter says, "Well, bro, you just gotta wait a second." This laid-back English voice answers, "Well, I need to come in for just a minute." Finally, Walter lets the guy in, after we've cleaned up a bit. He tells the woman something, and ignores us. Then Ray starts introducing us as though this guy wants to meet these people who were messing up his bathroom. Ray was being his gracious self, but almost nodding out from the dope we'd been doing. Fortunately, the guy was a fan of Walter's, and that chilled everything out.

Walter began to become a real drag around this time, though. Up till then, he had been a regulation dope fiend; all of a sudden, he turned into an acid head, and that's a totally different trip. On our first or second gig in the States after getting back from England, Walter took acid and just wandered offstage and into the crowd in the middle of the gig. He just disappeared; we lost Walter for a week.

Walter could get so fucked up sometimes, he looked like the wolfman. On some occasions, he was an angel; others, he acted like the devil. Yet he was one of these space cats who had so much fun and played so well you had to do your best to forgive them. He could test your patience; he'd run up a two-hundred-dollar tab on a break with people he'd met, and stick me with the bill later. I'd come down on him, and he'd get all innocent and hurt. But he wasn't as good a con artist as Ray, because he was coming from his heart. I could bust him real easy—he was a lovable cat you could read right through.

Ray, on the other hand, had a terrible habit of ripping off anything that wasn't nailed down. He would burn all the dope fiends who were stupid enough to put money in his hand and let it get out of their sight. But he was such a good player (he played on tuba, baritone horn, trombone, and sometimes percussion with us), you had to let a lot of these things slide.

I'd first heard about Ray in connection with his LA band, Red Beans and Rice. I'd heard good things about these cats, and went over to their rehearsal one day. When I heard Ray play, I was impressed. He was bad. He was a charmer, too. I liked the guy, and we started hanging out.

He was the first tuba player I had ever heard who played bebop, blues, big-band jazz, and funk—all of it. The first time you met Ray, he was just as charming as a pair of newly shined shoes; you wouldn't see his other side, how he just took everybody off—especially all those right close around him, figuring those who were near him wouldn't get him busted. He caught a lot of ass-whippings over this, but ass-whippings were built into Ray's game.

When he first heard Ray, Didimus urged me to hire him right off. I told Didimus we couldn't afford him. Didimus said, "Well, fire somebody. We got to have him." I didn't do it, but about a year later, on our lamed-out tour of Europe, Ray popped up in the Netherlands. As fate would have it, I was dope-sick, and Ray was carrying some European methadone, real strong shit. He walked into the dressing room and said, "You don't look so good," with a big smile on his face. I said, "Well, what are you holding?" He broke out this big bottle of stuff and fixed me up. I hired him on the spot.

That first gig, he didn't even have a horn; he said, "I'll get something," but he showed up at the gig with just a beat-up old conga and a bottle to play. It took him about a week to get a tuba. He wrote killer arrangements for the band, but all the shit that went along with him was a nightmare.

Once, in about 1976, we were on a gig in Toronto, I think, when right in the middle of the date the trumpet and tenor players both punched Ray Draper and began to kick and stomp him right onstage.

Of course, right after we came off, I had to call a band meeting, which I hate to do because bad things always come up at band meetings. The sax player told me, "Well, fucking Ray burnt me." I said, "You should have straightened this out after the gig. You're fired." I was pissed. The trumpet player said, "I just lost my cool. When I saw him hit Ray, I just couldn't help it. I hit him, too."

The tenor player gawked. "Why aren't you firing him, too?"

"Well, he told the truth. You was jive about it. You could have ruined his lip."

"I'm reporting you to the union."

I said, "Fuck you. Now I ain't even giving you a two-week notice."

"Well, now I'm gonna make *sure* you get into trouble with the union."

By this point I was really steamed; the first thing on my mind was kicking this sax player's ass. And all the while Ray Draper was sitting there smiling, like he'd forgotten he'd just had his ass kicked. At just the right moment, he got up, a big shit-eating grin on his face, and said, "Look, guys, I can straighten this out." He turned to the trumpet player: "Look, I know I fucked you with the money. I'm going to make it good." But the trumpet cat just belted Ray again, just popped him good.

I started screaming at Ray: "Look, motherfucker, every time I turn around you burn some sucker in this band. I ought to fire you. But if they're stupid enough to give you their money, they deserve to get burnt."

Now both the horn players were mad at me. The trumpet player, who was a Spanish cat, started cussing me out in Spanish, calling me all kind of *putas* and who knows what else.

Up popped Didimus, who said, "Mac, what you ought to do"—he's the secretary of the meeting all of a sudden—"is fire this lame," pointing to the sax man.

I said, "Right, now what do I do with the other two?"

"Let them beat each other's brains out," Didimus said.

The whole band walked out of the room and left Ray and the trumpet player to do what they would. This was a typical Ray Draper story.

Another night, he came in and asked me to hold on to a bag of some sort. I put it down. Shortly after, one of our singers came in and asked if Ray had been there. I said yes he had, and asked why. "'Cause he ran off with my record player, tape recorder, and all my tapes. And you let him get out of here."

So we looked in the bag and found all her tapes.

There was a period of several years—Ray's last in the band—when he was always gaming on some loan sharks. He owed all these lethal lenders from New Jersey and New York big-time money. He'd play one off against another: "Look, I would tighten you today, but I gotta tighten Matty first, or something to that effect." Finally, they started getting hip to him, realizing he wasn't paying anybody off. Sometime after that, one of them blew his ass away.

* * *

James Booker was another of the special musicians who drifted in and out of our band in the seventies. I had lost track of Booker for a number of years during the sixties; then, when I was first traveling with the Dr. John show, I needed another keyboard player, and Hungry Williams turned me back in Booker's direction because Booker was in New York. In no time, I got Booker into the band, where he remained, off and on, until the late seventies. It was often his role to open the show for us, doing a medley of Little Richard or Ray Charles tunes. He'd set the house on fire, because he was always better than the opening act.

Booker could talk you to death about any subject. He was very spiritual; he'd studied deeply in many faiths. He always took time out to teach me things; it was Booker and Lloyd Glenn who taught me how to play piano like the great Harry Van Walls. On top of all that, all the while he was with our band he also was writing for a newspaper down in Mississippi *and* had an ongoing relationship with some monastery there. He used to go down there, take the songs we were doing on our gigs, and plug in a whole new set of lyrics (substituting *Jesus* for *Baby*) and turn out with the monks.

Booker did the driving when we went on the road, and before long he was driving us crazy. We might be leaving New York for Richmond, Virginia; I'd go to sleep and then wake up half an hour later to find we're coming back through the Holland Tunnel. I'd say, "Booker, what the hell's going on?" He'd say, "Oh, I just gotta make a little stop, then we'll cut out." Well, he would stop off someplace in Harlem to cop, and then we'd bust ass down to Virginia. Booker could walk into any drugstore anywhere and be able to walk out of there with two bottles of codeine cough syrup, even if he had to sign for it. No one else in the band could get away with this. I don't know what Booker said, but it must have been mighty persuasive.

In the early seventies, about the time the Dr. John band started doing a lot of TV shows, Booker and I ran into this guy who wanted to cut a set of Beatles songs. Booker and I had written some arrangements for the record, which was going to feature Eric Clapton, Jeff Beck, and a host of others. Booker went to collect our fees for the session; he got the checks copped and liquidated, then went right back to the people and somehow got the money again. We got paid twice. Then Booker called the people and put some story on them to the effect that we hadn't been able to cash the checks. They paid us a third time. Well, Booker figured if they went for this story three times, they would go for four, but the fourth time a big guy who was one of the Beatles' bodyguards—I still don't know exactly what he had to do with the session—laced Booker up so bad he lost an eye.

After that, Booker got even stranger. He became convinced that if he lost the other eye, he'd be able to play as well as Ray Charles or Art Tatum. About this time, I got on his ass because he was doing strange things like wearing a glass eye or a calf-skin eye patch, and a glass eye on his necklace on our gigs.

A little later on, we did a TV show with the Dr. Hook band. Booker got weirded out heavy by Dr. Hook, who also had an eye patch. He walked right up to Dr. Hook, without winking his eye, and said: "You show me yours, I'll show you mine." Dr. Hook wanted nothing to do with this, so later, during the taping of the show, Booker took his eye patch off his bad eye and put it on his good eye. When he sensed the camera was off him, he put the patch back the right way round. It was all a bizarre little performance for Dr. Hook's benefit.

Another night at a gig, just as the MC was announcing me, Booker jumped out before me dressed up like Cleopatra and slipped in with the background singers. In those days, he had it in mind that he wanted to upstage me whenever possible. He'd say things like, "Mac, I have a great idea. On the next gig, I'm going to get up and say, 'Dr. John, you stole all my music. I challenge you to a duel.'"

I looked at him like he was crazy. "What kind of duel? Pianos? Swords? What?"

He just looked at me and changed the subject. Another

night, when we was playing the Aragon Ballroom in Chicago, I kicked off the set and Booker didn't show on the stage. Suddenly, this big mountain of sound began to swell beneath us; we looked down, and there's Booker playing this big theater organ down in the orchestra pit. It was just roaring; the whole stage was moving. The pipe organ isn't an easy instrument just to sit down and play; he sat down and cranked it up like it was nothing.

When he'd do those little things, he'd never fail to blow me away. The spark was there and it was strong. When he had his solos, he sparkled and spangled. People would come backstage and say, "Man, that was great. Who was the organist? The piano player? Who was that guy?"

I'd say, "That's James Booker."

They'd say, "Never heard anything like him before."

With the band I had at the time, I used to get real arrogant about our thing. We'd be opening for some famous act and I'd start trashing them to their face. "Man, you think you're bad, motherfuckers? I'll challenge you to a battle of the bands if you think you're so bad." Nobody ever took us on because the cats in my band might cut them to ribbons, musically, mystically, or, if necessary, physically. I mean, I felt like I could have taken on Duke Ellington or Count Basie with our little seven or eight pieces, which sometimes grew to ten or eleven.

At the time, Didimus was such a fiery conga player that he and Booker were the perfect combination: They romped when they played off of each other. Didimus was determined that Booker wouldn't outplay him. The rest of the band had to scuffle to keep up. For my own part, if I didn't feel up to what Booker was laying down, I was glad I could double on guitar with Shine, because I wouldn't feel so bad as when I had to play piano while Booker was stuck playing the organ. Sometimes he just overran me, left me in the dirt. I encouraged that from him, too, because he inspired things out of me that wouldn't have come around otherwise.

Naturally, Booker's frantic pace kept the level of musicianship in the band high. Soloists wouldn't dare play a second chorus unless they really had something to say, because if they wasn't happening, Booker would come out with a solo that would just blow them off the stage and disgrace them. Booker wanted everything to peak and peak and keep peaking until we reached the stars. We never wanted it to peak and come down, like most bands do; we believed if we just took off and kept going up, at some point we would hit another galaxy, and that would be the end of the set. This made for a lot of two-hour sets. Usually, the club owner would tell us to play an hour and a half, but we'd ignore him and play till we peaked. They loved it anyway.

This took a toll on guys who weren't at that caliber. We had a young tenor player who came into the band, a European guy who was a good player but not right up there with Booker, Didimus, Ray Draper, and the rest. After a while, he attempted suicide, and soon after that left the band. Later, he told me he couldn't handle the pressure of the musicianship and the road. Other guys came through the band who had less intense reactions but who had to quit, too. A horn player usually loves working with a good rhythm section, but James Black or John Boudreaux or Freddie Staehle coupled with Didimus were better than just good.

Toward the end, Booker was lost. Melvin Lastie had died; his mother died; then, finally, his sister passed. He began to lose it.

One night after a gig, about 1975, Booker pulled me aside and said, "Mac, I saw a sign from God today."

"Oh, yeah?" I said. "What was that?"

"Coming in from the airport. It said, 'Fly the friendly skies.' Fly the friendly skies, Booker. Fly your ass out of here. I saw a U-Haul sign, said Booker, you haul your ass outta here."

He was telling me he was getting ready to leave the band.

We were playing in Detroit, and Booker got us in deep heat

with the motel management over his habit. I gave him two weeks' pay, and sent him back to New Orleans. Booker immediately went to Joe Tex and got two weeks' pay to join Joe's band; he went to Marvin Gaye and copped two weeks' money to join him; he went to Fats Domino and got two weeks' money from him. Then he took all the cash, copped a bunch of dope, and got busted. They sent him to the parish prison, where he sweet-talked the sheriff into bringing a piano in and giving him his own phone. In return, he entertained the sheriff.

We made a tape over there one day at the parish prison. We had the whole band, with Booker playing piano. Booker didn't last too long after that. He died while I was in Scotland in a hospital, suffering with a blood clot in my leg from shooting dope. Nobody told me when he died. I don't know if they thought I'd have a blood-clot-ism and croak or what, but only much later did I learn about Booker's lonely death. He had been taken and left in the Charity Hospital, where he was dumped in a wheelchair in the hallway, having taken too much cocaine. It stopped his heart. He lay in the wheelchair for a half hour; his body was still warm when they finally found him. But by then, it was too late.

Booker could play it all—stride piano, butterfly, boogie, all the other New Orleans styles, the Chicago styles, the Memphis styles, the Texas styles, the California styles, bebop, avant-garde jazz, classical, even pop! He'd sit down at the piano and play knock-out versions of all kinds of tunes—everything from Malagueña boogie to Bach fugues. There were just too many things Booker did that were so outrageously beautiful that I just can't see how he ended up like he did. I consider him to be a genius. If I was ever blessed to meet one, James Carroll Booker was.

CHAPTER TWELVE

FESS

You got too much extortion in your amp.
Boys, I want to see you frolic when I hit the vamp.
Let me hear your foot propedeller,
And those horns spew
"Tra la oh la mala walla"
When Fess sing the blues.

—*Mac Rebennack*

Through much of the 1970s, Roy Byrd, whom everyone knew as Professor Longhair, lived in New Orleans with his wife, Alice, in a pad on Erato (the muse of poetry) Street, between Carondolet and Dryades, later by the Masonic Temple near Jackson Avenue. Maybe that's where his home-grown mystical poetry came from. Fess didn't get around as much then as he had when he was younger and healthier, but he would get his share of visitors, and I stopped by to see him whenever I got a chance.

In that house, he had a special room he had wired for kicks. In the middle of the room was a big easy chair with a panel of buttons on one of the arms. Fess would settle down there if he was in the mood for entertaining and entertainment. He'd sit back in the chair and fire up a big reefer. Then he'd push one of the buttons on the panel. In the four corners of the room, discreet puffs of roach spray would be shot into the air. This smell helped to disguise the aroma of marijuana—his wife didn't approve of him smoking reefer at the house—and maybe even accidentally killed a few roaches, too. After the roach spray fusillade, he'd hit another button that wafted the room with ozium, then a third that activated a spray of some kind of cologne. A fourth button turned on the lights; the fifth activated his tape recorder. By then he'd be deep in the chair, telling you about the music on the tape; he received lots of recordings of his music from fans around the world, to which he added his own personal tapes. If you was real honored, Fess would hit the sixth button, which turned on an electric piano and tilted his chair so that he was set up to play for you. This fonky, Fesserized remote-control paradise expressed the essence of the man—playful, inventive, with a touch of magic, and hisself pure and simple.

Later, you might be sitting out on the stairsteps: a dark New Orleans night, deep and heavy, the streetlights trapped in a cage of thick mist that rolled off the river. Nothing moving on the streets, for a long time nothing said. Until, after a while, Fess pulled a maxim out of the fog.

"You know," he'd say, "it's so dead on the streets tonight, there ain't even no second-story men out."

Professor Longhair was the guardian angel of the roots of New Orleans music. He was a one-of-a-kind musician and man, and he defined a certain style of rhumba-boogie funk that *was* New Orleans R&B from the late 1940s all the way through to his death in 1980. All New Orleans pianists today owe Fess. He was the guru, godfather, and spiritual root doctor of all that came under him.

I first worked with Fess back in the late fifties at Cosimo Matassa's studio. A bunch of us—John Boudreaux on drums, Eddie Hynes on trombone, Morris Bachamin on trumpet, myself on guitar, and Otis Deverney on bass—fell into a session with him, during which he gave us a taste of his fonky genius.

We began recording his song "Hey Now Baby, Hey Now

Honey Child." For starters, Fess sat down on John's drums and played what he wanted John to play. Fess was very specific about what he was looking for in the drums; John played it to death, and Fess was content. When we got to "Mardi Gras in New Orleans," Fess turned to the horn section and said, "What's y'all doing? I want y'all to make a 'spew.' " Eddie Hynes and Morris Bachamin looked at Fess, and I did, too, because I was playing a lick with the horn section. "Fess," one of us said, "what the hell is a 'spew'?"

Fess vocalized it for us, singing the horn line to illustrate what he meant. At the end of the line, he said, "Speeewwww!" and we got it. What he wanted was known as a "fall-off" by the horn section. And we said, "Oh, you want a fall-off."

"No," Fess said, real good-natured and sweet, "I want a spew." We ran through the number again. Hynes and Bachamin trailed the note off, and he was happy.

A little later, on another take of the same tune, Fess turned to John Boudreaux and said, "John, that ain't what I want you to play on your foot propedeller."

John said, "My whaaat?"

Fess said, "You know, I want you to propel the groove with your foot propelacter."

Man, he would change it every time he called the foot pedal's name.

Then he turned to me. "Max," he said, "I want you to distend your volume a little bit."

I just stared at him.

"You know," he said, "I want you to get more bass tonalities."

I added some bass, and he said, "No, that's not what I mean," and we fiddled and played with the guitar for another few minutes till the sound corresponded to what he had going on in his head.

Finally, when it seemed we had "Mardi Gras in New Orleans" nailed, we were doing one last take when Fess suddenly changed one whole part of the song. He added a baroque embellishment to the chart that looped a loop and callioped right back into the main melody.

Naturally, the band all blew it, had no idea that was coming.

Fess said, "Yeah, that's what I want. I want y'all to make the double-note crossover."

So we ran that down with him till we got it; now the whole band knew it was coming, and he did the turnaround like that every take, just for us.

See, Fess was the type who might play an unforgettable little piano signature just once on a gig, and never do it again. But at a recording session, he would do it again and again, till we got it cold. We all loved working with him. He threw directions at us left and right, but in a way that got the band looser and looser rather than uptight. Turned out that take of "Mardi Gras in New Orleans" we cut with Fess is the classic; it's the one you hear every year, and it's my favorite of the several well-known versions floating around.

I really got to know Fess well before I ever played with him, when he worked for a bit at the One Stop Record Shop on South Rampart Street. This was in 1954 or 1955, around the time I first started gigging in bands.

Fess had just gotten busted on a reefer charge during Mardi Gras. Fess, who loved reefer, gave a deck to this character named Beatnik who turned out to be a narc. The upshot of this piece of law 'n' order was that Fess couldn't work clubs in New Orleans for a while, because the club owners caught too much heat from narcotics agents on account of his problem. In order to work, Fess was forced to take dates around Biloxi and other places in Mississippi, which he hated. In short order, he quit this and turned to making a living at card games back in the city. He'd go play Piddy Pat and Coon Cane all night, and in the afternoon he'd work the One Stop Record Shop, filling out cards for the jukeboxes, which was hilarious because of the way he spelled things. He loved to type, because it reminded him of playing the piano, but he'd spell these songs all cockeyed, and his versions would turn up on jukeboxes all over town. Joe Assunto, who owned the One Stop, got a kick out of it, and let the cards go out the way Fess had typed them.

In the back of the store, Joe had this old piano. During down times, when there was nothing to do, I'd go sit back there with Fess. I'd play him a little tune I'd written, and Fess was so hip—he'd build my spirits up, say, "Play it again," as if he was intrigued by something I was doing. But he would do that just to get me charged. I'd run through it again and he'd listen, then he'd say, "You know, if you do this . . ." then he'd turn my song into something hip. I'd get all excited, watching what he was doing like a hawk. After that, he'd sit down and play me a version of "Tipitina" because he knew that was my favorite song. These versions came out like concertos rather than the stomp-down boogies he'd do on a gig: He'd make a gorgeous thing and then he'd say, "Now let me see you play that one part." I'd try and he'd say, "No, now look, Max, you got to do this and that," and he'd make it real clear to me.

Fess showed me other tunes he was writing, too. He had this one composition he never recorded that astonished me. He worked on it for years, turning it into a long-running improvisation of amazing depth and virtuosity. I kept urging him to record it, and he'd say, "One day I will, but I'm going to do it with eight banjos, two tubas, and a trombone." He wanted to use the eight banjos as a kind of snare drum–like battery, popping out a stringed syncopated rhythm. The brass would make elephant calls. He'd howl them out to me. He even went so far as to take my guitar, stick a pack of cigarettes under the strings, and pluck out the chords so the guitar sounded like a banjo. I'd ask him, "Why don't we just use guitars to do it?" He'd say back crisply, "No, it *got* to be banjos; that's my snare." He had it sussed out that the banjo is built like a snare drum; you can pop the strings of the banjo and get not just the snare tap but also have the tones of the banjo strings. It was a thing that should have been recorded, but Fess wasn't going to cut it unless it was done in exactly the way he imagined.

There was another little piece he'd always play me, his version of butterfly piano that grew into his songs "Rum and Coke" and "Crawfish Fiesta." This one had a kind of rapping lyric, which he'd belt out:

> I want everybody to come over,
> and we'll have a catfish party,
> but I want you to bring your owns along . . .
> Hey, bartender, give everybody a drink
> on the house . . .

And he'd do a run on the piano and rap another lyric. Then he'd explain the instrumentation. As with his major opus, he wanted banjos, bass drums, and tubas, plus a cornet, three saxes, and two clarinets. He had it all in his head.

What was amazing about Fess's orchestration—there's no other word for what he was explaining to me—was that he couldn't read music. If Fess was in the key of E flat, he'd say he was in E minor—or "E minus," as he called it. It was part of his own way of expressing himself.

When I was working for Ric and Ron Records, I tried to persuade Joe Ruffino to cut these songs of Fess's, and it was terribly flusturating to hear Ruffino come back at me: "Man, that Fess is crazy. He's been smoking too many of them muggles." I'd say, "Joe, this is serious. This is something Fess is really onto; he wants to do it." Joe would say, "You been smoking too many of those muggles along with him. Now get the fuck out of here." Now, if Joe had acts he thought might be able to make money recording, he'd ask me what to do. Yet when it came to something I was dead serious about, he told me to shove it. But I didn't give up there. I even went to Joe Caronna at Ace, but Caronna said he couldn't touch the idea because Fess was signed with Ruffino. I kept pushing for a recording of these songs throughout the sixties and all the way through the seventies. Still, nobody was interested. Even Bruce Iglauer, during the recording of Fess's last album, *Crawfish Fiesta*, looked at me like I was crazy when I tried to persuade him to record these songs. The game ended when

Fess died in January 1980, four months after we finished up *Crawfish Fiesta*.

When I was probably seventeen or eighteen, I first started seeing Fess around town more often. He was a charter member of a little clique of characters, and all them cats had their own oola-ma-walla-malla language, which Fess incorporated into his song lyrics. It was a wholly worked-out street Pig Latin patter, his "shallawalla oola mallawalla make me wanna holla" jive that shows up in "Tipitina" and a lot of his other recordings. This language was based on the tricks of street characters, who wanted to disguise what they were talking about when they were around squares. For instance, if you were discussing jail, you might not necessarily want to give yourself away, so you might say "jaoolla-mallawallaila." He could stretch one little word into a freight train. That's how he'd talk among the cats so the narcs and the vice and people he didn't trust would never know what the hell was going down.

Fess and his partners were into reefer, and not just for kicks but as a sacred thing, part of their roots. Fess spent a lot of time rolling decks of reefer at this one guy's apartment. There'd be three or four guys rolling up a whole small warehouse full of the stuff. Each roller had his own signature roll and tuck, so much so that out on the street these decks of gage sold because of these identifying tuck marks, which were guarantors of quality and authenticity.

He was also into his all-night card games, and he used to get my friend Cubano to drive him around town for card games or gigs. Once, I got a call from Fess to come pick him up from a card game around five-thirty or six in the morning. We'd talk a lot while cruising around town, and gradually I got a picture of how he got into the game.

Fess had started off in show biz as a dancer, and used to tap-dance at some joint with a troupe of shake dancers. Jack Dupree and a piano player named Kid Stormy Weather played piano at this joint. Fess danced for a while, but he always wanted to sing. He had this yodeling thing he always used to do. He told me he always liked to sing the hillbilly sound à la Ivory Joe Hunter, but he liked to sing it with the "groove" so he could "frolic" with the hillbillies. (Fess had a thing about getting high on reefer when he played. When he was high as a pine and feelin' fine, he would be ready to "frolic.")

Finally, he told Ivory Joe Hunter or somebody that he wanted to learn the piano. Ivory Joe or Jack Dupree or Brother Eurreal Montgomery or Kid Stormy Weather showed him a little something, and he took it from there, figuring out his own approach to the piano as he went along.

Remembering these early days, Fess used to tell a great story. Somebody would ask, "Say, Fess, what did you do during the war?" meaning World War II.

Fess would say, "I served behind enemy lines."

"Where was that, Fess?"

"In Shreveport."

After we finished making our stops, Fess and I would head on back to his house. The tone of the conversation shifted now, and I'd realize he had figured me in on an angle to get back in good graces with Mrs. Byrd.

We'd come to the front door and she'd be waiting for him. "Fess, you been out there all night. You gonna be out all day, too?"

"Well, Max is hungry," Fess would say.

She said, "He can come in and eat, and you welcome if you're hungry."

He'd say, "Well, Max say he don't want to eat unless I'm at the table."

It would go on and on, until finally Mrs. Byrd would give in, and that would be the end of that. Fess loved to "festoon," as he called it, even at home.

Fess used to have a regular card hustle going near the Gladstone Hotel. Fairly often, when he was near ready to leave the game, he'd slip out and make a call to me and a cabdriver named Freddy, who was a friend of his, asking us to wait for him outside.

I remember one night he came out of there beaming and gleaming, and I knew he'd done some serious scheming. He had come in there and really won big-time.

I said, "Where we going now, Fess?"

This was in the days of Jim Crow, when whites couldn't ride in a black cab, and vice-versa.

Freddy drove us around and Fess made a few stops here and there to pay off some people he owed money to. By this time, it must have been around ten at night. Fess gave Freddy directions to a part of town I didn't know then, and don't know now. We ended up at a place near the Pimlico in a very white part of uptown near Broad Street and Washington.

The joint had a piano in the dining room. We walked in there and it seemed like everybody in the place came up to Fess to say hello. I was proud to be with him. We sat down and the owner laid out food for us; after we ate, Fess sat down at the piano and played four or five songs. One customer came over and put some money in the kitty, and Fess just sat there waiting until it filled up; then he played a few more tunes, took the money, and left to a buzz of appreciation and excitement. Outside, he peeled off a Jackson, slipped it into my shirt pocket, and said, "Let Freddy get you home." Then he walked down the street and disappeared around the block.

Other nights, Fess used to give me long lectures about narcotics. "Quit shooting that dope," he'd tell me. "You'll get high enough from reefer without getting all messed up. All you do now is you shoot that stuff to keep that sick off your back. What you get out of that?"

He'd preach to me and I'd get angry with him, but down deep he'd hit me some kind of way in my heart. I'd hide from myself the hurt and shame that Fess tagged me with. He hurt me to my heart because he knew me so well. I would never tell him, but he knew he'd gotten to me.

He'd also give me these band raps. He'd say, "I hear you

boys trying to play jazz, all that big band. Why don't you just stick to something you know, try to expand on that? You can't stretch out on something you don't know. You playing over your head."

He was dead-on wise about this. When he said we was playing over our head, he meant we was trying to showboat, playing from our heads and not our hearts. This kind of advice came as a blessing to me, and helped me see clear of a lot of jive I was wading through at the time.

When my father died in the 1960s, Fess stepped in and became even more like a father to me than he had been already. He just took me under his wings so many times when he knew I was fucking up radical, and he'd talk to me like a son.

He was real blunt about the race shit, too. Fess knew what the deal was—that a lot of cats thought he was Tomming, because he played a lot of white joints, and played the games he had to in order to work. True, he'd have one front he'd present at some of these places, different from what he'd run down at a black joint; he'd wear a tux with tails, a turtleneck shirt, a medallion around his neck, white gloves, and an army fatigue cap on his head with a watch and watchband pinned onto the cap. He'd go up there, order a plate of crawfish or chicken, eat it on the piano, with his gloves on. Then he'd take the gloves off, play the piano, and run through a rap with the white folks that he dropped when he played the black joints. Some chumps came down on him for this, but what he was doing was keeping his gig. It was all still pure Fess.

Now it was a different story when he worked the other joints, the buckets-of-blood. There was a place like this way out in the middle of nowhere in Mississippi, somewhere near Pascagoula. It was out in the woods, way off the road, a little shack, no houses or people around. But come showtime, that place was packed—word spread fast that Fess was playing—and he'd play a smoker of a *black* set, rocking straight ahead.

Fess just didn't give a piss what the people who were bad-mouthing him thought. He knew where he was coming from. He also knew some of them thought his action was raggedy because he smoked that herb, but he came to marijuana from a whole 'nother perspective. He didn't smoke herb to get high. He said he smoked herb to "frolic" with the band. And when he wanted to frolic, he'd tear up a piece of paper bag and roll a joint about ten inches long, just sit there and roll it until it looked like a cigar. He'd light that up and smoke it to the end. When he got through, you knew the band was going to frolic. Later, when he bought a metronome, he hipped to the word *presto*, which described the fastest tempo. After that, his cope word was, "Come on, boys. Let's frolic presto." He kept me in stitches with his turns of phrase, but frolicking was serious business for him, and when he dropped the command on you, he meant it.

When he came back into a joint after smoking one of those bomolatchees, you'd better watch out: He'd go into his "over and unders," elaborate playing action with his hands. People ate it up. And that wasn't his only unorthodox maneuver: The club owner had to put a board up under the piano, because Fess kept time with his foot. If you didn't put the board up under one of those old uprights, Fess would kick a hole in it. A lot of times he would play with just a couple of other guys, one playing the maracas, the other a snare drum. Fess's romping foot was the bass drum; it was part of the show.

You just never knew how Fess was going to be turned out for a gig. At the fonkiest gig in town, he might show up wearing a tux. For a real fancy gig, he might appear in shirts sleeves and pants. One day, he'd have his army fatigue cap; another, he'd be wearing a turban. One week he'd have real long hair; the next, he'd be almost bald.

For a time during the late forties and early fifties, his band was called the Shuffling Hungarians; earlier they'd been the Cha-Paka-Shaweez, later they were known as the Blues Scholars. All over town you'd see them featured on posters: Professor Longhair and the Shuffling Hungarians. I'd always been curious about the origins of the name "Shuffling Hungarians," so one day I asked him about it.

"Well," he said in classic Fessese, "I had this guitar player who was Egyptian, so he hipped me to the name."

"What's that got to do with the Shuffling Hungarians?"

"Well, I knew that the Egyptians come from Hungary."

It took me a many a year to figure out the "Egyptian" he was talking about was a gypsy.

Fess took me to play a gypsy wedding on Melpomene, between St. Charles and Carondolet Street. We got there and they had a fourty-four piano. Half the regular keys, and even these hadn't been tuned in a long time. Fess sat down and got so much house from these gypsies. The king of the gypsies laid a beautiful gold pendant on Fess and tried to short Fess on the money. Fess parlayed a deal with the gypsies to play another set, passed the kitty, got the money, and kept the pendant.

Fess was experimenting, coming up with tricks and unorthodox figures no one else could touch. One of my favorite things that he used to do was a lick he played on a Paul Gayten song, "Hey, Little Girl." He'd get to the five-chord of that song, and in the bass line he'd play a minor note with his left hand against a major chord with his right, which totally reversed what anybody else would be doing. If the bass player turned it around and played major against Fess's minor, Fess would stop the band. He wouldn't point out who'd messed up, but he would make us all go over it till the bass player finally snapped and realized, Oh, God, he's playing that minor. He had a way of letting you know it was you who'd fallen out without coming right out and nailing you and hurting your feelings.

As much as he'd say that his playing came out of Champion Jack Dupree or Little Brother Montgomery, I never could see their influence on Fess. The closest thing I could ever find to his style among the earlier cats was a guy named Joseph Spence, who was a guitar player from the Bahamas who played rhythms like Fess. I've never heard any piano players flow into Fess's groove. Fess was Fess. Before him was the void; after him, we're just whistling in the dark.

It's tough for me on a gig to play Fess's songs. For instance, I've probably heard him play a hundred different versions of "Tipitina" over the years. I incorporate a little of this one, some of that one in whatever I do. But in the end, I try to play it the way I think he would, and leave my other business out as much as possible. The man had a deep brand on me; for the longest time, his playing became a dominant part of how I thought about the piano. I think this has happened to all the New Orleans piano players who followed him: Huey Smith, Allen Toussaint, Jake Myles, James Booker, and a gang-and-a-half more.

By making music the spontaneous way he did, Fess created something extraordinarily different and special. The shame of it was that he just didn't realize exactly how different it was. His songs were deeply felt spirituals with a rhumba-boogie beat, incantations to the jollamallawalla gods. I miss the man and feel blessed that he passed through my life and left the blessings of Saint Cecilia on everybody he touched.

WHAT GOES AROUND
COMES AROUND

There was a time when the earth
Was at peace, but along came man;
He began to change the plan.

In the end you gonna win whether you lose,
whether you raise, or whether you call.
Live your life to the full, and when the
chips may fall
In the end the ground and the grasses gonna
gather it all.

—"Snake Eyes,"
Mac Rebennack

During the filming of *The Last Waltz*, Martin Scorsese's tribute to The Band, I became friendly with Van Morrison. While we was hanging out, Van mentioned to me that he wanted to do a record of the old R&B stuff that had inspired him. We threw it around for a while, and later he called to hire me as producer and asked if I could get a rhythm section hooked up to come to England. I managed to hijack part of Stevie Wonder's rhythm section—Ollie Brown on drums and Reggie McBride on bass, plus Ray Parker, Jr., on rhythm guitar, along with myself on piano. These guys were absolutely happening at the time; they'd just finished recording Stevie's *Songs in the Key of Life*, and were considered one of the hipper rhythm sections.

We flew over, went up to meet Van in Oxford, and we were sitting at the table eating when Ray Parker started getting nervous 'cause his guitar hadn't come through customs. A high-strung person, Ray began to laugh, which is how he acts when he gets in a new situation that sets him at angles. At one point, Van got the idea that Ray was laughing at him—he'd missed the origin of Ray's hilarity. We wound up the next day with Van firing Ray Parker. Now, this was a time when Ray was playing on sessions with Diana Ross, Marvin Gaye, and heaps of other stars. He'd canceled stuff like that to come do the gig with Van, and Van shot him down before he even got started. Suddenly we ain't got a guitarist, and Ray's pissed with me because I'm the one who contracted him.

I told Reggie and Ollie, "Look, guys, we're going to make this record no matter what," and even though they were a little weirded out, they stuck it out because they wanted to go through with it. We all hung in there because Van just draws in musicians on account of his powerful singing; he may not have the best personality to deal with people, but the mystical quality of his voice could make you go through hell in dealing with him.

During the session I have strange memories of him auditioning a lot of guitar players—a group that included many of the premier players of England, who had driven up from London to Oxford to make the gig. There were players all over the studio; I'd give one guy a downbeat, he'd hit one note, and Van would cut him off—"Next!" It went on and on like that: The whole Chris Barber Band came there to play on a tune, and they all got axed real fast, too. It was one long continual confusement, and it all came out of the Ray Parker fiasco. We never did find a steady player, so Van and I ended up splitting the guitar duties ourselves. We finally used Marlo Henderson, who along with Reggie and Ollie was a member of Stevie Wonder's recording band. Marlo recorded his lead guitar parts during overdubbing sessions later in LA.

The same troubles hampered our work throughout these sessions. I had written some horn charts for the album and came to the studio ready to do the horns, but Van had fired most of the horn section! We had to wing it with just Jerry Jumonville and Joel Peskin on saxes, a sudden change of direction that made the horn charts useless, because I had written them for six horns.

I shouldn't have been surprised at all this. I'd heard stories about how difficult Van could be from Stuart Levine and Joe Sample and the Jazz Crusaders, who had collaborated with Van on an album not long before. At the time, the Jazz Crusaders were the premier band in the land, but whatever went down, apparently it wasn't right on the nail enough for Van. After they finished the record, Van changed his mind, decided he didn't like the album, and erased it.

He's probably one of the few guys that I ever felt like punching out in the middle of a session, but I didn't do it—not because I didn't feel like it but because I respected his singing so much. I really did get that mad at him sometimes; he's a very hard guy to deal with, but he has a thing about him that I just dig. His music is powerful. He's a mystical cat and I got to respect that in him. I figure the more talent there is in people, the bigger pain in the ass they usually are. But there are guys like Eric Clapton who disprove my rule: He has that kind of talent, but he's an easy-to-deal-with cat, a real sweetheart. He's always contributing, never in the way—the total opposite of Van.

Not too long after my mystical locomotion with Van Morrison, I hooked up with two other one-of-a-kind cats—Henry Glover and Doc Pomus.

I'd known of Henry Glover since my time with Johnny Vincent and Ace Records way back in the fifties. Johnny's biggest competition was Sid Nathan and his King, Federal, and Deluxe records, based in Cincinnati; with people like James Brown, Hank Ballard and the Midnighters, the Five Royales, Little Willie John, Freddie King, they were tough rivals. Henry Glover was a songwriter and producer who worked for Sid Nathan; he was a legend because of all the hit songs he penned for these acts. He wrote so many killer tunes it makes your mind bend. I used to get every new Federal and Deluxe record, and almost every one of them carried the songwriting credit *Glover*.

Later, when I finally met Henry Glover himself, it was as if I knew him already because I knew his music so well. One of my jobs at Ace was to listen to all the records that King and Federal were putting out and lift ideas from them. I knew his stuff inside out.

In the seventies, Henry used to have a little spot in a Chinese restaurant in New York near the Musicians' Union. Whenever I went to Times Square to cash my session checks, I'd drop by the restaurant to hang out and just talk shit with Henry, which is how I first got to know him well. Henry held court in this joint for years and talked and talked, but never ate anything—we drank the free tea they gave us, but never placed an order, no chop suey or nothing. Henry would hang there with some of the other old-timers, and I heard some great stories—more than a few of them about Henry himself.

I remember one of the old cats telling a cold-blooded story on Henry. Apparently, somewhere back in the game, Henry had been hanging out in Ray Charles's dressing room after a gig; Henry got drunk and started aggravating Ray about something or other. Ray kept coming after Henry and got an ear bead on him that knocked Henry on his ass. After that, Henry Glover became known as the man even Ray Charles could knock down.

When I first talked with Henry, he told me a story about how he wrote "I Love You, Yes I Do," which became a kind of black national anthem for a while (at the same time the white national anthem was "That's My Desire" by Frankie Laine). Henry was at the Dew Drop Inn in New Orleans and he overheard this guy tell some chick, "I love you, *yes* I do, baby." He took them seven words, worked the song around it, had Bullmoose Jackson, a Federal Records singer and saxophonist, cut it, and he had himself a national hit. He also penned "Drown in My Own

Tears," which was first recorded by Lula Reed on King and then picked up by Ray Charles, who made it his anthem for a number of years. These were songs that really were strong within my heart.

Henry liked complex tunes—not just your regular twelve-bar blues. His songs were always full of extended structures, with complex forms and hip changes and movements, and little touches he laid down on the production. For instance, the first R&B hit record in which I remember hearing a drummer playing brushes was a song Henry produced called "Fever," recorded by Little Willie John. They made the drummer play a back beat with brushes on a snare, and got it to sound like a stick. Henry was willing to try all kinds of different elements of things, mixing jazz and blues and gospel to come up with some innovative stuff.

Henry and I worked on Levon Helm's RCO All-Stars album. Henry and I were in Woodstock and started rehearsing these tunes of Henry's, and the tunes that Henry brought in inspired me to write some tunes, à la Henry, of my own.

At a certain point, the record people watching over the RCO All-Stars project got nervous because Henry was exerting so much influence over the record, and they decided to pull the plug on his involvement with the band. The word around the industry at the time was that he was overproducing; supposedly, he had done so on a Paul Butterfield record. But taking chances was Henry's style. I know you could say that he might have "overproduced" some of Little Willie John's stuff back in the fifties. Occasionally, he would put strings and a chorus of voices on his records. But he was into making commercial hits. Sometimes his approach didn't work, and he ended up with an eccentric record (which was interesting in itself). But a whole lot of times, he laid it right in the groove and the record just exploded into a monster hit and entered the arena of classic tunes. As far as the RCO All-Stars project went, I know that Levon and the other guys felt that a lot of the energy went out of the recording effort after Henry was gone.

I used to blow into New York and meet Henry Glover and Doc Pomus at the Sherry Netherland (we called it the Sherry

Never-Never Land) in New York. Henry had a little electric piano set up there, and we would all play each other's stuff while we were trying to work up some songs. My kids would wander in; Doc's kids would wander in; we'd order up room service and time drifted away sweet and gentle. Nothing ever seemed to get finished there, but the feeling was great. There was no pressure from anybody, just the fun of swapping song ideas with two great songwriters.

I knew about Doc Pomus, just as I did about Henry Glover, from his reputation. Doc had written some of the most famous rock and roll songs to come out of the fifties and early sixties— "Save the Last Dance for Me," "Suspicion," "Young Blood," and "Lonely Avenue," to name a few.

Doc and I had met a couple of times at gigs, but I had never worked with him until about 1977 or 1978. I was working at lots of sessions for Atlantic during those days and consequently was in New York, which was Doc's hometown, quite a bit. Joel Dorn, who at that time was at Atlantic producing people like Bette Midler, Roberta Flack, Roland Kirk, and Les McCann, got us together to write a song, a new national anthem, for a movie he was backing. I've still got a fond spot in my heart about that project because Joel used to talk about having Fathead Newman, one of my closest partners, dribbling a basketball with one hand and playing his sax with the other during this national anthem. But the movie never went down.

Anyway, a lot of this stuff was written at Doc's pad. We might have an idea for a new song, and Henry and I would get going on it; at a certain point, even if Henry had to split, Doc and I would keep on writing and writing and didn't stop till we had written three or four songs—all in one sitting. We just got on a roll. I hadn't written with anyone like that in a fistful of years, and it was a real spiritual thrill for me.

I remember one of the songs we were fooling with at that time we titled "There's a Better World Somewhere." Later B. B. King picked up this song and used it as the title song for his *There Must Be a Better World Somewhere* album. The song came out of this old hymn I knew from New Orleans called "This Earth Ain't No Place I'm Proud to Call Home." The next time I saw Doc after we had begun fooling with the song, he had finished up all the words, and all I had to do was work up the music. I felt proud of that song, which to me represented one of the peaks in writing I had with Doc.

Sometimes I wonder just what I'm praying for.
I win the battle, but I always lose the war.
Keep right on searching in this no-man's land out there.
And I know, yes I know, there's a better world somewhere.

There was something very special about that tune. B.B. won a Grammy for it; he won the Black Entertainer of the Year and Black Man of the Year award that year, too. The song also meant a lot to Doc. Before the record came out, B.B. sent Doc a picture of the album cover and Doc, who usually threw stuff like that away, hung it on the wall.

This roll led to other things, and eventually Doc and I got hooked up on a deal with Tommy LiPuma, who was working for A&M's subsidiary Horizon Records. Prior to my coming in on the deal, the only record Horizon ever had that did anything had been a Hugh Masakela/Herb Alpert collaboration. But because Tommy was over there, Doc and I decided to follow, and we wrote up a batch of songs that ended up on my album for Horizon called *City Lights*.

Doc and I used to argue a lot when we were working together. Like Fess, he would get on my ass about cleaning up, but he would do his little marijuana thing, too, and I'd say, "But, Doc, why you coming after me like this? You have your herb and I got my little issue. I don't see the difference." Then he'd argue back, but in a way that always had a good heart behind it. He'd get me caught up in these peculiar little things that he did, such as meeting him in tucked-away juke joints like Kenny's Castaways in Greenwich Village. I'd go down there and all these people would be hanging around Doc, and I hated most of them. I'd be meeting all kinds of stars and semi-stars—all these people I heard of but didn't know—and they were all there because of Doc's spark.

By this time, just prior to the *City Lights* record, Doc and I had probably written forty to fifty songs. All this time, I had never gotten back with Henry Glover, who had kicked off some of the song ideas in the first place; he'd gone off onto something else in the meanwhile, so Doc and I just had to wing it. The album ended up having a nice Doc Pomus stamp on it. "Dance the Night Away with You" is a good example of this, a real Docism tune. The experience left me feeling good: I had worked with two of the great songwriters of my time, giants, idols of mine—people who wrapped up my past and present in a real hip way.

This album got me hooked up solid with more songwriting deals with A&M Records. I'd go back to California and write songs with Alvin Robinson, then shuttle back to New York, where Doc would put his touch on them and finish them off. We put together a band of guys who were also on Horizon to promote the record: Hugh McCracken, Neil Larson, Buzzy Feiten, David Sanborn, Herman Ernest, and Rafael Cruz were in this band, cats who were primarily studio musicians, and we had a lot of fun. It was a loose-knit, kind of jazzy band that was into taking music all over the place. A lot of the songs lent themselves to their kind of interpretation.

One of the best parts of the *City Lights* experience was working with Tommy LiPuma, who I'd first hooked up with when he was working for Liberty Records in LA. This was during my Mercury period, when I did what I had to do to keep body and soul together; I tried to dump some half-assed masters on him, but he talked me out of the quick-buck route, and took me into the studio to make something out of my little songs. Right away, we were into something hip.

From that moment on, I knew Tommy was all right. As a musician himself, he really knew music from the inside; as our relationship went on, I realized he was dedicated to trying to put out the best music he could. There's a story that shows what kind of ears Tommy had: In the late seventies, he took me down to

CITY LIGHTS

City Lights was a record that came out of my collaboration with Doc Pomus and with Tommy LiPuma's move to Horizon Records. Because Tommy recruited Neil Larsen, Buzzy Feiten, and Hugh McCracken, guys who were special to me, I knew he was going to try to put together an interesting label.

I had an idea at the time of making the album tell this loose story about some guys who had gone to New York from New Orleans and were trying to make their way back and wound up going all through the country. It was a rambling sort of thing, like what had happened to me and a lot of other musicians, explaining how life is on the road and how you can get caught up in various tricks. Doc used to call each song a vignette, a story based on things we had talked about while we kicked around song ideas.

One of the songs on this record was a tune called "Rain," left over from my session with Van Morrison. I always wanted Van singing the damned thing, but that just didn't happen, so I cut it myself.

Rain

Come on down lightning
Come on down thunder
Come on down raindrops
Don't leave me to wonder
Life ain't worth livin'
Love ain't worth havin'
Without you

Come on down heartaches
Come on down pain
Come on down teardrops
Fallin' like rain
Life ain't worth livin'
Love ain't worth havin'
Without you

In any event, the album came out nice, and so did the title song, to my mind:

City Lights

Too many city lights
Too many midnights
On the wrong side of life
Too many honky-tonk-never-happen women
Gave me no time to find
A good wife of my own

All my yesterdays and tomorrows
Are startin' to look the same
All the places are filled with people
Without faces, without names

Too many city lights
Too many midnights
Make me die some every day
Too many never-was-never-will-be partners
Never gave me time to find
A real friend along the way
Never time to find a good wife
Never time to find a real friend

This pretty much expressed my connection with Doc at the time—we'd seen too much of juke joints, too much of the road, of everything a musician sees. Doc and I both had our own distorted viewpoints on life's little struggles and tribulations.

some little club in LA to hear this young singer he was crazy about by the name of Rickie Lee Jones. Rickie was working with a duet—singing and playing guitar, with another guitar accompaniment. I had a little office with Shine Robinson on the A&M Records lot, so after a gig we all made tracks over there. I got on the piano and Rickie ran through some of her tunes. Tommy sat in and listened. After Rickie left, Tommy turned to me and said, "She's tough." And she was. Within a year after that, she had busted out of the pack and was on her way to the top.

Everybody he ever touted me on was like that. His ears were that good, and he would never be shut down by a musician's joneses and twitches. He was always giving, always full of heart. Another thing I always liked about Tommy was that he attracted the old-timers. I remember when he did the first hit album that featured George Benson's singing, rather than just his guitar playing. It was a real breakthrough for George, and Tommy was the cat who, in a wild way that was real cool, helped George blossom into a more pop (and more money-making) direction. Strangely, the song that was a huge hit off this album was an instrumental called "Breezin' "; after years of George's instrumental career, Tommy turned an instrumental into a hit on what was being touted as a vocal album. I always thought that had a nice touch of poetic justice to it.

Doc Pomus never performed with the *City Lights* band, of course (he'd been a blues singer early on but had quit performing back in the early sixties). The most I ever got Doc to perform was one gig at the Lone Star in New York, when the band played a Joe Turner song. Doc, who was an old crony of Joe's, sang a couple of verses and quickly threw the mike back to the bandstand. He had a real good voice, though: Late at night, we'd be writing songs and there would be nobody else around, and Doc would loosen up and sing melodies in his à la Chuck Willis voice, which had gone unused for a lot of years and was a little uneven but was a real pleasing bluesy tenor. But most of the time we spent together, we spent writing.

This is how Doc wrote: We'd go sit down at his pad and start talking shit about what was happening or had happened in our lives. The next thing you know, as if by magic, Doc would write something down, and a song had begun.

Doc had suffered from polio as a kid, and sometime in the sixties he had taken a fall that had aggravated his condition, so he had to use a wheelchair to get around. He'd be sitting up in his bed a lot of the time, or sometimes I'd go to his Wurlitzer piano after we'd listened to some old records he had been talking about, and he'd suggest, "Maybe we'll try something like this on this song," and he'd come with a lyric and lick capping the sound we had just listened to. We'd float back and forth between lyrics and music. After we'd been writing songs together for a while, he'd just give me maybe one line of a melody to start, leave the rest to me. Before the night was over, Fathead Newman, Doc, and I might be all in it together. Fathead might play something; I'd write something; no matter what, songs would come out of it. We'd all be jammed in his bedroom, smoke thick as fog; by three or four in the morning, we'd be writing songs out of things that had been set off by the conversations we had, or phone calls we'd make. We used to write till one of his neighbors started beating on the walls or ceilings. I'd be stomping my foot and playing the piano; everyone was playing a little groove.

After a while we decided to get Barbara Becker, who later became the road manager, over there to record what we were doing on Doc's old tape recorder, which I never could run; we'd tried to record earlier, but half the time I'd forget to turn on the mike for the vocals, so we'd end up with a tape full of nice chords and no melody. This happened more times than I could tell you, which was a shame; most of the songs I had to rewrite later, because we just couldn't remember what the hell we'd started with.

This effort with Doc led to another album with A&M called *Tango Palace*. Doc really wanted more of the tunes we'd cowritten on this album than had appeared on *City Lights*. Around the middle of the session, people began to come by asking, "What's the single? When are we going to hear it?" Finally we wound up choosing one of my tunes, "Keep the Music Simple," and Doc got all bent out of shape. But the rest of the album is all stuff Doc and I wrote, and I always felt very proud of *Tango Palace* because of that, even though the label went under almost as soon as the record was released (and consequently the album ended up doing nothing commercially). It was a real good time for me.

I was being managed by Freddy DeMann at the time, and he came to me during the middle of the *Tango Palace* sessions and told me not to finish the album. He said it was going to go down bad (which, in fact, it did), but I told Freddy I couldn't screw Tommy LiPuma, who I'd known for a long time. When Freddy saw I wasn't going to take his advice, he fired me as an act. I respected Freddy for that; he gave me good advice and stood by it. At the time, he was managing the Jacksons and Gladys Knight; he didn't need me, but he took me on and told me straight what he thought I should do to further my career.

Doc and I wrote some really fun tunes for *Tango Palace*. "I Thought I Heard New Orleans Say" was a sideways tribute to an old song called "I Thought I Heard Buddy Bolden Say." Our song came out of something Shine Robinson and I wrote called "Brougham Dreaming," which was about dreaming about being a millionaire when you ain't got a pot to piss in. Doc and I also wrote a tune called "Louisiana Lullaby," which has parts of a lullaby that my father used to sing to me and that I used to sing to my kids when they were young. I tried to capture the mood of the lullaby more than the exact lyrics:

> *Fé dodo mon petit bébé*
> *Crabe dans cal al lou*
> *Maman li couri la revière*
> *Fé dodo mon petit bébé*
>
> *Go to sleep my Cajun cutie*
> *You're my special kind of American beauty*
> *I'll sing you to sleep*
> *Till your tears run dry*
> *With a Louisiana lullaby*

We had a lot of great singers singing on that album: Tami Lynn, Brenda Russell, Ronnie Barron, Petsy Powell—all really killer voices. Harold Battiste did charts for the voices. My favorite song on the album is the title song, "Tango Palace." It paints a picture of a guy and a chick who lived to go out and hit the sleazy juke joints, look sharp, and dance hot. I had an image of a couple who almost looked like dance instructors, they danced so well. But as the song goes on, you see they work at a beauty parlor, and their lives are a bit jaded and faded. It was a thing I had observed in joints over the years, and the song came off as something really special to me.

> *Every town's got a tango palace*
> *Old timers chasing broken dreams*
> *Living out B-movie themes*
>
> *Every town's got a tango dancer*
> *Pretending Latin ancestry*
> *Born somewhere on Main Street*
> *Low branch of the family tree*
>
> *He's got a patent leather hairdo*
> *To match the high style of his shoes*
> *Tho' he swears it's called the tango*
> *It's just another small-town blues*
>
> *Got a special tango partner*
> *Friend of twenty years*
> *She's the stylist in his beauty parlor*
> *Their dancin' messed up two careers*
>
> *Never goes out disco dancing*
> *Don't try no rock 'n' roll*
> *Says that kind of dancin'*
> *Just ain't got no soul . . .*

Doc and I was burning and turning with these songs. We were in sync about seeing the world from our slightly sick viewpoints, and the songs I wrote with him are more loaded with autobiographical detail than others I've done.

This was such a right time in my life. The brew of creation was running rich, even if commercially my career was in a slump. On top of working with Doc, I was gigging with Fathead and

Hank Crawford—two of the key arrangers/players from Ray Charles's great classic 1950s band—here and there under the name of Swamp Jam. Fathead, Hank and I had played on B. B. King's *Better World* album, so we were just continuing in that groove. Music is always growing in different ways, and sometimes it can be like a bad seed has sprouted; with this combo, though, the energy was high and the music was right. It was a good time to be breathing in the vapors and feeling the bricks under your toes on sweet Mother Earth.

CHAPTER FOURTEEN

SETTING THINGS STRAIGHT

When the battle is over
Who will wear the crown?
Who will it be? Who will it be?
Who will it be you,
Will it be me?

—"When the Battle Is Over,"
Mac Rebennack and Jessie Hill

Around 1980, while on the road somewhere around Washington, D.C., I met Jack Heyrman of Clean Cuts Records, a small outfit in Baltimore, through Calvin Rhodes, my road manager at the time. After the gig, Heyrman cornered me and hit me with the idea of doing a solo recording for his label, which was something I immediately dreaded because it reminded me of my greatest professional nightmare—that I'd end up a solo-piano lounge act, staring at Holiday Inns or bowling alleys for the rest of my natural life. I told him I would do it, really just hoping and expecting never to hear about the project again. But, as always, one thing led to another, and eventually Heyrman ran me down and set me up in a studio, all alone with the keys.

I probably prepared less for those two Clean Cuts albums—*Dr. John Plays Mac Rebennack* and *The Brightest Smile in Town*—than for any other I'd ever done. I just had to go in there and wing it; because of my fear of performing solo, I knew if I thought about it too much, I'd have frozen. It was a weird thing for me to approach, because all my thinking as producer and musician has always revolved around bands and how to make them work. I've never thought of myself as a solo performer, only as a member of a group. Solo music is just not something that normally gets my spirits up; I even liked Phineas Newborn better when he was playing with a group.

One thing I was happy to cut during those sessions was a tune by James Black called "Monkey Puzzle." This was a song I'd known for years; Roy Montrell and I had planned to cut it as one of our guitar duos for AFO in the early sixties, until the shooting incident that screwed up my finger. I always remembered it, and for years I had played it because I liked it so much; it made for a real hip duet. On *The Brightest Smile in Town*, the second solo album, I finally cut it on the piano.

James Black's music meant a lot to me. He was writing some of his best stuff—R&B with a nice jazzy feel—at a time when I was learning some of my first jazz pieces back at Cosimo's studio in the early sixties. James was heavily involved then in the New Orleans jazz and R&B scene. He was tight with Red Tyler and other jazz players at AFO, and was beginning to make his mark as a drummer and composer.

In a funny way, my recording "Monkey Puzzle" turned James Black against me. The first time I went to New Orleans after the record came out, I ran into James and he said, "Oh, man, you cut my tune. That's great. Give me a copy of the record." I told him I would and I forgot about it; and for months I forgot again and again, until finally he came up to me one night and said, "You motherfucker, where's my record?"

"I forgot it," I said, feeling real embarrassed.

"Listen here, sucker, you've been telling me that for the last two years."

"I'll go buy you a copy," I said.

"No, man. I want you to send me that record in the mail properly."

By the time James died in August 1988, I still hadn't gotten him the record. He must have gone out pissed off at me. I've had great intentions but short memory for things like this all my life.

The city of New Orleans recently planted trees in Congo Square in memory of the great musicians who came out of New Orleans. Ten musicians were chosen. Five were chosen from the old days—Jelly Roll Morton, Lee Arapola, Paul Barbaran, Louis Armstrong, and Mahalia Jackson—and five from the recent past. I was glad to see the city make the real hip choice to include the great drummer and songwriter James Black, along with James Booker, Professor Longhair, and the others.

Black and Nat Perrilliat, a tenor player who was also honored at Congo Square, were two of the guys who turned New Orleans music around by mixing music by people like John Coltrane up with the New Orleans feel. This approach fonked up the more abstract northern jazz sound. You can find this sound both in their own compositions and in their interpretations of other people's songs: It comes across clearly on Ellis Marsalis's first AFO record, recorded in that early-sixties period, an album titled *Monkey Puzzle* that had the song of the same name as one of its centerpieces.

I remember Nat especially well from the days when he was working in Houston for Don Robey's Peacock label. At that time he was working with the Al T.N.T. Bragg's band, backing up Junior Parker, Bobby Bland. He had a beautiful tone that always stopped me in my tracks. He could play funky, and yet he could stretch like an eagle on some sensational, more abstract jazz material. He could have been the next John Coltrane. Unfortunately, he died very young, before he had a chance to take off. But in his time, he had already contributed so much to changing New Orleans music. He was one of the many musicians who have come along and taken the music where nobody else has been before.

A few changes came out of my two Clean Cuts records. Tommy LiPuma, who'd moved on to Warner Brothers, dug the

DR. JOHN PLAYS MAC REBENNACK

This album came about, ironically, because I had no recording deal in the early 1980s. At that time, I was playing gigs here and there with Swamp Jam, and not necessarily looking for a deal with a new label.

What happened was that a small company, Clean Cuts Records, found me. I was wary of doing a solo turn at first, because I didn't want to come across as a rum-dum cocktail act, but when I saw that Clean Cuts had some respectable jazz acts, I realized the label was hip.

Even though I was leery of working solo, I was glad to record some of the tunes on *Dr. John Plays Mac Rebennack* and its follow-up, *The Brightest Smile in Town*. I wrote "Dorothy," a ragtime tune, and "Big Mac," a New Orleans–style boogie-woogie, for my mother and father, respectively. "Big Mac" is in the style of songs that my father, who owned a small record store back in the 1940s, liked. The left hand, which rolls between pairs of eighth notes and dotted sixteenth notes, is a 2/4 shuffle and creates a loose, slightly irregular groove. The right hand basically embellishes on what the tenths in the left hand are doing.

I wanted to mix up the styles as much as possible on this record—a little Latin beat here ("Delicado"), some gospel ("Saints"), boogie ("Mac's Boogie," "Honey Dripper," and "Pinetop"), standards (Hoagy Carmichael's "The Nearness of You"), and all-out Fessisms ("Memories of Professor Longhair") there.

The thing I enjoyed most about these sessions was that they confirmed a turn I had been taking in my music—mainly, that I was on to doing more sophisticated music, not just the same old Mardi Gras or Gris-Gris stuff that I had been doing before. The audiences loved these earlier songs, but I found they were also ready for music on a higher plane, sounds that appealed to a spiritual awareness, not just that lowdown meat level.

But I tried to keep the old street-side New Orleans flavor in there, too; "Touro Infirmary," recorded for *The Bright-*

est Smile in Town but not released until the CD reissue, is a
pain-filled sayonara to a partner
long gone:

Touro Infirmary

I went down to the Touro Infirmary
Lord knows, and I found my runnin' partner there
He was stretched out on a coal-black table, yes he was
With a DOA sticker to wear

He was gone, he was gone, he was gone, don't you miss him?
A better hustler than him never be found
All the characters on the street all around here
They all know he laid his burden down

He said, when I go, when I go, wearin' ten-dollar gold
    pieces in my eyelids
Lord knows, I want loaded craps in my shoes
I want the finest whores off of Bourbon Street
And I want to hear Professor Longhair sing the blues

I went down to the Touro Infirmary
Lord knows, and I found my sweet runnin' partner there
He was stretched out with a DOA sticker
With a .32 special in his hand

        alternate lyric:
(It was a cold black nite last winter
Five cold black horses on Prytania Street
Five cold black ho's all dressed in leather
Waitin' by the Touro Infirmary)

You know they said, Chief Giarusso warned him
Son, you can't win this game
But they never stopped him as long as he was livin'
Hey, Lord, you can't hold the boy to blame

Let him go, let him go, let him go, let him go, straight to
    heaven
I know none of you dirty rats expect him there
He was a better man than all the ones that expect to arrive
From that Touro Infirmary—he don't care . . .

The hardest thing to do is
let the spirituality flow *and* turn
the meat on. Doing that is creating art, radiating the 88s. When
you do that, you've achieved
something.

standards I did on the records, which led eventually to my hooking up with Warner for a new album, *In a Sentimental Mood*. As always, the path from conceiving an album to final product was a twisted road.

Around 1987, I wrote a couple of tunes I thought Atlantic might like to hear, with an eye to expanding them into an album. I talked with Ahmet "Omlet" Ertegun and he told me to go to Allen Toussaint's studio to lay two tunes down, which I did. I got back to New York and he said, "This one tune is great, but it's not for you. It's for Lynyrd Skynyrd!"

The person at Atlantic I really respected was Tommy Dowd, who was the hardest-working guy at the place. I watched Tommy produce records where later Ahmet or Jerry was given credit for production. Jerry and Ahmet, by contrast, would pop in periodically, then leave for long chunks of time. Every now and again, though, Jerry'd come up with a good record; I have to give him credit for doing a really good job producing my *Gumbo* album. Omlet used to come in like gangbusters and leave. But in spite of it all, I still have a soft spot for them both because I know how much both of them love New Orleans music. In the fifties they had cut Professor Longhair, Big Joe Turner, and Ray Charles in New Orleans, because they loved the roots of fonk.

When I went to see Tommy LiPuma later on about something else, I told him what had happened; we got to talking about Louis Jordan and veered in the direction of doing an album of Jordan tunes. We cut "Saturday Night Fish Fry," "Don't Let the Sun Catch You Crying," and "Beware, Brother, Beware." What I originally had in mind was a fistful of funk arrangements of these tunes, but unfortunately the sessions were being cut in Los Angeles and we just didn't have the right combination of musicians to do them the way we would have if we'd been in New Orleans. This became painfully clear when we cut an unhappening version of "Saturday Night Fish Fry."

But at some point I threw in "My Buddy," an old ballad that wasn't a Jordan tune, and the album tilted from being a Louis Jordan tribute to a collection of standards, which I think came out all right. Tommy LiPuma, as always, was a joy to work with, as was Al Schmitt, who, along with Tommy Dowd, is one of my favorite engineers. Plus, I loved working with the arrangers Ralph Burns and Marty Paich.

I think, without my even knowing it at the time, *In a Sentimental Mood* marked a deepening of something I was already onto with my Clean Cuts records—that is, I was broadening the kinds of music I was doing on record. I had always dug jazz and the standards, but this wasn't how I played, even though my band, from the 1960s on, had been into playing live sets all different kinds of ways—often as not taking the music out of rock and roll and into jazz. *In a Sentimental Mood* did this in a real open way by including standards such as Cole Porter's "Love for Sale," Duke Ellington's "In a Sentimental Mood," and a couple of Gus Kahn/Walter Donaldson classics, "My Buddy" and "Makin' Whoopee."

We asked Rickie Lee Jones to duet on "Makin' Whoopee," and we came up with a nice combination of ingredients on it. Rickie's drop-dead cool voice had a breezy ironical touch to it that I liked; we ended up getting a Grammy for best jazz vocal duet for that song, and the album, which was marketed as a jazz album, ended up being one of the top-ten-selling jazz LPs of 1989.

Late that year, I ran into Art Blakey again. My road manager, B.B. (Barbara Becker), was a friend of Art's, and she got him hooked on the idea of cutting a jazzy blues album with me and Fathead Newman. Things progressed quickly from concept to cutting on that album, which was called *Bluesiana Triangle*: Before I knew what was going down, I was in a limo and on my way to the studio with Art. We hadn't talked about what we were going to cut or how we were going to cut it. The two of us just rapped, and by the end of the ride we had a good start on the session.

Doing that album was a real kick for me, because I had looked up to Art Blakey since I was a kid. The sessions came off very naturally. Art was sweet enough not to mention the way we'd first met, when Walter Davis, Ray Draper, and I tripped through his darkened pad on our way to cop in the early seventies. We cut some fine tunes: Somehow, I found out Art liked the songs of the New Orleans songwriter and piano player "Cousin" Joe Pleasant, so we decided to do Cous's song "Life Is a One-Way Ticket," mainly because we both dug Cous's line about "never seeing an armored car at a funeral yet." Once we got rolling, Art suggested we do a jailhouse tune, so we cut my fonked-up version of "Shoo Fly." We also cut one of Fathead's tunes, "Heads Up," and another standard, "For All We Know," written by Fred Coots and Samuel Lewis. "For All We Know," on which Art played piano and sang, and Fathead laid down a beautiful solo, and I played a little guitar, was a poignant farewell:

> For all we know, we may never meet again
> For all we know, this may only be an end
> We won't say good-night until the last minute
> I'll hold out my hand, and my heart will be in it
> For all we know, this may only be a dream
> We come and go like a ripple in a stream . . .

Within six months after we cut the record, Art died of the lung cancer he may have known he had at the time of our sessions.

Bluesiana Triangle marked a step for me into the jazz world. In 1991, I followed it up with another album in that vein, *Bluesiana II*, which reunited me with Fathead, the trombone player Ray Anderson, and several other musicians. I wish Art could have heard it.

In 1989, after thirty-four years of off-and-on—but mostly on—use of heroin, I began to get a handle on my addiction. I had never been in the narcotics game with any intention of quitting; my attitude had always been that I'd go into rehab periodically to cut down on the money I was spending on narcotics, but if the price of dope came down and the quality got better, I was off and running again. That happened again and again during my halfhearted rehab attempts: I straightened up for a while, but sooner or later I ran into some Chang Moi rocks and it was off to the races, another four years of getting strung out like a fucking guinea pig.

What changed it all around was an experience I had when I wound up in a cardiac ward. I had been suffering some chest pains, which later proved to be nothing major, and I was lying in this bed, hooked up on tubes and wires, when I noticed that the guy in the bed next to me was getting shots of Demerol and morphine every couple of hours. I pulled all the wires and tubes out of myself and began planning how to follow the nurse, with the intention of knocking off the narcotics box. I knew I'd get busted if I did it, but that was the last thing I was worried about.

But just as I was about to put myself in gear, this one particular spiritual nurse walked in with a bag of tangerines. She saw I'd pulled all my tubes out, but she was cool about it—she didn't say a word. Instead, she asked, "Want a tangerine?"

I took it.

Until that time, nothing had stayed in my stomach since I had been in the hospital. But I bit into the tangerine, and it tasted so good. And it stayed down. I ate three of them, and they all stayed down. And it was something about just those sweet, juicy tangerines, at just that moment, that made me decide to try to square up and clean up my act.

And every time thereafter, when my roomie got his Demerol and morphine, this nurse would pop up with her tangerines and good company. I never got a chance to reconsider.

Bit by bit I found out more about her. I discovered that her old man worked at a drug-rehab place. Shortly, I found myself there, and I owe it to them that my decision stuck. They started me on a twelve-step program, and, like all good addicts, I thought I could get it all at once. I wound up in the psych ward, and ended up being heavily medicated on lithium for almost a year. My hands began to shake and I got nosebleeds from that stuff. This came at a time when I was doing a lot of solo gigs as a result of my two Clean Cuts albums, and it was no fun for me; not only did I miss the interplay with other musicians, but it's very lonely playing solo, and it was a little scary during the first flush of rehab. I'd be trying to play and my one hand would start shaking, while my other one was rocking. I had to ice that out real quick by turning down the volume of the medication the doc was giving me. All in all that kind of episode made me want to play solo even less.

Finally I went to another doctor in New York, who took me off the lithium and straightened me out. See, when I was smoothed over on narcotics, I always had this fear that if I ever tried to quit, some croaker would put me on some other drug and make me into his guinea pig. When my doctor took me off the lithium, I felt my life had really started up in a new way. I began to hang out with people who shared the same kind of experiences that I had gone through.

I learned a few humbling things about myself, too. I remember that when I was in the psych ward I called my friend Gene. I said, "Man, I think something went wrong here."

He said, "Before you try to run, maybe you should learn to walk." As an addict, you're out of control and all fucked up. You just have to learn things like that before you can go on up the ladder. True to the addict personality, I thought I could jump over the Grand Canyon and rewrite my life in one day. Didn't work out that way, though.

Looking back on the game, I can see now that I couldn't have been such a happy kid; the narcotics crutch was my way of somehow keeping myself from being more psychotic than I would have been straight. If that is what it was, it didn't work that well. I've spent my times here and there in psych wards, and, having been on both sides, I can see that I like being clean. I enjoy it.

I used to ask myself what life would be like without narcotics, and, in truth, I couldn't come up with much of an answer. I believed that heroin would preserve me, that I would live until the croakers figured out a way to freeze me and bring me back. So I didn't see too much future in not doing heroin.

Methadone was a whole 'nother bag all to itself. The time I spent on methadone was like putting the dog to sleep in the kennel. I first tried it in the late 1960s, during an earlier half-hearted attempt at cleaning up, but it did nothing for me. Methadone just shuts you down, and I spent most of the time I was on it sleeping—a ridiculously abnormal number of hours.

Between the heroin and the methadone, over the years I missed out on a lot. But back then, I would never have copped to admitting that I was missing out on nothin', even if I had known it. During thirty-some years of being a dope fiend, you'd think I would have wised up, but I had what you call denial, and there ain't no river in Egypt that could wash that clean. I thought of myself as being a different animal from street junkies, because I was a working, gigging dope fiend. I didn't have to go stick somebody up; I worked. It was all rationalizing jive, but that's what kept me at it.

One of my major MOs was to lie. Anyone who told me, "Man, you strung out! You sick!" would have caught it from me, real indignant: "Not me! What, you crazy? I just been up all night." I was down with my bullshit in everything I did—at home, in the studio, on the streets. I hustled people by creating sympathy. I could con anyone out of the first hit of his dope by saying, "I'm so sick, I think I'm going to die." The guy would react and give me the first hit and I'd be thinking, Oh, he's fucked now—this guy's a mark.

These days, I got to laugh about that. No question now, my brain works better. I enjoy little things in life today that just went by me before. Before I got clean, I lived in a tunnel-vision world, a ripping and running jungle where there was no time for the enjoyment of life. It's hard to put a finger on exactly what the difference between my old and new self is, except to say it's a matter of attitude. It's not like the things I do every day are different from before—it's just that now it's like someone has turned on the lights, so I can see the many little details I missed out on. Some of them might be things I might not want to see, but that part comes with being clean.

y, the difference comes in trying to be as emotionally
ı myself and with others as I can be, which is hard.
_____ ad channeled my emotions into my music, and there
wasn't a whole lot left to go around to anybody else. Now, especially with the help of some friends who've been there, I'm trying
to get the touch back with the other important people in my life.
I don't have a good nose for it yet, but I'm trying . . . I'm learning.

The whole turnaround of coming clean was nothing I
planned on; it just happened when it happened. God looks out
for chumps and assholes. That's what makes life interesting.

Anyway, I don't believe you can go back. Life just doesn't
work that way—or it shouldn't. One of the things I did learn
from the reverend mothers was that we all must struggle in our
spirituality, so that by the time we reach that point in life when
we're about to croak, we'll be all leveled off.

If you take the road going down and you come to the
crossroads of death, you got a lot of climbing to do real fast. Most
people can't make it back to the right place then; all their climbing
comes too late. The reverend mothers were down heavy on the
cycles of life: Every seven years, you go through a life cycle, and
if you get enough sevens behind you, you're on your way out of
this place.

No matter how far away from New Orleans I've gone and
what I've done, sooner or later I always want to come back to my
hometown for a roots recharge. LA and New York are cool, but
neither holds the spell for me that New Orleans still does.

In New Orleans, everything—food, music, religion, even
the way people talk and act—has deep, deep roots; and, like the
tangled veins of cypress roots that meander this way and that in
the swamp, everything in New Orleans in interrelated, wrapped
around itself in ways that aren't always obvious.

You can hear this hard-to-describe New Orleans quality in
the way people talk. Because of the peculiar accents you'll hear
around town, "Where's y'at, darling?" sounds different in the

Ninth Ward from the way it does in the mouths of society people, but they both use the same slang. The language is bastardized here: The Creole patois has enough Spanish, Italian, and other languages thrown in with the French and English that it's strictly a New Orleans thing. You couldn't speak New Orleans Creole to a Haitian or a Nigerian or a Frenchman and expect them to understand more than a few words here and there.

And of course you can hear the New Orleans essence in the music. One of the great things about New Orleans music is that whether it's brass bands, progressive jazz groups, traditional jazz groups, spiritual church singers, sanctified church players, gris-gris and santería hymns and chants, even pop, rock, country, and soul—if it came from New Orleans it has a flavor all its own, a sound distinguished by the beat and, if the song has lyrics, by the attitude. In the music, it's fonk, a syncopation on and around the beat. In the lyrics, it's a mixture of street smarts and soulfulness. If you want to know it, listen to Satchmo, Mahalia Jackson, the Meters, Irma Thomas, Allen Toussaint, or Earl King, to name a few. You'll find it with them, because they all got it.

Things have changed a lot in the New Orleans music scene since I was a little up-and-coming weed-hopper from the Third Ward trying to play a little music. Back then, the money was okay; now, thirty years later, the money hasn't gotten better, which means it's poor and there's not too much incentive for young musicians coming up. It's one thing to play around when you're making some money; it's another thing when you can't make ends meet and you're just playing around.

When I came up, there were places to have gigs all over town. You didn't have to leave New Orleans to support yourself. Now all the string of strips and clubs are long gone. Sure, there are a few places around town, but nothing like the twenty-four-hour, nonstop action that existed when I was a kid. Now Tipi-tina's, a New Orleans club, has a Monday-night performance benefit, sponsored by Tulane University, to help put on New Orleans music. Way back when, you didn't need no university to help support musicians. You had club owners with hard-nosed,

GOIN' BACK TO NEW ORLEANS

My last album was a tribute to the music of my hometown, and in a way it is complementary to my earlier album *Gumbo*, which had the same goal within a narrower time focus. *Goin' Back to New Orleans* covers a whole history of New Orleans music, including songs that are much older and have a much more mysterious origin than the tunes on *Gumbo*. Songs like "Didn't He Ramble," "I'll Be Glad When You're Dead, You Rascal You," and "I Thought I Heard Buddy Bolden Say" are real roots music.

"I Thought I Heard Buddy Bolden Say" is a tribute song by Jelly Roll Morton to the first great New Orleans jazz trumpeter. Even though Jelly Roll claimed to have invented jazz, that honor probably belongs to Buddy Bolden. Buddy never got any of his stuff on a disc, though; he flipped out early and was committed to a mental hospital. It wasn't until several years after this happened that the first jazz discs began to be cut, so we'll never know what that earliest jazz sounded like. Buddy got out of that hospital alive, but he never played again.

Street-side action, real life—that's what New Orleans music has always been about. It's usually up music, but underneath there's gravity, too, a soulfulness that gives it its color. "Didn't He Ramble" is a true-to-life street-side love lament that could describe the fate of a lot of guys in New Orleans, past and present. It's about a guy who robs and steals, whores and loves maybe the wrong women, and in the end has his style of living catch up with him—all of this to a syncopated second-line beat.

Didn't He Ramble

Ashes to ashes, dust to dust.
If the brown whiskey don't kill him
Then his woman must.

Chief Giarusso warned that boy
Time and time again,
"You're holding a losing hand, and you're playing a losing
*   game.*
When you play, you got to pay,
And you got to pay the one that lays.
And when you do, the groundhog will be shakin' your
*   hand."*

Didn't he ramble, didn't he ramble
Ramble all around, in and out of town
Didn't he ramble, didn't he ramble
Ramble till the butcher shot him down

His head was in the marketplace, and his feet was in the
*   street*
The lady was passin' by, she said "Look at the market
*   meat!"*
He tried to lift her pocketbook, and said "I wish you well."
She pulled out a .32, said "I'll see you first in hell."

Didn't he ramble, didn't he ramble
Ramble all around, in and out of town
Didn't he ramble, didn't he ramble
Ramble till the butcher shot him down

Now he snuck into the cathouse, made love to the stable
The madam caught him cold,
*   he said "I'll pay when I'll be able"*
Six months done passed, she'd stood all she could stand
Said, "When I'm through with you,
*   the groundhog gonna shake your hand"*

And he ramble, didn't he ramble
Ramble all around, in and out of town
Didn't he ramble, didn't he ramble
Ramble till the butcher shot him down

Ashes to ashes, dust to dust
If the gamblin' didn't kill him
All the ramblin' must.

real-life reasons to have rocking bands working 'round the clock in their places. Music just flowed and blossomed from that economic base.

Furthermore, because the music used to be played twenty-four hours a day, a lot of musicians back then could support themselves by playing an after-hours gig, and still have other parts of the day and evening for experimenting on their own music. Now, without the all-night scene, too many musicians are forced to take day jobs or take gigs elsewhere, and because of this the sheer volume of musical experimentation and creativity has diminished.

As a result, 95 percent of the most successful New Orleans bands have got to take gigs all over the country and the world—and hardly ever make it back to New Orleans. This just ain't what the city traditionally was about. It's always been a poor city, but when you consider that thirty years later bands are making the same money as when I was starting out—and that the best bands have to leave home to make it—obviously there's a problem.

Yet another symptom of this condition is the state of the recording industry in New Orleans. There are a couple of good studios but no one has the kind of state-of-the-art equipment they have in Los Angeles or New York. There's just not enough work coming in to raise the money to keep up with the others. And performers who ought to be on major labels—people like Johnny Adams, Chuck Carbo, Snooks Eaglin, and Irma Thomas—find themselves on small labels like Rounder and Blacktop. It's nice that *someone* is recording these artists, but in my opinion these labels are not worthy of this kind of talent.

The only hope I can see to help turn all this around is the reappearance of gambling in New Orleans, which is in the early stages of coming to be. Still, for better or worse, New Orleans remains its own strange self, and more than a little bit out of sync with other places in the United States. This is one of its charms, but it's also a curse.

These specific New Orleans twists and turns are what made me come back here to record my last album, *Goin' Back to New*

Orleans. I wanted to do what I could both to pay tribute to this fascinating history and to update and fonkify the music in my own way (and also throw a little work to local New Orleans musicians, who were the best cats to perform the songs I had in mind). The album was made up entirely of New Orleans songs, everything from "Careless Love" (which dates from way back in the 1800s) and "Indian Red," an old Mardi Gras Indian freedom song, to "Since I Fell for You," one of the songs that made me fall in love with Annie Laurie back in the fifties at Paul Gayten's Brass Rail Club.

Of all the songs on the album, though, the one that probably gave me the greatest kick was "Litanie des Saints," my compa-fonkilation of two pieces of music, Louis Gottschalk's classical "Bamboula, Danse des Negres" and the chants I have heard at various gris-gris churches over the years. After I had cut the song, I brought the tape around to play for some of the gris-gris people. One of them, a santería devotee, broke into tears when he heard this piece. When I saw the tears, I knew I had gotten it right, had stamped my own little groove into something that meant a lot to me. I was back in the gumbo, where there ain't no way of telling the ending from the beginnings, completing a circle of some kind, stacking up the sevens. This made me feel good about what I'd done and where I was from. At that moment, New Orleans sure enough felt like home to me.

CODA

So I've survived. I've made it through the last several decades as a functionally evolving musician, arranger, artist, songwriter, and record producer; I've been in and out of the record, film, and TV industries, and the jingle jungle, with all their downs and ups, offs and ons, always hurrying up to wait on the shifting moods of the times.

At the moment this little book of rememberations hits the bricks, my new album—*Television*—will be coming along too. It's my first record on MCA/GRP, a hip company with their soul in jazz, and with me they're dipping their feet in the fonk. MCA/GRP gave me the green light to cut a funky thing with them because they wanted to let a hard-to-categorize artist like me work without the fear of being misjudged or misguided by artistic direction or discretion.

After the roots-rompin' flavor of *Goin' Back to New Orleans*, I wanted to hit a new dance chord, and I think *Television* nails it; it's a true representation of fonknology. So I think I'll leave you blessed with this request: If you're hooked by this book, and you're looking for a new blast of funk, you better turn on the *Television*. It's what there is to say about Dr. John today.

INDEX

Morrison, Van, 224–226, 231
Morton, Jelly Roll, 14, 243, 251
Myles, Big Boy, 82
Myles, Jake, 223

Nathan, Sid, 226–227
Nelson, Lawrence (Prince La La), 84
Nelson, Louis, 21
Nelson, Walter "Papoose," 20–22, 47, 148
Neville, Aaron, 81, 190
Neville, Art, 36, 67–68, 190–191
Newborn, Phineas, 240
Newman, Fathead, 229, 235, 238, 245–246
New Orleans Musicians Association, 131
Night Trains, 46
Night Trippers, 146
Nilsson, Harry, 197, 201
Nocentelli, Leo, 190–191

O'Jays, 126
Oliver, King, 12
O'Neil, Leo, 81

Paich, Marty, 245
Palmer, Earl, 72, 83, 187
Parker, Charlie, 201
Parker, Frankie, 28
Parker, Junior, 46, 69, 83, 132–133, 243
Parker, Ray, Jr., 224–225
Parks, Van Dyke, 152
Payne, Richard, 85
Peaks, Donald, 127
Perrilliat, Nat, 85, 243
Peskin, Joel, 226
Pickett, Wilson, 133
Pleasant, "Cousin" Joe, 246
Pomus, Doc, 226, 229–238
Poppa Stoppa, 70
Porter, Cole, 245
Porter, George, Jr., 190–191
Powell, Petsy, 236
Pozo, Chano, 104, 146
Prado, Pererz, 12
Presley, Elvis, 83
Preston, Billy, 148
Price, Lloyd, 67–69, 76
Prima, Louis, 29

Quezerque, Wardell, 152

Rabini, Mike, 127
Radle, Carl, 178
"Rain," 231–232
Randi, Don, 127
Randolph, Boots, 110
Raye, Sonny, 141
Rebennack, Barbara "Bobbie," 6, 14, 19, 160
Rebennack, Lydia Crow, 41, 55, 94–98, 100–102, 107, 113–114
Rebennack, Pauline, 141
Red Beans and Rice, 178, 203
Redd, Pharaoh Al, 75
Redding, Otis, 193
Reed, Jimmy, 58
Reed, Lula, 228
Remedies, 173–175
Rhodes, Calvin, 239
Ricardo, Ricky, 54
Richards, Keith, 182
Richards, Marcel, 129
Richardson, Jack, 164, 167
Richberg, John, 80
Ridgley, Tommy, 57, 81
Roach, Max, 201
Roberts, Howard, 127
Robertson, Robbie, 181
Robey, Don, 44, 83
Robinson, Alvin "Shine," 130, 132–133, 139, 141, 146–148, 182, 185, 208, 233, 236
Rolling Stones, 182–183
Ruffin, Riff, 82
Ruffino, Joe, 69, 81, 216
Rupe, Art and Lena, 82
Russell, Brenda, 236
Russell, Leon, 183

Sahm, Doug, 190
Sample, Joe, 226
Sanborn, David, 233
Sansone, Johnny, 106
Santina, Herbert, 20
Schmitt, Al, 245
Scott, Joe, 83
Seals, Mother Catherine, 160–161, 165
Shadows, 46
Shannon, Mother, 163–164

Shuffling Hungarians, 221–222
Silver, Horace, 63
Sims Twins, 69, 126
Sinatra, Frank, 29
Sinclair, John, 195
Singleton, Shelby, 77
Smith, Huey, 21, 47–48, 55, 70, 72–74, 76, 78–80, 183, 223
Smith, Jimmy, 56, 124–125
Smith, Pinetop, 14
Sonny and Cher, 127–128, 141–142
Soul Stirrers, 125
Soxx, Bob B., 125
Spades, 36–37, 42
Specialty Records, 36, 66–71, 79, 82
Spector, Phil, 125, 127–129, 196–197
Spence, Joseph, 222
Staehle, Freddie, 175, 185–186, 209
Staehle, Paul, 46, 50–51, 53, 105, 186
Stanley, Earl (Earl King), 44–45, 54, 59, 69, 76, 79, 94–96, 106, 151–152, 183, 185
Starr, Ringo, 197
Stax, 131
Stone, Brian, 172–175, 179, 181, 189–190, 192
Stone, Roland, 52
"Such a Night," 191–192
Sugar Boy and the Cane Cutters, 58, 185
Sugar and Sweet, 54
Sun, Moon and Herbs, The, 177–180
Sundown, Lonesome, 82
Swamp Jam, 238, 241

Taj Mahal, 152
Talbot, Wayne, 81, 136–137, 149
Tango Palace, 235–237
Tate, Billy, 76
Tatum, Art, 12
Tee, Willie (Wilson Turbington), 85
Terroade, Kenneth, 179
Tex, Joe, 48, 72, 210
Thomas, Irma, 82, 254
Thomas, Tabby, 82
Thunderbirds, 46
Tillman, Eddie, 148
Toups, Boots, 164, 167–170
"Touro Infirmary," 242

Toussaint, Allen, 73, 80–81, 129, 185, 190–191, 223, 244
Troy, Doris, 178
Turbington, Earl and Wilson, 85
Turner, Joe, 9, 48, 234
Tyler, Red, 29, 72, 76, 84–85, 124–125, 240
Tyner, McCoy, 83

Underwood, Charlie, 153, 189

Van Walls, Harry, 206
Vaughan, Stevie Ray, 79
Vincent, Johnny, 66, 69–70, 72–75, 77–81, 226
Voco-Kesh, Abe, 135

Walden, Phil, 192–193
Walker, Junior, 83
Walker, T-Bone, 21, 67
Walton, Mercy Dee, 9
Washington, Richard "Didimus," 104–105, 130, 141, 145–147, 154–155, 157–158, 175, 182–183, 185, 204–205, 208–209
Washington, Raymond, 75
Washington, Tuts, 20
Watson, Johnny "Guitar," 130
Watts, Charlie, 182
Wells, Junior, 178
West, Willie, 68
West, Bob, 142
Wexler, Jerry, 82, 134, 141, 154, 168, 174, 179, 181, 183–185, 194, 244
Wilkerson, Don, 117
Williams, Charles "Hungry," 28, 83, 187, 206
Williams, Earl, 29
Williams, Joe, 178
Williams, Larry, 66–67, 130
Winter, Johnny, 69
Womack, Bobby, 125, 196
Wonder, Stevie, 178, 224–225

Zappa, Frank, 128
Zawinul, Joe, 85
Zimmerman, Roy, 106
ZuZu Man, 189–190